GW01336618

American Routes

American Routes
Racial Palimpsests and the Transformation of Race

Angel Adams Parham

OXFORD
UNIVERSITY PRESS

OXFORD
UNIVERSITY PRESS

Oxford University Press is a department of the University of Oxford. It furthers the University's objective of excellence in research, scholarship, and education by publishing worldwide. Oxford is a registered trade mark of Oxford University Press in the UK and certain other countries.

Published in the United States of America by Oxford University Press
198 Madison Avenue, New York, NY 10016, United States of America.

© Oxford University Press 2017

All rights reserved. No part of this publication may be reproduced, stored in a retrieval system, or transmitted, in any form or by any means, without the prior permission in writing of Oxford University Press, or as expressly permitted by law, by license, or under terms agreed with the appropriate reproduction rights organization. Inquiries concerning reproduction outside the scope of the above should be sent to the Rights Department, Oxford University Press, at the address above.

You must not circulate this work in any other form
and you must impose this same condition on any acquirer.

CIP data is on file at the Library of Congress
ISBN 978-0-19-062475-0

1 3 5 7 9 8 6 4 2

Printed by Sheridan Books, Inc., United States of America

CONTENTS

List of Figures and Tables　　*vii*
Acknowledgments　　*ix*

Introduction: Louisiana and the Advent of a New America　　1
1. Racial Systems and the Racial Palimpsest　　19
2. St. Domingue as Training Ground: Color, Class, and Social Life Before Louisiana　　51
3. White St. Domingue Refugees and White Creoles in Nineteenth-Century Louisiana　　68
4. St. Domingue Refugees and Creoles of Color　　94
5. Twenty-First Century Remnants of a White Creole Past　　120
6. Into the Twenty-First Century: Creoles of Color Finding Their Way　　154
7. Conclusions: Racial Palimpsests and the Transformation of US American Regions　　188

Appendix I: Notes on Methodology　　211
Appendix II: Cajun/Creole Survey Results　　221
Appendix III: St. Domingue/Haiti-Louisiana Interview Instrument　　225
Appendix IV: Creole Oral History Guide　　235
Notes　　239
Bibliography　　263
Index　　271

LIST OF FIGURES AND TABLES

FIGURES

I.1	The dances in Congo Square	9
3.1	Three municipalities: The schism of New Orleans	79

TABLES

I.1	St. Domingue Refugee Impact on New Orleans	7
1.1	The Two Layers of the Palimpsest	47
5.1	*Times-Picayune* Creole Family Search	150
7.1	Bonilla-Silva's Triracial Stratification System	195
A.1	Cajun/Creole Interviewees	213
A.2	White Descendants of St. Domingue	216
A.3	St. Domingue Descendants of Color	217
A.4	Oral Histories with White Louisianans with Creole Heritage	218

ACKNOWLEDGMENTS

The creation of *American Routes* has been a truly transformative experience. I could not have imagined when I started this project in August 2005 that I would be putting the finishing touches on it only in 2016. I launched the core stage of data collection just days before Hurricane Katrina hit the Gulf Coast and the levees broke, devastating the city I had come to love. I thought then that the project was dead before it had begun, but the city rallied and my respondents returned. Then in 2011 another storm threatened to ruin six years of work. My family and I were on our way to live in Princeton for the 2011–2012 academic year. The day we left a tropical storm hovered over our car and followed us up the East Coast. The day before we arrived in Princeton I discovered to my horror that the back of our minivan had leaked so badly that my cassette tapes and research documents were all soaked, floating in a couple inches of water. My husband Jonathan, who is a sound engineer, saved the day and is to be credited for saving the core data reported in *American Routes*. Thinking quickly, he instructed me to use a hair dryer to individually dry out each cassette tape. We then laid out every single page of every document across the room so that they could dry. When we got to Princeton the next day and settled into our housing, he set up the cassette recorder, connected it to my laptop, and transferred the recordings to the laptop to create digital files which we saved on our computer and burned onto CDs. His expertise saved six years of work.

Among others who have helped to bring this project to readers, I want to thank Ed McCaughan, who was the chair of the sociology department when I first came to Loyola University–New Orleans in 2003. It was he who encouraged me to consider doing a project that would connect my long-standing interest in Haiti with my newfound home in Louisiana. I am extraordinarily grateful for his suggestion. It is a very special thing to be able to dig deeply into the history and culture of the place where one lives, and to come to appreciate it in new and wonderful ways.

I am also grateful to the many local people who guided me and gave me entrée to the community as I felt my way along the path of this long and winding project. Augusta Elmwood, the founder of the St. Domingue Special Interest Group (SIG)—a subset of the Jefferson Genealogical Society—welcomed me heartily and introduced me to many SIG members whom I would eventually interview. Her knowledge and expertise have guided many scholars, and I am deeply indebted to her for all of her help and guidance.

Mary Anne de Boisblanc, who has passed away as of the time of this writing, is another to whom I feel a great debt. It was Mary Anne's heartfelt contribution during one of the St. Domingue SIG meetings that convinced me that I needed to include white St. Domingue descendants in my study rather than focusing only on those of color. It is to her that I owe the racially comparative nature of this study. Mary Anne was also extraordinarily warm and welcoming. She was in her early eighties when I first met her, and she had a passionate attachment to her ancestors and their experiences in St. Domingue and the Bayou Teche area of Louisiana. She was also an artist and she invited me early on to a talk she gave that integrated her love of history with her art. She invited me several times into her home, where she showed me her beautiful work and plied me with stories of growing up in Acadiana. Through her paintings, she channeled the lives of her ancestors and invited me to share their stories.

John Lawrence of the Historic New Orleans Collection (HNOC) deserves special thanks because he allowed me to set up a table at the 2006 Common Routes symposium sponsored by the HNOC so that I could sign up attendees who were descendants of St. Domingue refugees who fled to Louisiana in the nineteenth century. This kindness started me on my way with the critical mass of interviewees I needed to get the project going. Finding descendants of St. Domingue whose families fled the revolution in Haiti was no easy task, so John Lawrence's assistance and the cooperation of the HNOC were extraordinarily helpful.

I have also been greatly aided by Pat Schexnayder, the founder of LA Creole, a genealogical and cultural organization devoted to providing educational programming and research support on topics concerning Louisiana Creoles of color. Pat welcomed me to LA Creole events and introduced me to many who would become interview respondents. Pat was very generous in sharing her time with me and was an important guide during my early years working on this project.

I would also like to say a general thank you to the members of both the St. Domingue SIG and LA Creole. Members of both groups were very welcoming to me and to this project. When I returned from sabbatical in

2012, Augusta Elmwood invited me to do a presentation on my research during a winter meeting with the SIG. My research had been well received in Princeton, where I was on sabbatical, but I knew that the real test of the work would be the reception of these folks who were steeped in the history and culture I was researching. To my relief, they also received the work well and indicated that I was going in the right direction. This check-in was very helpful and encouraging.

I also count many colleagues and academic institutions among those who have supported this project. My own institution, Loyola University, has provided small grants that allowed me to hire research assistants who helped with transcribing interviews. This was an invaluable help. I was also part of a faculty reading group at Loyola which included Daniella Zsupan-Jerome, Artemis Preeshl, and Karen Rosenbecker as well as my sociology colleague Carol Ann MacGregor. They generously read and commented on early versions of some of my chapters. I am also grateful to all of my colleagues in the sociology department who have been supportive over several years. I would also like to remember Harold Baquet, Loyola's beloved photographer who succumbed to cancer in 2015. Harold allowed me to interview him and his was one of the most vibrant of interviews. Those who know him know that he can tell a great story, and I benefitted from this as he gave me insight into his life and community. We all miss him greatly.

A special thanks goes to the Institute for Advanced Study (IAS) in Princeton, New Jersey, which gave me the excellent opportunity of spending my 2011–2012 sabbatical year there as a member of the School of Social Science. This was an extraordinary opportunity to be surrounded by scholars from around the country and around the world who are at the top of their fields. Faculty members Joan Scott, Danielle Allen, and Didier Fassin cultivated an intellectual environment conducive to helping each scholar produce his or her best work, and I benefitted greatly from this. Joan Scott coordinated a weekly seminar group where we read and provided critical feedback on each other's work. I was privileged to be able to present twice to this group and to receive their invaluable critique and guidance. Those who were part of this group included the following: Celeste Arrington, Gail Bederman, Wendy Chun, Amy Kaplan, Judith Surkis, Sheena Kang, and Jessica Sewell. Outside of this faculty group, I also benefitted from Chad Goldberg's comments on early versions of my chapters. Chad was also in residence at the IAS during that time, in the School of Historical Studies. His support during the beginning stages of writing was quite helpful and encouraging.

I also benefited greatly from many conversations with IAS faculty member Danielle Allen with whom I had many talks about the idea and ideal of racial integration. Her book *Talking to Strangers* helped to inform my thinking about the efficacy of the different metaphors and practices we use to cross racial lines. Her work has been important to developments in my thinking about bridging racial differences. Finally, I am grateful to all the members of the School of Social Science who took part in the weekly lunch seminar and who responded so well to the talk I gave in the spring of 2012. Following that talk, Steven Lukes and Michael Walzer took time out to meet individually with me to provide insight and guidance on my work.

During the final stages of writing this project, I had the privilege of being part of a faculty reading group made up of faculty from several New Orleans universities. This group included Ashley Howard from Loyola, Rosanne Adderley and Guadalupe Garcia from Tulane, and Nikki Brown and Andrea Mosterman from the University of New Orleans. As the only sociologist among a group of historians, I was incredibly grateful to have their insights into the historical dimensions of *American Routes*. When I presented to them in late 2014, they perceptively urged me to dig deeper, sure that I was on the verge of something greater than I had yet to fully articulate. Their critique helped to push me to examine my data more carefully in order to come to analytical insights I had not yet brought out in the manuscript.

Wendy Roth, based at the University of British Columbia, provided invaluable insight and suggestions on the revised version of my manuscript after I had responded to reports of anonymous reviewers. Hers were the final eyes on the manuscript just before I turned it in to my editor. Her excellent work on race and immigration in Puerto Rico, the Dominican Republic, and the United States has informed my own, so I was extremely grateful that she was willing to take the time to read the revised manuscript and to provide comments. Her critical insights led me to make some changes that are woven throughout the book in order to clarify and strengthen the argument. It is also a pleasure to be both a colleague and friend of hers today, more than twenty years after we both graduated from Yale with undergraduate degrees in sociology. Who would have imagined that we would both end up doing work on race and immigration focused on Latin America and the Caribbean? Her support has been inestimable.

My editor at Oxford University Press, James Cook, has been wonderful from the time we first met at the 2012 meeting of the American Sociological Association in Denver. He has provided excellent guidance and ushered the manuscript adeptly through many levels of consideration and review. He selected a group of reviewers who provided very helpful and carefully considered comments. I am grateful to these reviewers for the thoroughness of their reviews, and *American Routes* has been greatly strengthened by their work.

Finally, I thank my family for their extraordinary patience with me through what have now been eleven years of work on this book. My mother Linda and sister Carla have listened to hours of talk about the challenges and triumphs of working on this project. My father Larry and his wife Debbie, and my grandmother Climmie have all been supportive of my work, as was my grandfather Rex who passed away before the book was published. During these eleven years my husband Jonathan and I have added our two daughters—Madeleine and Julia—to our family. Jonathan deserves the award of the decade for most supportive and flexible husband and father. He willingly uprooted himself and our two small daughters to go live in Princeton for the 2011–2012 academic year. Having my family with me during this time was a source of great comfort and strength. During that time, Jonathan took on the bulk of parenting duties as the girls romped through the Institute woods and discovered the joys of snow for the first time. All three of them have endured the ups and downs I have come through in getting this manuscript ready for publication. We all rejoice that the time has come to put *American Routes* out into the world. To all I say, "Thank you."

American Routes

Introduction

Louisiana and the Advent of a New America

At this moment an event occurs which will be attended with moral and political consequences much to be deprecated, which will rivet upon us a decided and irresistible preponderance of French influence—and thus prevent us for many years to come from considering this in heart and in sentiment as an American country—Many of the unfortunate French are arriving daily from Cuba about two thousand are expected they bring with them negro slaves & free people of Colour I pity their distress . . . but I sincerely wish that they had gone to some other part of our extensive Continent.
—Secretary Robertson to the Secretary of State, *New Orleans, May 24, 1809*

By 1809 the terrors of the revolution in St. Domingue had passed, giving way to the newly independent country of Haiti.[1] But in New Orleans, the full repercussions of that revolution were only just beginning. On the shores of the city stood vessels containing thousands of St. Domingue refugees who had been forced to flee their first refuge in Cuba. Now they were demanding entry to New Orleans.

A young W. C. C. Claiborne, appointed governor of the newly American Territory of Orleans, faced perhaps the largest quandary of his life.[2] This quandary, which Robertson alludes to in the letter excerpt in the epigraph, was multifaceted and would require that the Anglo-Americans adjust their expectations of what an American territory should look like racially and culturally. First, the newcomers included enslaved blacks whom most whites feared, assuming they carried the revolutionary fervor of St. Domingue with them. Second, all of the ships' inhabitants were French speaking and overwhelmingly Catholic—this would reinforce the Territory's already existing French language and culture and stall the efforts of Anglo-Americanization. This was of particular concern because the Americans had only just bought the Territory from the French six years earlier—the process of Americanization had not yet had time to take root. Third, the ships contained a large group of free people of color, a troubling intermediary group that did not fit well into the two-tiered racial system of the Anglo-Americans. This two-tiered system recognized black—usually enslaved—and white, little or nothing in between. Finally, by the time the 1809 exodus came to an end in 1810, the refugees would have nearly doubled the population of New Orleans. The result of this migration was a reinforcement of Louisiana's Latin/Caribbean racial system and a decades-long delay in the solidification of Anglo-American racial practices.

This book traces the nineteenth-century St. Domingue/Haiti to Louisiana migration case over the course of two hundred years to examine how the layering and relayering of racial systems created a palimpsest that transformed everyday life in southern Louisiana. A *palimpsest* is created when a new layer of writing or painting is placed on top of a preexisting layer. A *racial palimpsest* occurs when a preexisting racial system is almost fully eclipsed by a new racial system that comes into place as a population that lives according to a different racial logic begins to numerically or administratively dominate a region.

With any kind of palimpsest, traces of the original layer continue to be visible beneath what is superimposed on top. This is what occurred in nineteenth-century Louisiana. The Latin/Caribbean triracial system of French and Spanish Louisiana was challenged by the binary Anglo-American system that began to establish itself after the Louisiana Purchase of 1803. Then before the Anglo layer could become fully entrenched, the Latin/Caribbean system native to Louisiana was reinforced by the large influx of St. Domingue refugees in 1809 and 1810. Finally, over the course of the nineteenth century and into the twentieth, the Anglo system came to dominate as the Anglo-American population grew and their racial practices asserted increased pressure on the Latin/Caribbean system. But while the Latin/Caribbean racial system was weakened, it held strong for decades longer than would have been likely without the St. Domingue refugee influx, and even today traces of its influence are still visible in the lives of southern Louisiana's people.

The establishment of a racial palimpsest disrupted earlier, taken-for-granted understandings of race in Louisiana and imposed new social and political challenges and opportunities for those living under its influence.

As we travel across these two centuries and examine the ways white and black refugees and their descendants negotiated these changes, we begin to understand how living under the influence of this palimpsest has shaped racial categories, identities, and opportunities in Louisiana in ways that ricochet from the nineteenth century into the present.

This book aims to do much more, however, than tell the story of racial change in one US region. For the more we learn of the history and influence of the racial palimpsest in Louisiana, the more we see that similar processes are at work in other regions of the country that have recently experienced a large influx of immigrants from Latin America and the Caribbean. At the top of this list are Miami, New York, and Los Angeles, three areas that have received many immigrants from these areas over the last fifty years. Although many analysts have intensively studied these cities with an eye to understanding how processes of integration are unfolding there and how immigrants and locals are adapting to the new normal of racial and cultural mixture, none have compared these recent migrations with the case of St. Domingue/Haiti migration to Louisiana—perhaps the only historical US case that closely mirrors these contemporary experiences where large numbers of people of color from Latin America and the Caribbean settle into US American cities. Instead, sociologists of race and migration either explicitly or implicitly use the experience of European immigrants as points of comparison when assessing contemporary immigrants' experiences with racial and cultural integration.[3] This reliance comes from the strong influence of classic assimilation theory, which emerged from theoretical reflection on the integration experiences of European immigrants.

This reliance on the experience of European newcomers is problematic, however, because those migrations posed very different issues than do the current migrations of people of color from across the Americas. Although it is true that many European immigrants had to endure discrimination and struggled to become "white," it is also the case that their lighter skin color eased their gradual transition into whiteness.[4] This is an advantage that many current immigrants of color do not have. For this reason, the experiences of European immigrants from the past yield limited benefits when used as a reference point for understanding the social and political complexities of current migrations.

In response to the inadequacies of the assimilation framework and its foundation in the experience of light-skinned European immigrants, an increasing number of scholars are calling for the explicit racialization of immigration study.[5] Saenz and Douglas, for instance, call for more scholars to develop a "counternarrative to immigration analysis that disproportionately focuses on the experiences of European immigrants."[6] The call for racialization is a call to place the process of racial formation, the negotiation of racial boundaries, and the realities of racism at the center of our understanding of immigrants' experiences. This is in contrast to assimilation theorists for whom the study of racial inequality remains at the sidelines of inquiry on immigrants' integration.[7] This sidelining of race is understandable when we consider that the intellectual foundations of assimilation theory are rooted in the experience of light-skinned European immigrants. But when we decenter the experience of European immigrants, and instead pay renewed attention to the historical experiences of immigrants of color, the salience of race and racialization becomes clear. This is the benefit of examining what Saenz and Douglas call "less told historiographies."

But to incorporate these submerged historiographies, we must be aware of them. The near absence from the sociological literature of nineteenth- and early twentieth-century migration cases featuring large numbers of people of color has meant that the major analytical tools used to understand the integration of today's immigrants of color continue to be rooted in the quite different experience of European immigrants in the United States. The unique and understudied experience of the St. Domingue/Haiti refugees of color that is featured in *American Routes* fills a significant gap in our repertoire of historical immigration case studies that include large numbers of voluntary nonwhite immigrants. Furthermore, because the racial palimpsest concept was developed from a historical case study that more closely resembles contemporary social contexts—areas with large numbers of immigrants of color from across the Americas—it provides new and more relevant analytical lenses for understanding the short- and long-term implications of this kind of migration experience.

The argument to be made for using Louisiana as a historical touchstone for thinking through current issues surrounding immigration, race, and cultural difference in the United States is bolstered when we consider what the immigration picture looks like today. Fifty-three percent of immigrants to the United States have come from Latin America and the Caribbean.[8] In ways similar to what occurred in Louisiana's early nineteenth-century migrations, today's immigrants come with racial and cultural understandings that are quite different from what is found in much of the United States.[9] In addition, the earlier Louisiana immigrants also tended to cluster in the large urban area of their time: New Orleans. We see a similar kind of clustering among today's immigrants. Recent immigrants tend to be concentrated in certain states: California has 25.8 percent of immigrants, Texas 14.2 percent, Florida 13 percent, and New York 10.2 percent.[10] These are the states where the encounter between local and immigrant racial and cultural understandings is likely to be most intense. These issues are further intensified when we look at the city level. In Los Angeles 38.8 percent of all residents are foreign born and in Miami the figure is 51.3 percent.[11] Many of the immigrants in both areas are from Latin America or the Caribbean. The numbers here sketch an immigration portrait that has many resonances with what occurred in late eighteenth- and early nineteenth-century Louisiana—in each case, a racial palimpsest emerged that reshaped racial categories, identities, and opportunities.

The early nineteenth-century influx of St. Domingue refugees significantly bolstered Louisiana's foundational Latin/Caribbean racial system. Then, over the course of two hundred years, the Anglo-American racial system gained steady ground and gradually came to dominate the area. The resulting racial palimpsest created a situation where both the Anglo and Latin systems shaped everyday life, but with varying levels of strength and influence as the Anglo system strengthened and the Latin system weakened. The key point, however, is that the Latin system never completely died out and, indeed, aspects of it are still alive and well in twenty-first-century Louisiana. Similarly, in cities and regions characterized by a layering of racial systems today, we would expect that as immigrants from Latin America help to usher in racial practices more in keeping with a Latin/Caribbean approach to race, the foundational Anglo-American racial framework might weaken, but it will continue to exert its influence for generations to come. In this sense, the creation of a racial palimpsest does not spell radical transformation, but rather the emergence of a more complex sociopolitical system in the areas where a palimpsest does emerge. This more complex system will have significant implications for racial identification, racial classification, and for our understandings of how to identify and eradicate the structural and cultural roots of racism.

Because the racial palimpsest approach is rooted in a historical case study that includes people of color whose integration experiences we can follow over the course of two hundred years, its insights lead to ways of thinking about transformations in the US racial system that are quite different from what is common in current social science research. Within this literature, many scholars are debating whether or not the black/white color line is transitioning to become black/nonblack or triracial.[12] The underlying assumption in this work is that the traditional black/white binary is being replaced by a new system.

The St. Domingue-Louisiana case study will, however, demonstrate a more complex reality which will show that more than one racial system can operate at a time and that the strategic use of alternative racial logics varies by race. In the St. Domingue case, whereas white refugees and their descendants conformed to the Anglo-American binary system, becoming "white" in the traditional Anglo-American manner, those of color strategically held onto the tenets and logic of the weakened Latin/Caribbean system as a buffer against the extremes of the binary Anglo-American system. Their insistence on holding to this alternative racial logic bolsters studies that find that today's immigrants from Latin America and the Caribbean are resisting assimilation into Anglo-American racial categories that they find to be ill-fitting and/or disadvantageous.[13] Instead of such assimilation, we are likely to see that the layered racial terrain of palimpsest regions will allow for greater flexibility in racial classification and will provide for new forms of racial identification out of step with the traditional binary system of the United States. Thus, when we consider contemporary racial dynamics in areas with large Latin and Caribbean immigrant populations, our focus should be on how people will negotiate the logics of two simultaneously existing and layered racial systems, rather than on debating what the "new" color line will be. This room for flexibility and negotiation should not, however, lead us to the premature conclusion that racial inequality and the structural significance of race will attenuate. Instead, what we will learn from the fate of the St. Domingue refugees of color and their descendants will continually demonstrate the disadvantageous significance of race.

To begin to understand the social and political tensions between Anglo and Latin/Caribbean approaches to race, we need a basic understanding of how Anglo-Americans and persons of Latin/Caribbean origin in nineteenth-century Louisiana engaged in different kinds of racial and cultural practices. As we begin to understand the differences, it becomes clearer how and why a large influx of French-allied Caribbean refugees was of such great concern to US-born Anglo-Americans striving to govern their new Louisiana territory.

THE COMPLEXITIES OF RACE, CULTURE, AND INTEGRATION IN NINETEENTH-CENTURY LOUISIANA

Louisiana received several waves of refugees who fled the revolution in the French colony of St. Domingue. The revolution began in 1791 and ended with the establishment of an independent Haiti in 1804. Many of these refugees fled to surrounding colonies, including Jamaica to the southwest and Cuba to the west. Those who fled to Cuba settled there and established new businesses and plantations. All too soon, however, they were forced to flee again as a result of political tensions between France and Spain. These tensions arose when Napoleon Bonaparte placed his brother on the

Spanish throne and plunged France into a brutal war with Spain. For the French-identified St. Domingue refugees, this meant that their welcome in Spanish Cuba had worn out. As they sought a place to go quickly, many set their sights on Louisiana with its French colonial and cultural heritage.

Between 1809 and 1810, nearly ten thousand St. Domingue refugees fled Cuba and went to New Orleans, Louisiana. To get a sense of how upsetting this migration was for many in Louisiana, we must set the migration into demographic context. First, consider the figures on Table I.1, which provide total population numbers for Orleans Parish in 1806.[14] The 17,001 total is for urban New Orleans combined with surrounding areas. The urban population of New Orleans proper, however, was only about ten thousand in number. This is significant because the vast majority of the 9,059 immigrants who fled to Louisiana from 1809 to 1810 settled in urban New Orleans. This means that the city's population was nearly doubled by the migration.

In addition to the sheer increase in numbers, the migration had great racial and cultural significance. The area had just been bought from France in 1803, part of the historic Louisiana Purchase. Anglo-Americans had taken over the administration of the territory and were preparing it for statehood. In addition to providing political preparation, the Anglo-Americans were also interested in culturally Anglicizing Louisiana. This process had scarcely gotten underway when the virtual flood of refugees arrived in 1809. While this threw a wrench into the cultural project of Americanization, the racial implications were even more disturbing for white Louisianans: two-thirds of the new residents were people of African descent. Included among them was the socially ambiguous and politically problematic category of free people of color. This was an in-between racial grouping that did not have a clear parallel in the Anglo-American US experience.[15] The free people of color from St. Domingue were often well educated, cultured, wealthy, and in some cases had slaves of their own. Anglo-Americans did not know quite what to make of them but were certainly not comfortable with their increased presence. As Table I.1 shows, the population of free people of color in New Orleans was more than doubled by the 1809–1810 migration.

Table I.1 ST. DOMINGUE REFUGEE IMPACT ON NEW ORLEANS

	Whites	FPC	Slaves	Total
Orleans Parish, 1806	6,311	2,312	8,378	17,001 (urban ~10K)
Refugees, 1809	2,731	3,102	3,226	9,059
Orleans Parish, 1810	8,001	5,727	10,824	24,552

FPC, free people of color.

This demographic onslaught, with its reinforcement of the French and Catholic presence in Louisiana, expressed itself as a conflict between Creoles—those native to Louisiana—and Americans. Because the term "Creole" has a somewhat complex and often contentious history, it is helpful to distinguish between its ethnic-cultural and racial-structural dimensions. The ethnic-cultural dimension of Creole is best described as including peoples or cultures present in Louisiana before the Louisiana Purchase of 1803. These peoples and cultures were shaped by the French and the Spanish and would have been described as "Creole" rather than "American" in early-nineteenth-century Louisiana. When I say "American," I am referring to the people and cultures that fit within the Anglo social and cultural framework of nineteenth-century Louisiana. Although the St. Domingue refugees technically entered Louisiana after the Purchase, they had strong social and cultural affinities with the Louisiana Creoles who were there before the Purchase, and by the 1850s they had effectively dissolved into this larger Creole community.

Differences in the ethnic-cultural practices of Creoles and Americans are illustrated by their conflicting approaches to New Orleans' Congo Square. Figure I.1 is a sketch of Africans dancing in Congo Square.[16] This was an area where free and enslaved blacks would congregate to sell garden crops or other wares, as well as to dance and play the drums. Because Louisiana was a relatively poor colony, owners allowed their slaves some freedom to move around in order to provide for themselves economically. But this mobility also allowed enslaved persons to maintain cultural practices that would likely have died out were they under more intense supervision. When the Americans began streaming into Louisiana, they were flummoxed by the license Creole slaves were given. In his article on Congo Square, Jerah Johnson describes the reaction of traveler Benjamin Latrobe:

> Benjamin Latrobe's reaction was typical ... he betrayed his amazement and apprehension at the sight of five or six hundred unsupervised slaves assembled for dancing when he added, in a tone of relief, "there was not the least disorder among the crowd, nor do I learn on enquiry, that these weekly meetings of negroes have ever produced any mischief."[17]

Latrobe and others were also greatly troubled by the cultural practices of French-speaking Catholics. In another passage from his Congo Square essay, Johnson describes the reactions of English-speaking Protestant Americans:

THE BAMBOULA.

Figure I.1 The dances in Congo Square.

They had never seen anything like it ... the way French, Catholic New Orleans observed the Sabbath. After going to mass on Sunday morning, the Creoles made the rest of the day a festival, indulging themselves in public entertainments, going on outings and excursions, enjoying picnics and barbecues, shopping the street markets, and, on Sunday evenings, drinking and dancing. It struck the newcomers, mostly Anglo-Protestants accustomed to taking Sundays as days of grim abstinence and pious reflection, as near blasphemy.[18]

These cultural differences were compounded by different ways of organizing race. The racial-structural dimension of "Creole" refers to the ways Creoles' racial practices differed from those of Anglo-Americans. First, both native Louisiana Creoles and the St. Domingue immigrants who merged into the community were accustomed to a triracial system that included whites, free people of color, and blacks. In addition, both St. Domingue immigrants and Louisiana Creoles were more public in the crossing of racial lines in their social lives and intimate relationships. This meant that many whites were relatively open about their relationships with people of color in ways that would have been shocking for the typical Anglo-American. In addition, the Americans were unused to the relatively large and sometimes armed population of people of African descent who were not only free but also enjoyed high social status. White Creoles, in contrast, were accustomed to being surrounded by free people of color who were in positions of wealth and power.[19]

Over the course of the nineteenth century, the meaning of "Creole" has changed in significant ways and it is common for the ethnic-cultural and racial-structural dimensions to be confused in the popular imagination. For many outsiders to the community, the racial-structural understanding of Creole assumes racial mixture and thus nonwhiteness. This is the reason white Creoles were gradually forced to relinquish the identifier "Creole" so they could be accepted as unequivocally "white" according to the logic of the Anglo-American binary system. This relinquishing was part of an extended struggle that resulted in the changing definition of "Creole" over the course of the nineteenth century. When discussion in future chapters tracks these changes, we will signal whether and how the ethnic-cultural or racial-structural dimensions are at issue.

So, how did Creoles negotiate the very different racial and cultural frameworks they found in the newly Anglo-American Louisiana region? And what can we learn from the triumphs and challenges of this early group of immigrants that is of use in helping us to think through the challenges faced by today's black, white, and mixed-race newcomers and their descendants? In the first part of the book, we will glean our lessons from Louisiana by probing the experience of the nineteenth-century refugees. Once we have a foundation for understanding the past, we will fast-forward to the present, examining the ways descendants living today continue to be touched by racial and cultural tensions of integration from the past. Finally, we will consider the lessons the Louisiana case holds for us as we welcome new waves of immigrants of color from Latin America and the Caribbean. The following section provides a discussion of how this project came to be and outlines the methods used to produce the story that unfolds in the rest of the book.

AT THE MOUTH OF THE RIVER: HOW HISTORY, MEMORY, AND STORY FLOWED TOGETHER TO CREATE *AMERICAN ROUTES*

New Orleans is a place of characters, stories, and memories that are variously exhilarating, cautionary, and inspiring. When I moved here in the summer of 2003, the chair of my department casually suggested that I might want to explore the city's connections to Haiti since my most recent work had to do with immigrants coming from that country.[20] His suggestion was well timed as I had arrived in the city right at the bicentennial of the Louisiana Purchase. In 1803, Anglo-American US leaders struck an unbelievably sweet bargain with Napoleon Bonaparte and bought the large swath of land that now constitutes a good part of the present-day United States. The bargain was struck in large part because Napoleon was so desperately losing the revolutionary war being waged in his most profitable colony, St. Domingue. That year, following the battle at Vertières, the revolutionaries declared victory, named the newly independent country Haiti, and celebrated their independence on January 1, 1804.

As I came to know New Orleans during that 2003–2004 academic year, the suggestion that I look into the connections between Haiti and Louisiana continued to take root in my mind. I began to learn about the region's Creole community—many of whom, I was told, were likely to have ancestry going back to St. Domingue/Haiti. At that point, my experience was limited to Creoles of color. I learned about some Creole heritage groups and got approval from the institutional review board to do preliminary research starting with an online Creole heritage discussion group. I went from this to doing an online survey of the group and then completed in-depth interviews with a subset of the members. This preliminary work helped me to ease into what was, for me, the new world of Louisiana Creoles. By the beginning of 2005, I was becoming well acquainted with some of the pressing issues and debates occurring within Creole of color communities concerning race, culture, identity, and positioning vis-à-vis Anglo–African

Americans.[21] At the same time, I confirmed that many Creoles of color do have ancestry going back to St. Domingue/Haiti. Indeed, given the doubling of the New Orleans population following the influx of St. Domingue refugees in 1809–1810, it would be likely that most native New Orleanians—whether white or of African descent—have some ancestors going back to that French-speaking colony if their families have been in the area for many generations.

The Creoles of color I spoke with were interested in Haiti, curious to know more about their ancestors' origins, and I initially had in mind a study examining how they thought about and identified with this history and memory. But then in the spring of 2005, I learned about an intriguing organization called the St. Domingue Special Interest Group (SIG)—a subset of the Jefferson Genealogical Society. The people attending SIG meetings are mainly white, and all of them have ancestors they can trace back—often with voluminous documentation—to revolutionary St. Domingue. I was attending my second SIG meeting and sitting next to a sweet older woman named Mary Anne de Boisblanc. Mary Anne was a painter, and she was intensely attuned to her family's St. Domingue and early Louisiana history. I had just settled down to learn more about the group when Mary Anne made an extraordinary comment that forever changed the trajectory of the project. She told the group a heartfelt story about how her ancestor had been killed by Toussaint L'Ouverture. She was visibly upset as she told the story. Then, recovering, she explained that she had written a letter to L'Ouverture expressing her feelings about the bloodshed of the revolution, apologizing for her ancestors' slave ownership, and forgiving him for killing her forbears. I was, quite honestly, speechless. But as her story sank in, I realized that I had to broaden my project to incorporate white Louisianans, including the SIG members who—like their counterparts of African descent—also knew of and were intrigued by their family connection to this former French colony whose revolution had transformed the Atlantic world.

I was just solidifying my grip on this new project when Hurricane Katrina struck on August 29, 2005. I and my potential research participants were scattered across the country for several months. But New Orleanians have an indomitable spirit. By February of 2006, I and many of those I was to interview had returned and I met some of them at the Historic New Orleans Collection's "Common Routes" symposium, which was dedicated to examining the role of the St. Domingue refugees in shaping the newly Anglo-American territory of Louisiana. I was able to recruit many research participants at that symposium and used those interviewees to find others who were not at the symposium.

Over the course of three years, I carried out participant observation with the Creole of color group LA Creole and with the St. Domingue SIG. Attending meetings and events and getting to know members of both groups helped me to better understand the cultural distinctions between Creoles of color and Anglo-blacks, and helped me begin to understand why white Louisianans have, for the most part, stopped calling themselves Creole. White Louisianans told stories of how they or their older family members struggled to make Anglo-Americans understand that one could be both white and Creole. And Creoles of color struggled to identify with their unique history and culture without offending Anglo–African Americans who felt that this group was trying to avoid being identified as "black." At issue in both cases is the fact that the category "Creole," inherited from French and Spanish–controlled Louisiana, is rooted in Latin/Caribbean racial and cultural understandings that are in conflict with Anglo-American assumptions.

The racial-structural dimension of Creole identification was traditionally rooted in a Latin/Caribbean approach to race where public social interaction between whites and people of color was relatively common, and where the triracial system provided at least two separate categories for persons of African descent. Creole ways of thinking about race thus have much in common with a Latin/Caribbean understanding where appearance rather than "purity" of blood determines whiteness, and where a mixture of appearance and status determines various ways of categorizing blackness. Historical and contemporary Creoles' dissonant experiences with race and cultural identity resonated with what I knew of current immigrants of color from Latin America and the Caribbean who express similar kinds of frustration with a US racial system that clashes with their own characterization of themselves.

In addition to the participant observation, I completed fifty-six in-depth interviews. These interviews are divided into two categories. The first is a group of forty white and black respondents who were researching their family ties back to St. Domingue/Haiti. Of these forty interviewees, nineteen were white and twenty-one were of African descent. Because of the nature of racial inequality and the particular ways this inequality is reflected in historical documents, my white interviewees who were researching their connection to St. Domingue/Haiti generally had much more substantial documentation of this connection than did those of color. In some cases, participants of color did have a good deal of documentation, whereas in others, no written documentation had yet been identified, but there was family oral history connecting the respondent's ancestry to St. Domingue.

The second group of interviews is a supplementary collection of sixteen oral histories—nine with Creoles of color and seven with white Creoles—who do not necessarily have St. Domingue/Haiti heritage but whose ancestors struggled with the strictures of the Anglo-American racial system in the same ways as St. Domingue refugees and their descendants. Because the St. Domingue refugees blended into the larger Creole community by the 1850s, it was important to develop an understanding of the Creole population's struggles with Anglo-Americanization. This attention to Creoles' experiences vis-à-vis Anglo-Americans was necessary in order to track evolutions in the social and political effects of Louisiana's layered racial systems from the nineteenth century to the present.

The supplementary interviews with white Creoles were particularly important because most of the white St. Domingue/Haiti descendant interviewees came from families that had become so integrated into Anglo racial and cultural norms that they had no memory of their family's Creole heritage and no experience of the clash between Latin/Caribbean and Anglo-American racial assumptions. They were—depending on one's perspective—the beneficiaries or victims of Anglo-American assimilation that chipped away at Creole identification over the course of the nineteenth century. And yet understanding the white Creole experience and how it has interfaced with the US system of race and ethnicity was crucial to understanding the complexities of racial and cultural integration over the last two hundred years in this region of south Louisiana. The seven oral history interviewees were selected specifically because they had held on to their Creole identification.[22]

These oral histories supplemented the interview accounts of white St. Domingue descendants who held on to their Creole heritage and provided the important and underrepresented perspective of white Louisianans whose families did *not* fully assimilate. Their families' resistance to assimilative forces meant that they had to grapple with Anglo-American misunderstandings of the ethnic-cultural and racial-structural dimensions of Creole identity. The St. Domingue/Haiti interviewees of color differed from the white respondents in that most persons of color in the study identified as Creole or came from Creole families. The nine supplementary oral histories with Creoles of color were included because those interviews provided a deeper understanding of how many Creoles of color have struggled with the logic of the Anglo-American racial system and attempted to use the existence of overlapping racial systems to their advantage when possible.

All interviews included filling in an extensive family tree as far back as possible. Where the documentation was particularly good, interviews were followed by trips to various archival sites in New Orleans where I was able to learn more about participants' ancestors by reading through letters, baptismal certificates, newspaper articles, obituaries, and so on. Overall, the combination of participant observation, in-depth interviews, oral histories, and archival work has provided a wonderful comparative and multi-generational portrait of how the struggle for racial and cultural integration has unfolded over the past two hundred years in south Louisiana.[23] The concluding section provides a brief outline of the book.

THE DISCUSSION TO FOLLOW

In this opening chapter we have had a brief introduction to the St. Domingue/Haiti-Louisiana migration case and have begun to consider how it helps us to think through the complexities of racial and cultural integration today. Chapter 1 provides an in-depth introduction to the Anglo-American and Latin/Caribbean racial systems—the two layers of the racial palimpsest that exists in southern Louisiana. The conceptualization of these two racial systems emerges from an in-depth, comparative analysis of the ways racial categories and practices changed over time in the United States and across the Americas. This discussion lays the conceptual foundation for the racial palimpsest concept, which is then applied to material in the chapters that follow.

The second chapter provides an in-depth look at the historical context of revolutionary St. Domingue and examines the ways refugees' experiences there shaped the understandings of race, politics, and culture that they brought with them to the United States. This background helps us to understand how the refugees and their descendants would have experienced the new racial and cultural context they found in Louisiana.

Chapter 3 follows white St. Domingue refugees as they integrate into Louisiana's white Creole community and struggle against the tide of Anglo-Americanization during the nineteenth century. The St. Domingue refugees had a great deal in common with white Creoles native to Louisiana. As the refugees blended into the Creole community, they felt the consequences of the racial and cultural assumptions Anglo-Americans made about Creoles. The most damaging of these was the suspicion that—because of their higher tolerance for publicly acknowledged interracial relationships—all Creoles, whether they appeared to be white or not, were really racially mixed. This racial handicap became particularly dangerous after the fall of Reconstruction and the rise of Jim Crow. At that point, identifying as Creole became a serious social liability for white Louisianans. This chapter explains how and why most white Creoles eventually let go of their Creole identity and blended into Louisiana's white Anglo-American community.

In Chapter 4 we examine the experience of St. Domingue refugees of color across the nineteenth and twentieth centuries. We focus on the experience of refugees and their descendants who were free people of color. Like their white counterparts, members of this group also integrated into Louisiana's already existing Creole community. Their French-speaking, Catholic background and free status contrasted greatly with that of Anglo-blacks who were English speaking, Protestant, and more likely to be enslaved. This variation in background led to enduring differences between Creole- and Anglo- blacks in Louisiana, so much so that one prominent Creole of color of that era—Rodolphe Lucien Desdunes—wrote a public letter to W. E. B. DuBois comparing what he called the Latin Negro to the Anglo-Negro.[24] We examine this group's struggle across the nineteenth century to position themselves with respect to Anglo–African Americans. As was the case with white Creoles, Creoles of color faced intense pressure with the rise of Jim Crow to take a stand on one side or the other of the starkly drawn black/white border.

Although they were officially categorized with black Anglo-Americans, Creoles of color in the late nineteenth and early twentieth centuries continued in many ways to operate according to a Latinized racial system that allowed them to differentiate themselves socially from Anglo-blacks. Many were able to maintain their own Creole of color social institutions in the form of schools, churches, and social clubs. These social institutions were important resources because many of the Creoles who founded and frequented them were descended from free people of color who had been free—and often well educated—for generations. In this way, they were able to place something of a buffer between themselves and the worst of Jim Crow oppression. Thus, in contrast to the white Creoles examined in Chapter 3 who blended into white Anglo-American society, many Creoles of color saw a benefit in preserving their Creole identity because it provided a way of resisting the degrading racial effects of the Anglo-American racial system.

Next in Chapter 5 we fast-forward to the experience of white Creoles in the twentieth and twenty-first centuries where many have blended into the mainstream white Louisiana community. For this group, the Anglo-American racial system overpowered the Latinized system known to their ancestors. This Anglo-American triumph has, however, come at tremendous social and cultural cost. Most white Louisianans fully lost the connection to their Creole identity. Some, however, were able to hold on to it, and others are beginning to rediscover it. Even in these cases, however, the racial cloud of Anglo-American assumptions about Creoles' racial impurity continues to hang over them so that few would call themselves Creole unless they were with others who understood exactly what they meant. These stories emerge from rich interview data with white St. Domingue/Haiti descendants and from oral histories with white Creoles.

In Chapter 6, we compare the contemporary experience of white Creoles to that of Creoles of African descent. Whereas Creoles of color were slower than whites to adopt an Anglo-American approach to race, changing conceptions of blackness during and after the Civil Rights and Black Power movements challenged Creole identity and made it more difficult for some Creoles of color to see themselves as distinct from other black Americans. This changing political landscape also led many Creoles of color to take a more critical stance toward issues of color, class, and inequality within black communities in the United States, and to identify themselves as black. We explore these tensions by examining the stories of Creoles of color as gathered from interviews and participant observation with Creole cultural organizations. In effect, compared to white Creoles, it took nearly one hundred more years for the logic of the Anglo-American racial system to significantly weaken the hold of the Latinized system under which they had operated. Even so, Creole identification among many of African descent continues to remain strong today and has been reinforced by the creation of new online and place-based Creole of color organizations that have established themselves within the last ten years. What has also remained, however, are underlying tensions between Anglo–African Americans and Creoles. Part of the reason for this has to do with the former's sense that Creoles of color try to distance themselves from the US experience and category of blackness. The chapter concludes by considering similarities between Louisiana's Creoles of color and Latino immigrants of color who have experienced many of the same tensions and misunderstandings as they have struggled with Anglo-American conceptions of blackness.

In the final chapter we bring together the threads of the previous discussion and consider what we can learn from Louisiana's past that is of use as we address our contemporary experience with migration from Latin America and the Caribbean. Here we will see that the current experience of Latinos bears many similarities to that of the St. Domingue refugees and their Creole descendants in Louisiana. From here, we consider the analytic contributions of the racial palimpsest concept for scholars who are studying the integration of immigrants of color and attempting to understand how they and their descendants are likely to fare over the next several decades. As we reflect on the different experiences of white and black St. Domingue/Haiti descendants and consider the ways current immigrants' experiences mirror them, the discussion reaffirms the importance of resuscitating alternative historiographies of people of color and of moving away from reliance on analytical tools originally developed to make sense of the situation of European immigrants. Finally, after considering the implications of the book for the ways we study immigration, we conclude by drawing some practical lessons for working toward greater racial equality within areas characterized by layered racial systems that contain alternative social and political logics.

CHAPTER 1

⚜

Racial Systems and the Racial Palimpsest

[Maria] Martins ... [is] a Brazilian who, for 30 years before immigrating to the United States, looked in the mirror and saw a morena—a woman with caramel-colored skin that is nearly equated with whiteness in Brazil and some other Latin American countries. "I didn't realize I was black until I came here," she said.

Jose Neinstein, a native white Brazilian ... boiled it down to the simplest terms ... "In this country [the United States]," he said, "if you are not quite white, then you are black." But in Brazil, he said, "If you are not quite black, then you are white."

Maria and Jose's experiences with race in the United States help to demonstrate the social reality of living under the influence and rules of quite different racial systems.[1] Given the disadvantages still associated with being black, Maria's discovery that she is perceived as black in the United States must have come as quite a shock. Her "transition" to blackness nicely illustrates Jose's explanation that a person who is "not quite white" may be categorized as black by the rules of the US racial system.

A *racial system* is a collection of formal and informal rules that order the ways color, phenotype, and status are "read" from individuals' bodies in a way that places them higher or lower in the social hierarchy which apportions resources and opportunities. In addition, a racial system provides formal or informal rules about how, if, and under what circumstances persons from different racial categories interact with each other. Finally, a racial system may fix these categories as flexible or firm. In the case of the former, an individual may change categories with relative ease, whereas in the latter, racial categories are generally fixed. As we will see, the Latin/Caribbean and Anglo-American racial systems provide very different approaches to each of these dimensions of race.

Whereas Maria's experience and Jose's insights help to highlight differences between racial systems in the United States and Brazil, the rest of this chapter will go further to argue that the rules of racial systems across a large swath of Latin America and the Caribbean are similar enough to each other in their major characteristics to constitute what I call a Latin/Caribbean racial system. When compared to the United States, the rules for racial categorization are so different in these regions that they make a distinctive contrast to the racial system that holds sway in the United States. I describe this US-based system as the "Anglo-American racial system," and though its influence was less uniformly in force in southern Louisiana than in other parts of the country, it has, for the most part, been the dominant racial system in the United States.

It is important to note at the outset that the Latin/Caribbean system described in this chapter applies most seamlessly to parts of the Americas that are similar to the United States in that the majority of the population consists of black, white, and some mixture in between. This includes countries such as Cuba, Haiti, the Dominican Republic, Argentina, Venezuela, Brazil, and the US territory of Puerto Rico, among others. The composite Latin/Caribbean system proposed here is a looser, though still relevant, fit for parts of Central and South America where there are very heavy indigenous populations such as Bolivia or Guatemala. Though the fit is looser, however, it is still relevant in that these countries are characterized by much less rigid understandings of whiteness and blackness, and by less clearly drawn color lines than is the case in the United States. The United States is truly an outlier in the severity and rigidity of its largely two-tiered, binary system of categorization and identification.

The argument concerning the existence and social significance of the Latin/Caribbean and Anglo-American racial systems is developed in two steps in the sections that follow. First, we put both racial systems into historical context by examining their emergence and transformation over several centuries.[2] Elites in both Latin America and the United States began with similar aspirations of keeping tight boundaries around the borders of whiteness and harbored similar hopes of creating majority white nations. They also began with similar tendencies toward limiting the population of free people of African descent and of equating blackness with enslavement. Racial systems in the two regions began to diverge, however, as social and demographic realities pushed elites in many Latin American and Caribbean countries to reevaluate the feasibility of strictly policing the borders of whiteness and encouraged transition toward a new strategy of valorizing the positive effects of racial mixture. Meanwhile, the United States with its larger white majority had a brief period of relative flexibility in racial categorization but ultimately held firm in cultivating an ever-stricter color line.

In addition to demographic differences that set the United States apart from other regions in the Americas, the influence of different legal systems would also result in differences between American societies' abilities to limit the population of free people of color and to equate having African blood with enslavement. The existence of the legal instrument *coartacíon* in Spanish-controlled colonies, for instance, allowed enslaved persons to buy their way of out slavery even against the will of their owners. Access to this option significantly increased the number and political power of free people of color in Spanish territories and made it less feasible to equate having African blood with enslavement—this in direct contrast to the United States, which had no comparable legal instrument and had a comparatively small population of free people of color. By the beginning of the twentieth century, the United States would triumph over other American regions in preserving a strict color line that limited the entrée into whiteness and expanded the boundaries of blackness to include nearly everyone with African lineage. This triumph in holding the color line culminated in the rise of Jim Crow segregation by the late nineteenth century.

After sketching this historical portrait, the second section of the chapter brings this historical work into dialogue with comparative sociological research on American racial systems and provides an outline of the major characteristics of the Anglo-American and Latin/Caribbean racial systems that are the building blocks of the racial palimpsest concept.

CHASING THE DREAM OF A "WHITE" AMERICA

Whiteness—its purity, its protection, and its deliberate cultivation—motivated the racial strategies of many colonial American elites. Initially, many Latin American elites brought with them to the Americas the principle of restricting full membership rights to those who could demonstrate "limpieza de sangre"—blood clear of racial taint from nonwhite ancestry. As Loveman notes: "the most consequential legal and social divide was between those with *limpieza de sangre*, on the one hand, and would-be risers and other castas afflicted with the 'stain' of impurity."[3]

Although the vision of *limpieza de sangre* or "pure" whiteness was more easily realized in the largely European-descended population of the United

States, and much harder to achieve with Latin America's more heavily African and indigenous populations, in both cases the supremacy of whiteness remained an unassailable ideal despite differences in how it was ultimately defined. Charles Mills nicely describes the cross-national flexibility of whiteness when he explains that persons are "designated by (shifting) 'racial' (phenotypical/ genealogical/ cultural) criteria ... as 'white' and coextensive ... with the class of full persons."[4] This definition allows for who is counted as white to change over time within one place and to vary in the same time period across places, while holding constant the understanding that, in all of its guises, whiteness bestows on its members exclusive access to full membership rights in a given society.[5]

But before demographic realities set in, elites in Latin America and the Caribbean expressed a clear desire to keep white blood "pure" by limiting miscegenation and/or by increasing the whiteness of their populations through European migration. José Antonio Saco of Cuba starkly described the stakes of the racial situation in that colony when he wrote in 1858 that mass immigration of Europeans was necessary in order to:

> neutralize to a certain degree, the terrible influence of the three million Negroes surrounding us, millions that keep on multiplying, and that may swallow us up in the not too distant future if we remain idle.[6]

Saco's voice was joined by many other leaders who lamented the darkness of their populations and who sought immigrants to whiten their colonies. Loveman notes that when the 1899 census in Cuba showed that the colony was one-third black and mulatto, the results elicited public demand for more European immigration—the most effective strategy whites could imagine for overcoming the seemingly catastrophic results of the encroaching blackness that surrounded them.[7]

The desire to protect the boundaries of whiteness was imperiled not only by demography but also by international differences in the understanding of *who* was white. In his book *Race in Another America*, Edward Telles describes the fallout of these international differences as Brazilian elites came to understand just how different their whiteness was compared to that of their European and North American counterparts. In general, Brazilian leaders shared key assumptions with North American and European intellectuals about the superiority of whiteness. They got more than they bargained for, however, when they called on international consultants to help them in crafting strategies concerning race and racial categorization. Telles describes, for instance, how Arthur Compte de Gobineau—an outside consultant to Brazil—brought his obsession with white racial purity to the colony in a way that threatened the local elite. Gobineau, who wrote *L'Essai sur l'Inégalités des Races Humaines* in 1856, was a vocal white supremacist who believed strongly in the inferiority of non-whites. Although Brazilian leaders shared his views, they were perturbed when he accused many elites themselves of being racially mixed. It quickly became clear that the Brazilian elite's understanding of whiteness clashed irreconcilably with Gobineau's.[8]

Later on, Telles relates another example that suggests ambivalence around how to draw boundaries based on color and social status. He describes the work of an official named Rodrigues who made proposals for defining and clarifying Brazil's racial categories. Rather than creating one "mulatto" category, he proposed creating subdivisions of superior, ordinary, and degenerate mulattos. In reflecting on Rodrigues's intriguing divisions, Telles notes:

> Rodrigues' ambivalence about the status of the mulatto and the need to distinguish them from whites may have kept him and other members of the elite from taking the extreme segregationist route chosen by the United States and South Africa in the late nineteenth and early twentieth centuries.[9]

In other words, policing the boundaries of "pure" whiteness, or even being too quick to lump most people of color into a single category, risked placing many elites on the wrong side of the color line.

The ambivalence which attended the drawing of lines between racial categories was also reflected in social and political questions about census development and interpretation. Mara Loveman's study of census making in Latin American countries affirms the uneasiness and misunderstandings that plagued partnerships between Latin American elites and European scholars and consultants who were experts in the counting of populations. Loveman's book *National Colors* tells the story of how such elites sought to model their societies on those of wealthier, whiter countries in Europe and North America. Part of becoming "modern" was developing a scientifically sound system for census making that would allow for an accurate enumeration of diverse populations. As in every country that keeps such statistics, the counting of racial groups is an inherently political process that highlights tensions concerning who "we" are as a nation and what "we" will be like in the future if current demographic trends continue. Unfortunately for Latin American census makers who sought to prove that their countries were modernizing, developing, and becoming more white over time, European and white North American outsiders saw the *majority* of the population in Latin America as nonwhite and racially degenerate. To make matters worse, it was a common practice for leading European and North American intellectuals to point *directly* to Latin American countries' economic delays as compelling evidence of the debilitating effects of racial mixture for countries seeking to develop socially and economically.[10]

At the root of Latin American elites' difficulties in pursuing whiteness and respectability within an international context was the undeniable preponderance of the African and indigenous populations in many Latin American and Caribbean countries. Several cases demonstrate the ways that demographic realities and widespread racial mixing undermined aspirations for pure whiteness across Latin America and the Caribbean. In a comparative piece that examines the differential construction of race in Cuba, Virginia, and Louisiana, Gross and de la Fuente write that in Cuba, "despite efforts to police an ideal caste system, extensive racial mixing and mobility undermined it."[11] The clear implication here is that an "ideal" system would have been one that maintained carefully and clearly marked categories where blackness and whiteness were well contained within their particular borders in such a way that racial mixing was rare or nonexistent.

Similarly, in her comparison of race in Louisiana and St. Domingue, Laura Foner discusses the difficulty of policing the color line in St. Domingue and contrasts that colony's experience with the comparatively successful project of racial separation in the United States. She notes that in the United States "white residents looked on their new home as a place to settle permanently ... [and] the population in the United States was predominately white, with large numbers of white women."[12] This was far from the case in St. Domingue, where before the revolution whites were outnumbered by people of color by more than ten to one. Telles and Flores's work also emphasizes the importance of demographic differences and contrasting approaches to European settlement in protecting the borders of whiteness. They write that "overall racial mixture was apparently greater in Latin America than in the United States where a more balanced sex ratio among whites emerged from a more family-based immigration in the colonial period."[13] As a result of these quite different demographics and immigration strategies, antimiscegenation was easier to enforce in the United States than in Cuba, French St. Domingue, and other parts of Latin America.

The force of these demographic realities put Latin American elites in a difficult position. Faced with this situation, what was a modernizing Latin American elite to do? As such leaders came to see that they must grapple with the demographic realities they had been dealt, the majority changed strategy so that rather than seeking to more strongly police and protect the boundaries of whiteness, they instead *challenged* the international consensus which assumed that racial mixing degraded whites and prevented nations from advancing.[14] In the nineteenth century, this new stance led to an explicit focus on race mixture as an ameliorative process that improved the society as a whole and moved it toward whiteness. Loveman makes note of Latin American officials' defiant stance against the international consensus that their mixed-race populations were doomed to backwardness and degeneracy. She explains:

> Contra the pessimistic pronunciations of international observers and their domestic adherents, Latin American census officials produced authoritative descriptions of populations moving steadily forward, not backward, in the race to progress.... Using statistics—the same internationally legible and authoritative language that lent credence to racial determinist tracts—Latin American census officials presented evidence that mixture, in conjunction with other "progressive" demographic dynamics, generated racially "improved" (which nearly always meant "whiter") populations.[15]

With this argument, Latin American officials set out to prove that rather than being swallowed up demographically by the black and indigenous presence in their societies, they would biologically mix their way to whiteness over time.

It is possible to discern two different versions of race mixing in Latin America: whitening and *mestizaje*—each the result of quite different racial projects. Here I invoke Michael Omi and Howard Winant's discussion of racial projects as "simultaneously an interpretation, representation, or explanation of racial dynamics, and an effort to reorganize and redistribute resources along particular racial lines."[16] At the root of every racial project is a vision of how one group or another stands to gain or lose from the way race is understood and practiced. At stake in the earlier version of race mixing as "whitening" was the desire to defend and restore the social and racial integrity of Latin American and Caribbean countries that were seeking entrance into the community of nations on equal footing with Europeans and North Americans. A second version of race mixing as *mestizaje*—a form of racial inclusion and acceptance where race mixture was seen as a good in itself rather than as a bridge to whiteness—would come later and be accompanied by new kinds of promises and benefits.

The ideological transition from policing white purity to racial mixture as whitening was attended by mixed social and political consequences. On the one hand, the shift can be seen as a kind of progress in that it acknowledged and worked with Latin American and Caribbean countries' demographic realities rather than wishing those realities away. On the other hand, however, early justifications for the desirability of racial mixing were quite racist and clearly reinforced white supremacist ideals. Now, rather than protecting whiteness or seeking to limit miscegenation, the idea was that racial mixing would help a country become whiter than it had been before. In this sense, the shift to embracing racial mixture was done in the hopes that African and indigenous influences would gradually be wiped out, or at least radically decreased.

Telles describes the eugenicist underpinnings of early proponents of race mixing as whitening when he notes that scholars who were shaped by eugenicist thinking:

> accepted the racist predictions of black and mulatto inferiority but thought this inferiority could be overcome by miscegenation. Based on their interpretation of eugenics, and their own sensitivities to theories about racial and tropical degeneracy, Brazilian scholars used a theory of constructive miscegenation and proposed a solution of "whitening" through the mixing of whites and nonwhites.[17]

The racist and eugenicist overtones of this racial mixing project come across in the language intellectuals used to describe the ameliorating effects of miscegenation. One Brazilian writer explained that:

> It is known that in the crossing of animals, the qualities of the superior race can be grafted little by little to an inferior race, in order to form, through successive selections, a new ethnic type, that possesses the most excellent attributes of the superior race.[18]

In a similar vein, we find the following:

> In this work of the aryanization of our people, there are more energetic collaborators than the immigration of white races from Europe, there are natural and social selection, which accelerate extraordinarily among us the rapidity of the process of reduction of the ethnically inferior elements.[19]

Finally, in her critical review of evolutions in the culture and politics of racial mixing, Lourdes Martinez-Echazabal cites Vasconceles who explains that "the lower types of the species will be absorbed by the superior."[20]

Although this racial mixing project began its ascendance within an explicitly racist framework, as Latin American and Caribbean countries moved toward independent nationhood, efforts to embrace the ideals of democracy and social equality brought about a change in approaches to thinking about racial mixture. Rather than being portrayed as a kind of racial cleansing, racial mixture was reinterpreted as a good in itself. This made it possible to see mixed-race persons—at least at the level of ideology—as full and equal members of the new nations.

Thus, rather than seeing race mixture as a way of eliminating racial undesirables, Martinez-Echazabal explains that:

> As early as the first decade of the twentieth century, in various parts of Latin America (Brazil, Mexico, Peru, Cuba), this new [mestizo] image began to flourish and with it a new rhetoric—one that for the most part no longer referred to "inferior" races and cultures.[21]

Loveman describes the transition as one where "census officials stopped portraying the *mestizo* as evidence of a population in transition. Instead they redefined 'mixture' as the inevitable and ideal demographic end state."[22] Similarly, Telles and Flores note that ideologies that had once emphasized whitening were "turned on their head and replaced with ideologies of *mestizaje*, or race mixing."[23] Perhaps the strongest or best-known incarnation of this new, more inclusive form of racial mixing is the idea of "racial democracy" in Brazil. According to this concept, there was no racial discord in Brazil because all races were mixed together in such a way that the very heart of what it meant to be Brazilian was to have racially mixed ancestry.

In his seminal work on race and culture in Brazil, Gilberto Freyre described Brazilianness as inextricably linked to Africanness—even for white Brazilians. In describing the Brazilian, he explained:

> Every Brazilian, even the light-skinned fair-haired one, carries about with him on his soul, when not on soul and body alike ... the shadow, or at least the birthmark, of the aborigine or the Negro.... In our affections, our excessive mimicry, our Catholicism, which so delights the senses, our music, our gait, our speech, our cradle songs—in everything that is a sincere expression of our lives, we almost all of us bear the mark of that [nonwhite] influence.[24]

The cultural embrace of African ancestry was so complete, in fact, that in the introduction to his critical examination of race and ideology in Brazil, Telles ponders:

> What about those white Brazilians who claim to find blacks and mulattos in their family albums? How common is this? Are such ancestors merely historical remnants? Or are such findings over-stated to project a culturally desirable pedigree of miscegenation?[25]

White Brazilians' desire to claim African ancestry brings us full circle—at the level of ideology if not practice—from the initial goal of defending *limpieza de sangre* among early white colonists and residents of Latin American and Caribbean countries.[26] Telles and Flores nicely summarize the completion of this circle when they note that across Latin America: "as generations of race mixture made *castas* unsustainable ... ideas of lineage were gradually substituted with informal discourses of physical appearance."[27] It is the transition from biological to appearance-based understandings of whiteness that makes it possible for white Brazilians to proudly claim African ancestry without being concerned that their essential whiteness will be challenged or stripped from them. This comfort with the idea of nonwhite ancestry contrasts quite clearly with US American notions of whiteness that still cling either consciously or subconsciously to the idea of whiteness as purity.[28]

In fact, this shift to an appearance-based understanding of whiteness constitutes a decisive difference between US and Latin/Caribbean approaches to determining who is white. This focus on appearance over biology, moreover, had implications not only for determining who was white but also for interpreting and categorizing persons with African lineage. As a result, across Latin America and the Caribbean, if having African blood was not enough to disqualify a person from being white, neither was it enough to make one entirely "black." Instead, these countries developed either a triracial or continuum system of racial categorization and identification based on gradations of discernible African, indigenous, and European heritage. This relative racial flexibility allowed free people of color in Latin American and Caribbean countries to move up and down the social hierarchy based on combinations of appearance—lighter being better—and status.

As Latin American and Caribbean leaders were coming to terms with and even embracing racial mixture, room for racial flexibility and fluidity in the United States was more fleeting and more complex. At the level of everyday discourse, "pure" whiteness continued to be elevated and racial mixture looked down upon. But at the level of everyday practice, miscegenation continued, and in some areas mixed-race free people of color were able to flourish despite a racial context that made them a social minority. Up until the mid-nineteenth century, there was room for some flexibility and fluidity in racial categories in the United States. But as the second half of the nineteenth century dawned and social and political tensions in the United States led the country down the path to civil war, the already fragile space for interracial relationships and intimacy, and for mixed-race persons themselves, was gradually but decisively closed by a tightening political and legal climate. The closing of this space of fluidity for free people of color was accompanied by a tightening of the boundaries of whiteness—so that "whiteness" demanded purity in lineage—and a corresponding broadening of the category of "blackness" to include everyone with discernible African heritage.

Whereas in the preceding sections we explored the ways demography helped to shape different outcomes in whiteness across colonial America, our comparative focus in the following section will explore differences in the construction of blackness and will demonstrate how blackness—defined broadly as anyone with African lineage—and slavery came to be so closely identified in the United States that there was relatively little room for blackness and freedom to coexist in the popular imagination or to flourish in most US American states. The evolution of this difference in constructions of blackness contributed significantly to the divergence of the Latin/Caribbean and Anglo-American racial systems.

THE NINETEENTH CENTURY AND THE CLOSING WINDOW OF RACIAL FLUIDITY IN THE UNITED STATES

The construction of blackness in the United States is quite distinctive compared to its construction across the rest of the Americas. The United States has long been characterized by what is called the "one-drop rule"—a person with any discernible amount of African lineage has traditionally been considered black in the United States.[29] In contrast, one could have light brown skin in many Latin American countries and not be considered black. Contrary to what one might assume, however, there is little evidence that early US leaders' approach to blackness was fundamentally different from their peers in the rest of the hemisphere. Instead, much as colonial elites across the Americas started out with a similar goal of holding fast the color line in order to preserve pure whiteness, they also generally shared the idea that blackness was inferior and should be closely, even exclusively, identified with enslavement. Central to achieving this identification between blackness and enslavement was limiting the size of the "free people of color" population so that having African lineage would become a kind of shorthand for enslavement. This approach links all people of African descent together under the umbrella of a single master status—the enslaved. It also serves, when combined with the preservation of "limpieza de sangre" through antimiscegenation policy, to create what many colonial elites saw as the ideal of a clear color line with pure whiteness on one side and impurity or mixture on the other. Had this approach to defining blackness and whiteness succeeded across the Americas, much of the hemisphere would have a racial system similar to that of the United States.

The United States, however, had several advantages that allowed it to prevail over other American societies in sustaining this strict color line ideal. First, it was a largely white country with a relatively large population of white women to balance out the number of white men. This led to a situation where race mixture was an option, but it was not seen as an absolute necessity. The result was that, although there were significant populations of free people of color—many of them mixed race—in the United States, their presence was not as widespread as it was in Latin America and the Caribbean. The lower prevalence of miscegenation resulted not only in fewer persons of mixed race but in fewer *free* persons of mixed race, thus strengthening the association between blackness/enslavement on one side and whiteness/freedom on the other.

Another factor that played a significant role in the number and status of free people of color in American societies was the differential impact of varied European legal regimes. The French, Spanish, Portuguese, and English took different approaches to the legal processes of enslavement and manumission. Legal diversity in colonial regimes was put forward as one of two major factors identified in the controversial "Tannenbaum Thesis," which was deployed by Frank Tannenbaum to explain broad differences between systems of slavery and routes to freedom in the Americas. In *Slave and Citizen*, Tannenbaum argues that we can understand differences in the treatment of slaves, likelihood of manumission, and the tenor of postemancipation race relations by examining the roles of the varied legal and religious traditions that characterized different European powers.[30]

Tannenbaum's thesis has been widely criticized for its suggestion that differences in cultural essence and moral values between European regimes account for different degrees of harshness in the structuring of enslavement across the Americas.[31] Passages like the following are among those that have sparked a good deal of criticism:

> this [denial of Negro moral status for legal freedom in the United States] did not occur in the other parts of this world we call new and free. It did not occur because the very nature of the institution of slavery was developed in a different moral and legal setting, and in turn shaped the political and ethical biases that have manifestly separated the United States from other parts of the New World ... the separation is a moral one.[32]

Tannenbaum's emphasis on the essential moral difference between English slaveholders –whose territories he characterizes as most oppressive to persons of African descent both free and enslaved–and the Spanish and Portuguese, who he sees as the most lenient, is problematic on a number of levels. First, even if we focus only on the English-speaking colonies and the independent states that came of them, the United States is quite different from Jamaica in the experience and structure of slavery and in the fate of people of African descent following emancipation. Secondly, ascribing moral essence to an entire colonial power is a sweeping generalization that on its face invites criticism.

But whereas the moral dimension of Tannenbaum's argument is problematic, his emphasis on the significance of different kinds of legal regimes is worth examining in some detail because variations in legal doctrines did have a significant impact on the occurrence and ease of manumission in different parts of the Americas. These differences, in turn, helped to account for wildly varying numbers of free people of color and affected the social and political power of this in-between population in the United States and in other parts of the Americas.

In their insightful comparison of legal systems and slave life in Virginia, Louisiana, and Cuba, Gross and de la Fuente clearly demonstrate the significant role legal systems played in shaping the lives of enslaved Americans. They note that although "efforts to permanently identify blackness with slave status took place in all three locations ... Virginia was the most successful, followed by Louisiana and finally Cuba."[33] Differences in legal codes were central to the varied abilities of officials in Virginia, Louisiana, and Cuba to keep blackness closely identified with slavery.

There has been much justified critique of the temptation to equate what is written in law with what occurs on the ground in everyday practice.[34] But, while we must acknowledge that it is impossible to determine the reality of social life in the past solely from the examination of laws, it is equally important to acknowledge that in many cases, laws have been crucial to paving the way toward freedom. In this sense, laws share much in common with roads and paths. When paths are blocked, then we are impeded from taking advantage of where they might lead us. At the same time, however, a blocked path nevertheless represents a kind of hope. If we are successful in toppling the obstacles, then it will be possible to use the path in order to get to previously inaccessible places. But where there is no path at all, there is literally no way to move forward. In this sense, laws regarding manumission have often been necessary but not sufficient mechanisms for escaping enslavement and realizing freedom.

The comparative case of Virginia, Louisiana, and Cuba is revealing as it shows changes over time in how blackness and freedom were constructed ideologically and practically and how officials in Virginia won, comparatively speaking, the effort to almost fully equate having some African blood to being enslaved. In this sense, Virginia stands in for most of the United

States—outside of Louisiana with its French and Spanish influence—where English law dominated the treatment of enslaved and free people of African descent. Nevertheless, it took time for Virginia—and by extension the rest of the Anglo-American United States—to develop its distinctive stance toward blacks and thus to distinguish itself in comparison to Spanish Cuba and French- and Spanish-influenced Louisiana.

In the beginning, officials in each of the three areas were more or less united in their stance on blackness and their efforts to impose a strict color line. In sixteenth-century Cuba, for instance, officials were diligent in their efforts to equate blackness with enslavement and to limit the population of free people of color. For those familiar with colonial Cuba in later centuries, this sixteenth-century state of affairs will be surprising because it seems like a racial picture more fitting to the US South than to Cuba, which was known to have a relatively large population of free people of color in the nineteenth century. Indeed, it runs counter to Tannenbaum's argument about the relative leniency and moral superiority of Spanish colonial laws. In contrast to the somewhat rosy picture that Tannenbaum paints of slavery and manumission in Latin America, sixteenth-century Cuba was clearly a hostile environment for people of African descent—whether slave or free.

Gross and de la Fuente cite a catalogue of policies aimed at establishing the permanently degraded status of blackness and of solidifying its equation with slavery. These policies included disallowing black men or women from living in a place other than their master's house; collecting weapons belonging to blacks; the sentencing of "negros" who cut down trees to three hundred lashes and ten days in jail; and confinement to jail for selling corn tortillas at an "unfair price." Many of these provisions did not make a clear distinction between "blacks" and "slaves." This slippage between being black and being a slave occurred in language that referred generally to "negros," but then followed this with the assumption that these "negros" also had masters.[35]

Indeed, Cuban officials took their project of equating blackness with enslavement so far that in 1557 they banned all free people of color from Havana. The stated reason was that their presence was "damaging." Reading beneath the surface, however, one can see concern about making the line between black and white, slave and free as clear as possible. But free people of color resisted the law, and we can imagine the surprise and dismay of Cuban officials when the Spanish government at Santo Domingo reversed the Cabildo's decision and soundly condemned it for the expense of bringing the case to trial.[36] This decision was a foreshadowing of the ways Spanish law would gradually but decisively counter colonial officials' racial ideals and eventually contribute to the creation of a relatively large free black population.

In the case of Virginia, the process of equating blackness with enslavement evolved over several decades and was a bit slower to take root than had been the case in sixteenth-century Cuba. In early seventeenth-century Virginia, there is clear reference to negro and European servants—not slaves—working together on what appears to be equal footing. In an interesting reversal of Tannenbaum's argument about the essential moral goodness of Catholic Spain, Gross and de la Fuente suggest that because of Spain's early history of enslaving Africans *before* the Trans-Atlantic slave trade, its officials had long-term experience equating Africanness with enslavement and had therefore developed a code of laws assuming and reinforcing their essential inferiority to Europeans. Gross and de la Fuente then argue that these assumptions of inferiority and of the slave-like nature of Africans were carried across the Atlantic and applied early on in Spain's American colonies. The English, in contrast, did not have such extensive experience with enslaving Africans, and thus officials in their colonies started out by applying to Africans the framework they were most familiar with applying to servile Europeans: indentured servitude.

Slowly but surely, however, distinctions were drawn between African and European servants, and these distinctions were decisively hardened by the mid-seventeenth century. In 1662, Virginia's General Assembly declared the following:

> Whereas some doubts have arisen whether children got by any Englishman upon a Negro should be slave or free, Be it therefore enacted and declared by this present grand assembly, that all children borne in this country shalbe held bond or free only according to the condition of the mother, And that if any Christian shall commit fornication with a negro man or woman, hee or shee soe offending shall pay double the fines imposed by the former act.[37]

This act laid the groundwork for cinching the connection between blackness and slavery in the sense that any child born to an enslaved mother would automatically be born into the status of slave. In addition to this biologically based way of connecting blackness and enslavement, Virginia officials passed laws that used cultural difference to ensure that blackness and slavery would be indissolubly yoked together. Whereas it was initially the case in the Virginia territory that being baptized as a Christian exempted Africans from slavery, by 1705 Viriginia law declared that any servant entering the colony who had not been a Christian in his or her native land would automatically be considered a slave upon entrance to the colony. Moreover, a conversion to Christianity following arrival would no longer make a difference in this enslaved status.[38]

While these events were occurring in Virginia, Louisiana was under the control of the French where the situation for blacks was equally dim. The French crown's concerns that freed blacks might unite with whites led to a ban on interracial marriage. In addition, freeing a slave was quite onerous. It required that the owner be at least twenty-five years old and that the manumission be approved by the Superior Council. These restrictions were followed by a plethora of new laws which further whittled away the freedoms of people of African descent—whether enslaved or free. Gross and de la Fuente note that:

> The new regulations aimed at . . . subordinating all "negroes," whether free or enslaved, to all white men in a variety of ways. "Negroes or negresses" were not allowed to assemble "under the pretext of dancing, or for any other cause; to be in the streets or public roads carrying a cane or stick without a pass; or to be "insolent" to white people. Any white person who met a black person in public, without a pass or carrying a stick, or considered the black person insolent in any way, was exhorted to whip the slave, or even to have him branded with a *fleur de lis* on his backside.[39]

This subjection of blacks to whites through intimidation and violence reinforced a situation where blackness was equated with inferiority and slavery, as was the case in early Cuba and Virginia. In the case of Louisiana, as with these other colonies in their earliest years, the population of free people of African descent remained small and their freedoms were steadily eroded. The situation would change markedly, however, by the mid- to late eighteenth century in Cuba and in Louisiana, where the Spanish took over from the French by 1769.[40]

One of the mechanisms that significantly opened up the divergence between Virginia, Louisiana, and Cuba was the difference in available legal doctrines that allowed people of African descent to make legal claims that Spanish colonial governments could not fully resist. In this sense, Havana officials' loss of the 1557 attempt to ban free people of color from the city foreshadowed the difficulty officials throughout Cuba would have with containing the spread of freedom and the growth of the free people of color population. Here Tannenbaum's emphasis on legal foundations bears fruit. Increasingly, enslaved persons in Cuba made use of the right to *coartación*: a distinctive legal doctrine which was absent in English territories like the United States, but which helped to add significantly to the population of free people of color in the Spanish colonies. The right to *coartación* allowed an enslaved person to pay her owner the market value for her freedom. In cases where the owner refused, it was possible for the enslaved person to petition the courts to determine a fair market price and to compel the owner to follow through on the self-purchase. Tannenbaum describes the practice as follows:

> The purchase of one's freedom was so accepted a tradition among the Negroes that many a negro bought the freedom of his wife and children ... and among the freed Negroes societies were organized for pooling resources and collecting funds for the freeing of their brethren still in bondage.[41]

In support of his discussion of the institution of *coartación*, Tannenbaum cites the observations of the Reverend Abiel Abbott, an American traveler to Cuba who described the system as follows based on his trip to the island in the 1820s:

> the free blacks are considerably numerous; the number has been stated to exceed 100,000. It is a redeeming circumstance in regard to the Spanish character, that their laws favor emancipation, and the government faithfully executes them. If the slave can present his value, nay, only his cost, his master, however reluctant he may be to part with the best body servant he has, or an invaluable mechanic, or skillful driver, he cannot retain him. If he attempt to evade the command, the captain of the Partido must enforce it, and evasion in either case is punished with high pecuniary penalties.[42]

Abbot then goes on to describe the ways enslaved blacks arranged to save for and purchase their freedom:

> A certain method is to raise a hog, which they can do, to a large size, by corn of their own growing. I have seen swine belonging to slaves worth two or three ounces, (forty or fifty dollars), and there are purchasers enough without their carrying them to market. Live hogs are at this moment sold here at eight dollars per hundred on the hoof.... This very week a splendid funeral was made for a black woman who paid for her freedom and has left behind her $100,000, collected by her industry.... From my chamber window I look down upon a family of freed blacks, who are my laundresses. They sell admirable spruce beer, and I know not what else; and the daughter amuses herself and the family and the neighborhood, by singing with a sweet and powerful voice of great compass, and accompanies her singing by the guitar.[43]

The Rev. Abbott paints quite a vivid and gay picture of life in the Cuban countryside with what appears to be a great deal of romanticization. Still, however, the institution of *coartación* did generally work in the way he describes.

When Abbott reflects on the system of Spanish Cuba compared to what he is familiar with in the southern United States, he explains that he "would hide [his] face for shame that in some of our republican states, a statute forbids manumission, even when the owner is disposed to grant, or the slave is prepared to purchase the blessing."[44] In this sense, *coartación* provides a compelling example of how colonial legal regimes did matter to the social life and potential freedom of the enslaved in different parts of the Americas.

The system is all the more remarkable in that slaves were able to buy their freedom in *installments*, and as their payments increased, so did the proportion of their ownership in themselves. Two cases in 1690 Cuba describe how the process worked:

> In 1690 ... the slave Juan, a seventeen year old creole, was sold four times, always on condition that he was to be freed as soon as he was able to pay the 200 pesos remaining for his total value. In practice, only a portion of Juan was being sold. He owned a portion of himself. Buyers were instructed that they could only "use" the portion of the slave that they were paying for ... [Similarly] when a mulatto female slave who had paid half of her price was sold in 1690, the contract stipulated that she was entitled to half of her labor and that the sale was "only on half of the said mulata."[45]

The ability to buy one's freedom in installments significantly opened up the possibility for freedom. Many enslaved persons could and did save slowly and painstakingly toward buying their freedom. An additional benefit of the system was that the increase in free time as one's ownership percentage increased theoretically allowed the enslaved person to invest more time working to save money and thus helped to speed up the time to full freedom.

Coartación was also used by many enslaved persons in Spanish-controlled Louisiana. This policy significantly helped to solidify Louisiana's three-tiered racial system before the Anglo-Americans' purchase of Louisiana. There was quite a significant jump in the number of free people of color in Spanish Louisiana compared to what had been the case when the French governed the colony. Kimberly Hanger documents the social and political legacy of the Spanish period in Louisiana and notes that it was "during the Spanish period that libres in New Orleans made their greatest advances in terms of demographics, privileges, responsibilities, and social standing."[46] From the time that the Spanish took control of Louisiana in 1769 until the early Anglo-American period in 1805, the number of free people of color jumped from 97 to 1,566—this is a sixteen-fold increase. When we compare this to an approximate doubling of the white population and tripling of the enslaved population over the same period of time, it becomes clear that the Spanish period in New Orleans made a definitive difference in the size of the free people of color population.[47]

Hanger affirms the significance of the shift from French to Spanish control when she notes that while "Louisiana's [French] code noir had permitted masters over the age of twenty five to manumit their slaves, with prior consent from the superior council.... Spanish regulations ... did not require official permission for a master to free his or her slave and even allowed slaves to initiate manumission proceedings on their own behalf."[48] Here Hanger refers directly to the practice of *coartación*, which the Spanish brought with them to Louisiana.[49] As in Cuba, enslaved persons in Spanish New Orleans could buy their freedom all at once or on installment. She describes the case of the slave Michaud, who used installments to secure his freedom:

> In 1791 a white couple manumitted their Moreno slave Michaut for one thousand pesos. At the time Michaut had already deposited installments of five hundred and one hundred pesos with his owners, and he swore to pay the remaining four hundred pesos at a rate of five pesos per month.[50]

There were also, however, cases where the enslaved paid all at once not only for their own freedom but also for that of other family members. This was the case with Maria Luisa:

> Maria Luisa, the thirty-two year old parda slave of a white army officer, requested her carta [of freedom] and that of her four children: Noel (seven), Joseph (five), Miguel (two and a half), and Francisca (three months). She paid five hundred pesos for their freedom.[51]

In cases where the owner would not agree to accept payment for a slave's freedom, the courts supported the enslaved by "[demanding] that a tribunal issue a *carta de libertad* at the slave's estimated worth." In these cases, slave appraisers were enlisted to determine fair market value.[52]

How did this flourishing of freedom in Cuba and Spanish Louisiana compare to what was going on in Virginia and other parts of the Anglo-American United States? As might be expected, the well-being and rights of free people of color varied by the community and laws under which they lived. In general, however, historical scholarship demonstrates that while there was some ability to secure one's freedom, and some space in certain communities for free people of color to increase their numbers, the space for such freedom and flexibility was often narrow and closed decisively by the mid-nineteenth century. This narrowed flexibility solidified the binary approach that is the hallmark of the Anglo-American racial system.

Ira Berlin compares and contrasts the situation of free people of color in the United States by drawing a distinction between those in the Upper and Lower South. According to Berlin, most free people of color in the Upper South gained their freedom as a result of the American Revolution, whereas those in the Lower South were more likely to receive their freedom as a result of paternalistic ties with owners favorably disposed toward their slaves.[53] Because of their ties of affection to their former owners, Berlin argues, free people of color in the Lower South tended to be better off financially and socially than those in the Upper South.

More recent scholarship finds greater variation than Berlin did in the lives and freedoms of free people of color in the Upper South, but even this work highlights the restricted nature of this freedom. In his critique of Berlin's position, for instance, Warren Milteer documents some space and freedom for free people of color in the Upper South by closely examining the lives of people of African and Indian descent living in a small North Carolina community. There, rather than finding rigid separations between different groups of people, he found some flexibility and fluidity in racial categorization over time. But then in the following section, Milteer describes a situation where, although there was some amount of freedom, it was within a fairly constrained social and economic context:

> Daily life for free people of color in Gates County entailed interactions with people of varying racial classifications, classes, and social positions. Many free people of color interacted with their wealthier neighbors, both whites and free people of color, from a subservient position. Landless and poor, they frequently found themselves in situations of dependence and servitude. Over generations, small numbers of free people of color achieved financial success and obtained considerable autonomy in their lives.[54]

Thus, while there was some freedom and flexibility for free people of color in Gates County, they were limited in their ability to gain wealth and security.

Part of the reason for this constraint was that the legal environment in North Carolina made for hard-going for free people of color in the early nineteenth century. In 1826, a state law declared that any free black person "in idleness and dissipation" could be arrested and hired out for up to three years. Then in 1827, free blacks residing in North Carolina who had been born elsewhere were given twenty days to leave the state. Otherwise, they would face a fine of $500, and if unable to pay the fine, would be forced into servitude for up to ten years. The law was not much better for native North Carolinian free blacks either, as any who left the state for more than ninety days were not allowed to return. These are examples of the kinds of laws that sought to tighten the linkage between blackness and slavery. Cuban officials in Havana had tried this in the mid-1500s and were rebuffed by the Spanish government. There was, however, no similar legal recourse to a colonial government for free people of color in North Carolina or other Anglo-American states that enacted such restrictive laws.

Despite the draconian nature of the law, some communities did afford greater freedoms to free people of color. Richard Rohrs, for example, finds that enforcement of the new laws was lax in Wilmington, North Carolina. He describes James D. Sampson and the Arts and Howe families as free people of color in the building trades who were "influential members of their community."[55] He also notes that the impact of the laws could be attenuated by relationships to white members of the community, as when some free blacks in Wilmington were able "through their labor or the financial support of white fathers" to accumulate property. Still, however, the opportunities were slim when compared to other parts of the United States with larger and more influential free black communities. Whereas the average wealth of free blacks in Wilmington was just $1,342, it was $4,268 in Charleston and $3,623 in New Orleans.[56]

Across the US South the situation for free people of color became even more fragile during the second half of the nineteenth century. Following the US war with Mexico, which resulted in the United States taking over a substantial amount of new territory in the West, the country was torn over how to determine the slave or free status of the new states being added to the union. As an intervention, the Compromise of 1850 was brokered in order to maintain a fragile political balance between slave and free states. While the Compromise achieved some short-term goals toward restoring political balance, part of the package of laws included in the Compromise was the Fugitive Slave Act—a piece of legislation that dealt a mortal blow to the fragile freedoms of free people of color throughout the country. The Act required that citizens and states assist in the capture of fugitive slaves and return such slaves to their masters. Those found to be supporting or giving sanctuary to fugitives were liable for high fines or imprisonment. Most disturbingly, the structure and implementation of the law created a danger not only to those who had escaped slavery by clandestinely fleeing their owners but also to free people of color who had acquired their freedom through legal means or who had been born free. The contours of the law made it very easy for *any* black person to be accused of being a fugitive and to be delivered to the person claiming ownership. When this happened, there was no effective legal recourse for the accused to pursue to plead her case because the Act had removed the right of accused fugitives to a trial by jury. Instead of a trial, contested cases were decided by a special commissioner. Here the decks were further stacked against the accused: the commissioner would be paid $5 if the accused fugitive retained her freedom but compensated $10 if the claimant in the case retained the "fugitive." As free persons of color—whether living free after an escape or living free as a result of legal channels—grasped the terrible reality of the new legal situation, many fled the country with thousands going north to Canada.

The assault against free people of color continued to intensify in many other ways throughout the 1850s as racial tensions increased exponentially and white Americans sought to purge their states of this in-between group of people that had the audacity to be both black and free. In *Slaves without Masters*, Ira Berlin sketches out the social and political context within which white Southerners sought to create a social space that consisted unambiguously of free whites and enslaved blacks. Berlin notes that despite the political tensions, the economic situation of the 1850s was generally good for many blacks. It was so good, in fact, that many free blacks were able to realize significant financial success that propelled them ahead of some whites. Berlin explains:

> During the 1850s, free Negroes prospered as never before.... In Charleston alone some seventy-five whites rented their homes from free Negro landlords, and one street took its name from the wealthy freeman who owned the houses that lined both sides of the street.... In 1860 Nashville boasted twenty-six free Negroes worth over a thousand dollars who had owned no property at all ten years earlier. Tax rolls and census enumerations in other Southern cities told similar success stories. Black wage earners also partook of the good times. In spite of numerous restrictions and growing competition from white immigrants, the general prosperity and the labor shortage drove wages up.[57]

Added to this success was the increased political activism of free people of color who began to agitate more aggressively for their civil and political rights. These economic and political gains were not in themselves cause for great concern among whites. Far more worrying was the increased attention and mobilization of free blacks around the larger political issues concerning the slave or free status of the states, and the growing movement for emancipation. Defenders of slavery were sure that free blacks were behind the increased success of fugitives and were also convinced that having more free blacks would fuel discontent and rebellion among those who were still enslaved.

White Southern fears of the militancy or potential militancy of free blacks led to an intensification of efforts to rid states all together of free black people. Proposals for removal included sending them to the North or West, or sending them out of the country through colonization efforts to Liberia or Haiti. In describing the situation of this "unwanted people," John Hope Franklin provides several examples from contemporary sources that attest to the great fear free blacks engendered in Southern whites. An 1850 citizens' petition in Lincoln County, North Carolina, declared that "It is desirable that you should adopt a course of policy, and pass a system of laws to induce, if not compel, the free Negroes of North Carolina to emigrate to the Abolition and Free Soil States." In 1852, fifty-five citizens in Sampson County, North Carolina, wrote to their legislators with a "desire to call your earnest and direct attention to the evils that exist in our midst, arising from the bad conduct and evil disposition of very many of the free negroes amongst us." The remedy proposed was to raise money "to be appropriated to their colonization in Africa, or by petition to the general government for a location for them in the far West." Finally, a Cleveland County Grand Jury concluded in 1858 that "free Negroes in general are a nuisance to society ... it would be expedient to have a law requiring them to leave the State."[58]

Similar stories of the repression of free blacks were repeated across the South in the 1850s leading up to the outbreak of the Civil War. In his work on free blacks in Norfolk, Virginia, Tommy Bogger contrasts the social and political situation of Virginia's free blacks at the beginning of the nineteenth century and the middle of that same century. He notes that Norfolk's free blacks began the century "amid great optimism" and with a sense that the world was open to them and their success was imminent. The opportunity was such that they "purchased slaves, granted deeds of emancipation, acquired land, and engaged in petition campaigns."[59] In addition to this, they were able to successfully go to court in order to defend their interests. Much of this initial optimism and political space grew out of the war with Britain and the freedoms it opened up for many blacks who fought to secure the nation's independence. As the nineteenth century wore on, however, it became clear that those were short-won gains. Bogger explains that:

> having begun the century with high hopes, free blacks had been side tracked down a road of hopelessness and despair by the 1850s. Manumission, the

process by which their numbers had been rapidly augmented in the first decade, was seriously restricted, and those few who still managed to gain their freedom could no longer remain in the city and enjoy it. The depth of their disillusionment was reflected in the revival of interest in an idea that only the most desperate embraced in the worst of times, African colonization.[60]

In addition to contemplating colonization, in some unthinkable cases, free blacks actually consented to choosing masters to whom they became enslaved or reenslaved. Here, Franklin provides examples of several free blacks who in 1860 and 1861 entered into a state of enslavement. These stories include that of Celia Lynch of Martin County, North Carolina, who felt that she would be better off as the slave of Dr. J. T. Watson rather than remaining free, as well as that of Ellen Ransom, who consented to become the slave of Leonidas Perry in order to have a secure home.[61]

Even in New Orleans, where free people of color had flourished during the Spanish period and well into the early period of the Anglo-Americans, new restrictions whittled away at their freedoms by the 1850s. Rebecca Scott describes this period leading up to the Civil War as striking in its reversal of the previous status quo:

> In the decades that preceded the Civil War, Louisiana's legislators systematically tightened the constraints on people of African descent, both slave and free, rural and urban.... The free population of color in New Orleans fell in size between 1840 and 1850, and in 1857 the Louisiana legislature prohibited all future manumissions.[62]

The denial of manumission was preceded in the 1850s by several other onerous measures that made life extremely difficult for free people of color. These included prohibitions against free blacks entering Louisiana from other states and mandating that any person freed in Louisiana leave the state.[63] Thus did the 1850s usher in a period across the US South of extreme intolerance toward the idea of a social space between white freedom and black enslavement. The starkness of this line between white and black, slave and free, which was solidified in the 1850s, laid the foundation for the stark racial divisions characteristic of the Anglo-American racial system.

Some might question the extent to which this crackdown on free people of color in the United States was unique. Indeed, it is true that similar repressions occurred throughout Latin America and the Caribbean during times of political tension. What *was* unique to the United States, however, was its comparatively large white population and a lack of manumission-friendly laws, especially when compared to Spanish America. Both of these factors contributed to the United States having a relatively small and politically weak free people of color population that had a very difficult time resisting repressive measures. In other parts of the Americas where political repression threatened the vibrancy and existence of free colored communities, the population had gained enough in terms of numbers and social stability to weather difficult times.

Following the end of the Seven Years War in St. Domingue, for instance, the colony received new waves of white immigrants. Increased competition between new white immigrants and free people of color who vied for similar positions increased racial tensions that culminated in the creation of repressive laws that restricted the liberties of the free colored population.[64] Though the repression was significant, the free population of African descent was nearly equal in size to the white population of St. Domingue and many of its members were well-educated property owners who could stand their own ground. They were able, therefore, to weather the repression and to continue to grow. Their continued presence and strength preserved the significance of their intermediate position in the colony in ways that were not true in the United States following the repression of the 1850s.

Extreme repression of free people of color also occurred in Cuba beginning in 1844 when authorities engaged in a brutal crackdown against free people of color who were alleged to have plotted to end slavery and colonial rule in what came to be called the Conspiracy of La Escalera. The actual existence of a conspiracy has not been established, but the official response to the *idea* of a conspiracy was quite clear and severe. Those accused of participating were imprisoned, exiled, or executed. Beyond those directly implicated in the alleged conspiracy, the general population of free people of color suffered significant political and economic setbacks as authorities limited their access to occupations and dismantled militia units that had once provided key opportunities for free people of color to move up the social hierarchy.[65] But while the rollback of civil, social, and economic rights was a significant setback for free people of color, Cuba's free colored population was large, organized, and had developed extensive social networks over many decades. Their relative strength in numbers was due in great measure to the legal instrument of *coartacion*.

Michelle Reid-Vasquez argues that the social capital the free population had amassed helped them, in the face of the Escalera repression, to "[petition] for the release of imprisoned family members, the return of confiscated property, and the reversal of expulsion orders."[66] The depth and extensiveness of the free population's resistance leads Reid-Vasquez to note that "any assumptions of their silencing in 1844 has been premature and is in need of revision." David Sartorius echoes this sentiment in his work *Ever Faithful*, where he also urges historians to reconsider the idea that free people of color were forever beaten into submission.

> Rather than ending the story of the militias—or of early nineteenth- century politics altogether—on a bleak note in 1844, extending the chronology allows for a different interpretation. The free-colored militias reappeared in 1854 as part of a broad attempt, in the words of one commentator, to "invigorate in the spirit of the population of color an unlimited adhesion to the political interest of Spain in the island of Cuba."[67]

Sartorius notes that while officials onsite in Cuba tended to disagree with the reinstallation of the militias, those in Spain generally applauded the move. The Spanish government saw the reestablishment of free colored militias as an important incentive aimed at securing the loyalties of subjects of African descent within the context of a colonial situation always vulnerable to moves toward independence. In the case of Cuba, therefore, the size, strength, and political savvy of the free colored population helped them to survive while the political interests of colonial Spain provided an alternative power structure supportive of free colored opportunities.[68] Neither of these situations existed in the United States of the 1850s where the population of free people of color had always been small and relatively weak, and where there was no countervailing colonial power with which to negotiate.

In sum, in comparison to St. Domingue, Cuba, and other parts of Latin America and the Caribbean, the demographic, political, and legal context in the United States contributed to an extreme dualism in the country's black/white racial divide in several ways. First, the unique demographic situation made miscegenation less of an imperative and thus made it easier to maintain the construction of whiteness as purity. At the same time, the flip side of whiteness as purity in the United States was that *any* African lineage was defined as "black." In addition, the legal climate made it difficult for most of the South—outside of French- and Spanish-controlled Louisiana—to create a large, stable, and prosperous group of free people of color. This, combined with draconian measures to drive the small population of existing free people of color out of Southern states and out of the country, tightened the connection between blackness and slavery. These factors combined to solidify the structure of the Anglo-American system. This linkage between blackness and enslavement was, moreover, solidified in the public imagination, for although free people of color and their communities continued to exist, the social space for *imagining* the coexistence of blackness and freedom as viable reality was quite small and shrank as the nineteenth century advanced.

Emily Clark makes note of the power of the public imagination in the United States to figuratively erase the presence and significance of black freedom, and particularly of mixed-race free persons of color who managed to exist in-between increasingly rigid social and racial boundaries. She argues that the tendency to symbolically erase the figure of the free, mixed-race person was in evidence at least as early as the eighteenth century. In her study of the quadroon in Philadelphia, she notes that Philadelphians in the eighteenth century had a remarkable ability to exoticize the figure of the quadroon as something nonnative to the United States, as an import from the Caribbean. She explains:

> [The] homegrown American quadroon was ... unacknowledged, both literally and figuratively.... Americans developed a complex symbolic strategy that kept her at an imaginative distance from the nation's heart and heartland.[69]

Then, when the quadroon *was* acknowledged as existing on US soil, her presence was limited to New Orleans—a place thought to be a kind of Caribbean outpost in the United States.

Sequestering the quadroon figuratively in the Crescent City shaped American identity and historical narrative in subtle but powerful ways, effectively turning New Orleans into a perpetual colonial space in the national imagination.[70] Therefore, even as law and social practice chipped away at the freedoms of free people of color and made it nearly impossible for enslaved persons to acquire their freedom, the very idea of free people of color as social reality was increasingly excised from the public imagination.

The demographic and legal situation in the United States, combined with this limited space in the social imagination for in-between social and racial statuses, created an environment conducive to the growth of a very broadly based "black" identity and organized "black" resistance to white dominance. Nowhere else in the Americas were the outlines for black identification and black organizing among *anyone* with some degree of African lineage so clearly drawn. This identification of even small amounts of African lineage with "blackness" is unusual compared to the rest of the Americas where intermediate groups are categorized according to a triracial or continuum system based on a combination of a person's color and social status. By contrast, although there was a brief period between 1850 and 1920 when the US Census included the category "mulatto"—with 1890 standing out for its inclusion of "quadroon" and "octoroon" as well—subtle color distinctions in legal documents faded altogether from public life by the 1930 Census, leaving the separate categories of black and white.[71]

Moreover, the US "victory" of maintaining whiteness as purity and blackness as the presence of *any* African heritage was strengthened following the Civil War.[72] With the *Plessy v. Ferguson* decision in 1896, which declared that "separate but equal" was the law of the land for managing race in public spaces, the relatively tight connection between African lineage and degraded social status that had obtained throughout much of US history was cemented into a postemancipation social and legal practice that equally sealed the fate of all people of visible African heritage.

Thus did the United States succeed where Cuba and other Latin American and Caribbean countries had failed—it managed both socially and legally to keep firm the boundaries between whiteness as purity and blackness as any hint of African lineage, of whiteness as freedom and blackness as enslavement. Although there were certainly exceptions to the enforcement of the rules—not least in Louisiana with its French and Spanish heritage—for the vast majority of the United States, black and white became clear, separate, and unequal statuses with nothing meaningful in between if a person had discernible African heritage. In the final section we compare and contrast the characteristics of the Anglo-American and Latin/Caribbean racial systems that form the two layers of the racial palimpsest.

THE LAYERS OF THE PALIMPSEST

Our historical and comparative examination of changing racial systems in the United States and across Latin America and the Caribbean make it possible now to sketch an outline of the two layers of the racial palimpsest concept. The characteristics of the Anglo-American and Latin/Caribbean racial systems are shown in Table 1.1.

Table 1.1 builds both on the comparative-historical analysis of the previous sections and on earlier attempts of social scientists to draw meaningful contrasts between racial systems in different parts of the Americas.

Earlier attempts to delineate different types of American racial systems have generally resulted in the description of two or more different types. In his work on the Caribbean, for instance, Hoetink describes the difference between a continuum-based and a tripartite system for categorizing racial groups. He makes this distinction by engaging in a contrast between French colonial St. Domingue and Spanish Santo Domingo. With this comparison, Hoetink theorized that the different bases of the economic system

Table 1.1 THE TWO LAYERS OF THE PALIMPSEST

	Latin/Caribbean Racial System	Anglo-American Racial System (United States)
Whiteness is generally determined by …	*Appearance*, with some nonwhite mixture and ambiguity allowed	*Ancestry*, with "purity" or nonmixture emphasized and low tolerance for ambiguity
African ancestry is categorized according to …	*A tripartite or continuum system* of multiple categories depending upon the ways African ancestry is expressed in phenotype, facial features, hair, and to some degree status. According to this system, many people of African descent are *not* categorized as "black."	*A binary logic*—any amount of apparent African ancestry makes one black and not white

in each colony led to demographic differences which helped to create either a racial continuum or tripartite racial system. He explains:

> In the Spanish colony of Santo Domingo, the economy [in the last quarter of the eighteenth century] might be termed one of self-reliance.... Without a plantation economy geared to export, and hence without a need for massive importation of slaves or their strict regimentation … a particular sociracial structure developed.... Whites … were clearly favored socially over blacks … but the vast majority of the population had amalgamated sufficiently to leave no room for fixed color lines.... The French colony of St. Domingue at the same time was an export-oriented plantation economy with a large majority of black slaves, a tiny minority of whites … and further minorities of free blacks and coloreds … Saint-Domingue was characterized by potentially explosive lines of division, not only between the oppressed slaves and their masters, but also between whites and coloreds.[73]

Hoetink argues that the differences in the proportion of the slave population and the dynamics of economic competition led to the creation of a continuum system in Santo Domingo, where "subtle differences in skin color, hair texture, and facial features were noted and essentially catalogued in an extensive vocabulary."[74] In contrast, what developed in French St. Domingue was a system where color lines were more firmly identifiable between the black African masses, the whites, and an intermediary group of often mixed-race persons of color. This is what is meant by a "tripartite" racial system.[75] Hoetink's work helps to flesh out the lower left quadrant of the Table 1.1, where the presence of African lineage in many parts of Latin America and the Caribbean is categorized according to one of these two systems.

Charles Wagley's comparative work bolsters the division between Anglo-American and Latin/Caribbean systems when it comes to highlighting the distinctiveness of the Anglo-American system for determining who is "black." Wagley uses the term "social race" for his analysis of distinct and varied patterns for categorizing persons in different parts of the Americas. He identifies what he calls three major "stocks" or groups of people who have populated the Americas: blacks, whites, and Indians.[76] Wagley argued that across the Americas, three major criteria are variously weighted to create distinct kinds of racial systems in different parts of the Americas: ancestry, physical appearance, and sociocultural status. Out of these differently weighted combinations, Wagley discerns three major logics for naming and organizing social races. One of these includes areas in Central and South America with large amounts of indigenous people.[77] This system bears the least resemblance to the United States in comparison to parts of Latin American and the Caribbean which are dominated by mixtures of black and white and which have less of an indigenous presence.

Of the remaining two types of social race, the first is one where appearance is the factor most strongly weighed in determining a person's racial group membership. This social race type aligns with the left two quadrants of the table—those that describe the Latin/Caribbean racial system. Here Wagley includes Brazil and much of the Caribbean. He describes a mixture of color, hair texture, and physical features that is "read" or interpreted in the process of informally assessing a person's race. These readings result in a fine-grained division of people into categories along "a continuum from Caucasoid through the various degrees of mixed physical appearance to Negroid."[78] He provides, as an example, observations from a Brazilian community where there were at least eight different racial classifications based on variations in skin and other features. At the darkest end was the *preto*, immediately followed by a *cabra* who had lighter skin, less kinky hair, and features that were slightly more European. Intermediate categories included *cabo verde*, which is described as "dark skin color, but straight hair, thin lips, and narrow nose," and *pardo*, which is "'brown' . . . closer to the white than a light mulatto." At the lightest end was the *moreno*, a person with very light skin, European features, and dark curly hair—this person is nearly white.[79]

Finally, Wagley defines the US approach to social race, which stands alone for its nearly sole emphasis on ancestry in determining who is black and who is white. After noting that there was initially some fluidity and flexibility in racial classification in the United States, he notes that by the late nineteenth century the color line had hardened so that:

> whites were able to establish a rule of descent based upon ancestry which states that anyone who has a known Negro ancestor is a Negro.... Thus, the system of classification of people by social race was reduced to a twofold castelike system of "Negroes" and "whites." Not even the fair-skinned individual with Caucasoid features with a remote Negro ancestor can be classed as a "white," although thoroughly adapted in occupation, education, social graces, and economic position to middle- or upper-class status.[80]

This strong reliance on ancestry or descent encourages a great deal of social distance between people who can claim to be "pure" white and those who cannot. This does not mean that interracial friendships and other forms of interracial intimacy did not exist in particular instances, but it did provide a foundation for people of a wide range of phenotypes who were defined as black to identify as a group that shared a common oppressive experience. Here Wagley's analysis supports the right two quadrants of Table 1.1, which describe the logic of the Anglo-American racial system. In the final section, we come full circle by bringing the racial palimpsest approach to bear on the experiences of Maria and Jose from the beginning of the chapter.

RACE, IMMIGRATION, AND THE PALIMPSEST

At the heart of the racial palimpsest approach is careful attention to the local and regional racial histories of particular places in the United States as these have developed in relation to flows of people and ideas from other parts of the Americas. While the Anglo-American and Latin/Caribbean racial systems have emerged from different regional and historical circumstances, large-scale migration from Latin America and the Caribbean to the United States is leading to the emergence of a palimpsest environment in areas where immigrants become a substantial enough part of the population that their varied approaches to race begin to challenge Anglo-American racial assumptions. This comparative-historical and regional approach helps us to understand how Maria's integration into the United States may differ based on where she settles in the United States. If she ends up in southern Florida or certain parts of New York City, she will be in areas where a racial palimpsest is in evidence. In these areas the Anglo-American system forms a solid foundation, but it is being challenged by a superimposed Latin/Caribbean layer that also exerts influence on her everyday life.

In the following chapters, analysis of the varied receptions of black and white St. Domingue/Haiti refugees in nineteenth-century Louisiana will provide a historical analog to Maria and Jose's experiences in the twenty-first-century United States. As we examine the different ways light and dark-skinned St. Domingue refugees and their Creole descendants experienced an Anglo-Americanizing Louisiana, we will glean insights into the ways an emerging palimpsest reshapes racial categories and identities while also shifting the sociopolitical landscape within which persons attempt to work toward inclusion and racial justice. To better understand the integration challenges faced by this early nineteenth-century group of refugees as its members made their way in Louisiana and sought to start new lives there, we begin by examining their lives and the racial system they lived under in colonial St. Domingue.

CHAPTER 2

St. Domingue as Training Ground

Color, Class, and Social Life Before Louisiana

The Good Lord who created the sun which gives us light from above, who rouses the sea and makes the thunder roar—listen well all of you—this god, hidden in the clouds, watches us. He sees all that the white man does. . . . He will direct our hands; he will aid us. Throw away the image of the god of the whites who thirsts for our tears and listen to the voice of liberty which speaks in the hearts of all of us.

—Declaration at Bois Caiman, *August 1791, St. Domingue*

We were attacked by a horde of assassins, and could offer only meager resistance. . . . After the first volley we took refuge in flight.

—Mossut to Gallifet, *September 19, 1791, St. Domingue*

The revolution in St. Domingue would upend the colony's social order and scatter many of its residents across the Americas.[1] The refugees who fled the revolution were forced to leave much of their property behind in order to rebuild their lives. But while they left land and material belongings in St. Domingue, what they brought with them in social practice, cultural expression, and political experience would make an indelible mark on Louisiana. First-generation refugees and their descendants from each of the three major social categories—whites, free people of color, and enslaved blacks—made distinctive impacts on the newly American territory. James Pitot, a white St. Dominguan, would become the first mayor of the newly incorporated city of New Orleans, serving from 1804 to 1805.[2] Louis Charles Roudanez, a free man of color born in Louisiana of a St. Domingue refugee mother, ran a radical newspaper demanding the rights of full citizenship for all people of African descent.[3] And as for the enslaved who accompanied their owners, many in the Louisiana Territory feared they would incite rebellion and revolution in their new home—they had brought one colony to its knees and it seemed reasonable to think they might do so again in a new country.

To assess how the refugees both influenced and were influenced by understandings of race in American Louisiana, we must examine the social, cultural, and political contexts that formed them before they arrived in the United States. The following sections flesh out the social and political context of St. Domingue by describing events there through the eyes of these different groups. It is only by understanding this background that we are positioned to consider what each group stood to gain or lose as they made their tumultuous transition to American Louisiana.

A LIFE OF CHARM AND STYLE: ELITE WHITES IN ST. DOMINGUE

In her book *From Saint-Domingue to New Orleans*, Nathalie Dessens outlines the lavish social and cultural life of St. Domingue compared to other French possessions in the Americas. Although Louisiana was considered a cultural backwater, eighteenth-century St. Domingue had a vibrant theater life; newspapers; a bookstore with a library; and a branch of the Société Royale des Sciences et des Arts in Cap-Français.[4]

In his prerevolutionary study of the colony, Moreau de St. Méry describes the theater at Cap Français as essential to social life in the city:

> It would be impossible not to take part in the theater at Cap especially once one makes a habit of it. There are so few people in this town and at least we are assembled if not united. The desire to please, to show off one's dress provides many women a diversion from their sedentary life. Foreigners, sailors especially, find in the theater a recreation that rescues them from boredom and from more costly pursuits. One can also take language lessons, and in a town where the promenades are not much used, where one fears the sun and after that the silence, the theater seems agreeable.[5]

The portrait of life that St. Méry sketches here is one of boredom intermittently relieved by various amusements to be found in town. As he briefly notes in this description, the theater at Cap did more than provide a place to stage plays. In addition to providing lessons, other parts of St. Méry's description highlight the many balls, dances, and operas that took place there. Central to all of this was the fun of having a place to go out in order to see and be seen.

According to St. Méry, the popularity of different kinds of dance events changed over time. When the theater was first established, a Sunday night ball was held every week from Three Kings Day until Mardi Gras. These balls would begin at six in the evening and go as long as the dancers could endure. But the all-night balls were tiring in a country where "staying up for a single night does real damage to one's health."[6] Because many found these Sunday night events unappealing, the decision was made in 1780 to replace them with less formal dances where many participants engaged in masking. In contrast to the Sunday night affairs, these less formal dances started promptly at 5 p.m. and ended at 9 p.m. just in time for the evening meal. Reflecting on these dances, St. Méry writes:

> One goes there to dance, to see dancing, to talk, and discuss business.... The prettiest faces, the most seductive grace, the most elegant clothing, everything ravishes, and on leaving these charming parties the soul is in a state of delirium.[7]

One can almost hear the music and see the fancy dress in St. Méry's lively descriptions.

But not all of life consisted of gaiety, ribbons, and lace for St. Domingue's white population. The hand of colonial rule weighed heavily on them—particularly for the Creoles who had been born in the colony and could call no other place home. The Creoles felt the time was long overdue to gain political and economic autonomy from France. In their minds, they were the ones who truly owned and thus should govern St. Domingue. Unlike the absentee owners in France who sought to profit without labor or sacrifice, they put up with the many difficulties of life in the colony. In addition, they chafed under the French policy called the "Exclusive," which required that they buy from and sell exclusively to the French. The policy made a mockery of St. Domingue's geographic and economic realities, located as it was just south of the United States, next to Spanish Cuba, and to the northeast of British Jamaica—three important non-French trading partners. The Exclusive policy—while good for France—was economically backward for the Creoles. Thus, when they learned of the opportunity to participate in the reassembled Estates General, they organized themselves to elect representatives to send to the talks.

In this sense, St. Domingue's white Creoles were quite different politically from those they would encounter in Louisiana. As a group, St. Domingue's Creoles were more organized and quite vocal in their demands for autonomy because so much was at stake in this wealthy colony that made fortunes for many. In Louisiana, by contrast, the relative poverty of the colony made the stakes much lower. Instead, the struggle for everyday survival absorbed white Louisianans much more than concerns about autonomy. Nathalie Dessens provides a concise comparison between the politics of St. Domingue and Louisiana Creoles when she writes that:

> [The St. Domingue Creoles] were accustomed to exercising self-government, to a large measure, and they put forward their claims with a boldness unheard of in Louisiana, where the Spanish mode of government had been much more centralized. They were also clearly ahead in civic awareness—as proved by the dynamic colonial press of Saint Domingue—compared with Louisiana.[8]

In line with this political savvy, as we have already noted, the first mayor of the newly incorporated city of New Orleans was not a native Louisianan, but rather a St. Domingue refugee named James Pitot. Many other St. Domingue refugees like him filled important political and civic roles once they settled into Louisiana.

In this sense, there are important similarities between white St. Dominguans and free people of color in the colony. St. Domingue boasted a wealthy, well-educated, and politically active group of free people of color, many of whom owned plantations and slaves in their own right. These free colored residents had their own place in the colony's expansive social scene and also sought greater political recognition and power befitting their levels of education and wealth. Both of these characteristics would make them unusual and potentially threatening to white Anglo-American Louisianans who were unaccustomed to such self-assurance and high status among people of African descent.

Before the Revolution, free people of color played a significant role in sustaining the cultural life of the colony. In his discussion of musical life in the major cities of eighteenth-century St. Domingue, Bernard Camier describes the lives of some prominent free people of color who were musicians.[9] One of these was a free woman of color named Minette, a singer who enchanted many. Her life of ease is confirmed, Camier writes, by the fact that she owned slaves and by the names of the prominent colonists who surrounded her. Another highly esteemed free musician of color was Joseph César. He lived and worked in Cap-Français and was a first violinist at the theater there. Soon after the Revolution erupted, he emigrated to Philadelphia, where he was well received.

People of color were not, however, restricted to the role of performer. Many also regularly attended concerts, dances, and plays. Across the major towns of the colony, people of color had their place—though it was a prescribed place. Among the fifteen hundred seats in the Cap theater, for instance, there were ten boxes that were reserved for people of color. St. Méry explains that seven of them were for mixed-race women described as *mûlatresses* and three were reserved for black women.[10] There is, as we learn later on in his discussion, quite an interesting history behind the three boxes reserved for black women.

Before 1775, black women were not allowed into the theater. In protest, they approached St. Méry and asked him to draft a letter on their behalf demanding that they be permitted to enter the theater to sit with their mixed-race daughters. Apparently, the daughters balked at the idea of their mothers sitting with them, so although the mothers were allowed in, they were restricted to separate boxes near but not right next to their daughters.[11] Why would the young women have been so averse to their mothers accompanying them? St. Méry provides his own interpretation when he describes the theater as an:

> Asylum for the young people of the town and the garrison because of the young women of color whose boxes are on top, conversation is sometimes established from bottom to top and top to bottom, and it is of the sort that could offend the ears, though harmless. At each intermission there is a great murmuring and shuffling and it grows between the two areas because the young women of color use this time to go out into the adjacent streets or onto the government promenade in order to get air, or that, at least, is the pretext they use.[12]

Although St. Méry insinuates that these young women may have had lax sexual mores, the mothers' successful petition to accompany their daughters suggests an alternative interpretation: that the young women may have been taken advantage of by men from the garrison without the protection of older and wiser female escorts. As these examples illustrate, the social and economic position of free people of color in St. Domingue was one that set them apart from the black majority of St. Domingue. They were free, educated, and sometimes wealthy. They had greater entrée to white society than did the enslaved majority.[13] In some cases, this entrée was achieved through *placage*—an informal system of partnership between white men and women of color.

This position in between that of whites and slaves also existed in parts of the Anglo-American United States, but in much weaker form. Although there were some free blacks in many parts of the United States, nowhere—other than in New Orleans—did they constitute such a well-established and well-off society of their own. For those free St. Dominuge refugees of color, therefore, arriving in New Orleans in 1809 was a fortuitous event. Whereas their background and experience made them different in some key ways from native Louisianans, in many other ways a path had already been carved for them. They would take their place and resist attempts at Anglo-American racialization that would threaten their freedom and position by lumping them into a larger category called "black." In this sense, the St. Domingue experience prepared them well to thrive in Louisiana.

And indeed, in 1789, when St. Méry was writing his manuscript, the time was not far off when many of St. Domingue's free people of color would need a place of refuge.[14] For beneath the lively cultural life available in St. Domingue lay deep and enduring social and political tensions that would ultimately be the colony's undoing. Though free people of color were among celebrated performers and many were well-off enough to own slaves and participate in the lavish entertainments on offer, their lives were not so carefree as these experiences might suggest—particularly after the Seven Years' War when France experienced a significant contraction in its colonial holdings.

With the loss of many of its American territories in 1763, St. Domingue became the centerpiece of France's colonial empire. The colony received renewed waves of French immigrants seeking to make their fortunes. The new arrivals fostered increased competition for land and employment, often pitting free people of color against poor and middle-class whites. As John Garrigus notes, this was a turning point in social and legal definitions of race in the colony that established "a deep and apparently permanent gulf between 'whites' and 'free people of color.'"[15]

Laura Foner confirms the transition to a heightened state of racial conflict when she writes that:

> A new influx of poor whites had come to St. Domingue in the last decade before the French Revolution, drawn by the extraordinary prosperity. When they arrived, they found that almost all of the good land was already taken up—much of it by free colored men. If they tried to find work as artisans in the towns, they also came up against the competition of free men of color.[16]

These tensions were accompanied by a series of new laws and social practices that institutionalized and guarded the borders of whiteness. After 1769, free men of color were forbidden to serve as militia officers, even over other men of color. To assure "purity," white militia members would engage in probing genealogical investigations meant to unmask a potential officer's mixed-race roots.[17] In addition, free people of color faced a laundry list of other restrictions, including the inability to use the same surname as white families; refusal of the titles "Sieur" and "Dame"; enforced segregation in public places; inability to practice certain professions; and the inability to wear fine clothing, jewelry, or ride in expensive coaches.[18]

The already simmering tensions between whites and free people of color were made more complex and more intense by the calling of the Estates General and the beginning of the revolution in France in 1789. This revolution across the sea opened up a space for dissent in the colony that members of every social status—free and enslaved—took advantage of. That space would soon explode into revolution in the colony itself and spur the flight of multiple waves of refugees who would take to the seas from the 1790s until St. Domingue was reborn as the independent nation of Haiti in 1804. It was these events that paved the way for the refugees of St. Domingue to make their way to Louisiana. We explore these developments next.

FAREWELL, ST. DOMINGUE

It was July 26, 1803, and the widow Lambert was still living in Cap-Français, St. Domingue's capital city, while the revolution raged around her. In the midst of this, she put pen to paper to write to her son, Pierre Antoine:

> Cap [Français], the 26th of July 1803
> My dear Lambert, your last letter announced the departure of your wife and of all that I hold dear which keeps me in constant anxiety, impossible to express. Send me news of yourself and of all your family. We are blocked by sea and by land. If we have the happiness to learn that you are safe, it will soften the cruel position that we are in. My sister and her husband and I tenderly embrace you all. Good bye my children. Put us at peace by writing. Good bye again once more.
> Widow Lambert"[19]

Madame Lambert was just one among thousands of white St. Dominguans who found themselves in this same situation—surrounded by revolutionaries and fearing for their lives. How did things come to such a pass? How was the beautiful "Pearl of the Antilles," with its cultivated social and cultural life, brought to its knees?

The colony's unequal social relations were like dry kindling that had long smoldered, nourished by discontent and eventually fanned into flame by events on both sides of the Atlantic. *Libérté, Egalité, Fratérnité* ... the cry of the Revolution in France echoed across the waters to the inhabitants of St. Domingue. The call spoke to the hearts of people in every social and economic stratum—but in different ways.

Having endured the tightened screws of racism over the course of the 1770s and 1780s, free people of color were more than ready to have their voices heard in the new National Assembly once the opportunity presented itself in France. Despite being educated, qualified to work in the professions, and, in some cases, plantation and slave owners themselves, free people of color were actively marginalized by white colonists who were intent on holding fast the color line. This was not, however, a group willing to cede power easily.

Julien Raimond, an extraordinarily wealthy and well-educated free man of color, negotiated on behalf of free people of color in Paris in the early 1780s. There, even before the revolution in France got under way, he sought political recognition and official voice for his group in St. Domingue. In 1789 he joined a group in Paris called the *colons Américaines* and became a leading member of the organization as it worked for the abolition of social distinctions between free people of color and whites. Another prominent member of this group was Vincent Ogé, a free man of color who was also a leader in the group. The *colons Américaines* made a formal request to send representatives to the French National Assembly on behalf of free people of color to petition for their rights, but their request was denied in December 1789.[20]

Ogé would later go on to lead an unsuccessful uprising of free people of color in the north of St. Domingue with a collaborator named Jean-Baptiste Chavannes. After being repulsed by the white militia, Ogé went into hiding in the Spanish part of the island. He was, however, found by the Spanish authorities, returned to French St. Domingue, and violently killed by being broken on the rack. Afterward his head, along with those of others who had been involved in the revolt, was placed on a pike to serve as a cautionary tale to others. This would not, by any means, however, mark the end of the struggle of free people of color to gain their civil, political, and social rights. Whereas leaders like Ogé had begun by simply requesting equality between whites and free people of color, as they faced continual and sometimes violent rebuff from whites in St. Domingue, many came to see that it was in their interests to ally themselves with the enslaved majority in order to take the island over entirely from white rule.[21]

This brings us to the enslaved majority. Although the events in France were of interest to the enslaved persons who knew about them, they needed no French Revolution to commit themselves to seeking freedom. Most of the enslaved in St. Domingue—about two-thirds—were Africans who had been taken from their homes across the water and forced to endure the deadly passage to the Americas. They remembered the sweetness of freedom and were determined to have it back. In pursuit of this freedom, several different groups of enslaved persons came together to launch what would become the Revolution. The first was an elite group that included slave drivers, overseers, coachmen, and others in positions of authority and trust. Before he achieved his freedom, Toussaint L'Ouverture belonged to this elite group. These elite slaves often had greater physical mobility and thus were able to travel between plantations to help spread messages and organize others who were not as mobile. Elite slaves also had access to key information about developments in the colony because of their proximity to whites. A second key group consisted of maroons, those who had escaped the bonds of slavery and fled to the mountains, where they created their own autonomous societies. Although it was risky, maroons would come down from the mountains to participate in planning the revolt that was set to take place in August 1791. Finally, there were the masses of enslaved persons, some of whom may have been involved in the planning and others who joined as the revolt spread and turned into a full-fledged revolution.

On the evening of August 14, 1791, two hundred or more representatives from several different plantations in northern St. Domingue gathered to launch the rebellion that would grow into revolution. They met at Bois-Caïman, near the Lenormand de Mézy plantation in Morne-Rouge, where, under the leadership of a Vodou priest named Boukman Dutty, they carried out a ceremony that provided a spiritual bond and strengthened them for the battle to come. They were rallied together by the exhortation to "Listen to the voice of liberty which speaks in the hearts of all of us." At that assembly they set the date for the revolt, which was to begin a week later.[22]

On that fateful day, the northern part of the colony was taken by storm. In *The Making of Haiti*, Carolyn Fick describes the quick and devastating inaugural events of the Revolution as follows:

> At ten o'clock, the slaves of the Flaville-Turpin estate in Acul, under the direction of one Auguste, deserted en masse to make their way to the Clément plantation, where they joined Boukman and combined their forces with the rest of the slaves there.... [they] proceeded to the Noé plantation, where a dozen or so of these slaves had killed the refiner and his apprentice, as well as the manager.... By midnight the entire plantation was aflame, and the revolt had effectively begun.... Armed with torches, guns, sabers, and whatever makeshift weapons they were able to contrive, they continued their devastation as they carried the revolt to the surrounding plantations.[23]

Over the course of the Revolution, what must have seemed like oceans of blood were spilled and the formerly elegant city of Cap-Français was burned to the ground.

This, then, is what the widow Lambert was referring to in her letter when she told her son that they were blocked by land and sea—Cap-Français was a port city. The colony was brought to ashes and cinder as thousands fled, desperate to save their lives and what slave and other property they could take with them. But how did things turn out for the widow Lambert? Her case does not, unfortunately, have a happy ending. On November 27, 1804, her son received a letter from his brother-in-law who was known by the nickname "La Fraise":

> Last March I was indeed at the Cape, my dear Lambert; yes, my dear fellow, I did everything I could to save your cherished mother, and everything I believed I had to do for myself. I offered money to the pilot of the Cape—I offered him 100 gourdes—in spite of the fact that I didn't have a sou; but I was certain I would come up with them, because Captain de Butts has promised them to me to secure you mother's passage and I was certain of the captain. Nothing could have saved your dear one, so dear to a son, I wanted to have her disguised as a seaman; she told me that she didn't have any money for her passage. I spoke immediately to Captain de Butts who told me that she didn't need the money in order to leave, that his ship was at her disposal if she wanted to leave right away. She told me that she had a few little things to sell; but that she would leave in ten days, if the captain wanted to wait. He was not able to do that as his ship was ready to leave and loaded. Therefore, I was compelled, my dear Lambert, to leave without satisfaction, but I planned to return to the Cape; and to have your mother depart from that evil country, but two weeks after my arrival in Alexandria I had the misfortune to be ill; that prevented me from following through with my intention unfortunately for me and for your mother. But—the Captain had promised me to bring her back on his return, he was unable to do it, because the fatal blow of Dessalines was carried out during the time of his crossing.[24]

Other St. Domingue colonists, seeking to avoid the fate of Madame Lambert, had fled the island much earlier, taking their slaves with them. In the next section we follow some of these refugees in their voyage first to Cuba and then to Louisiana.

JOURNEY ACROSS THE WATER

By January 1, 1804, the colony of St. Domingue was no more. In its place stood the newly independent and majority-black country of Haiti. Thousands of its former colonists were dispersed throughout the Americas and across the ocean. For many, the neighboring island of Cuba became a new home in the tumultuous year of 1803, when it became apparent to all that the revolutionaries would win. Thousands of St. Domingue refugees settled in the eastern part of that island, hoping to renew their lives and repair their finances. The transformative 1809 migration that doubled the population of New Orleans drew its members from the St. Domingue exile community that had fled to Cuba. Their path from St. Domingue to Cuba and then to Louisiana was one filled with intense suffering and struggle as the stories of the Dauberts and of Justine de Carle will illustrate.

Germain Daubert and Marie Claude Rigaud were a husband and wife who were among the many who fled to Cuba.[25] If they had had the means to do so, they might well have chosen to invest in the cultivation of coffee— a crop that, while less lucrative than sugar, had the potential to rebuild some of the fortune they had lost in St. Domingue. The Dauberts were not, however, among those who had the resources to invest in coffee. Instead, Germain Daubert took an alternative route that was a path used to sustain refugees of lesser means: privateering.

Privateering could be a lucrative pursuit. The potential for success in this area is illustrated by the experience of one Jean-Baptiste Lemonnier-Delafosse, who, in an 1803 letter, explained how he turned around his initial period of difficulty:

> When I arrived amidst this colony, I had neither friends nor acquaintances; and yet I had to eat. A Creole named Courjol, reduced to selling bread in a market for a baker, received one for every dozen sold; with his meager earnings, he fed his wife and sister; his beneficial generosity admitted me to the sharing of this bread with his family. But I had to put an end to this burden. A ship equipped for privateering, commanded by French navy officers, led by frigate captain Boucher, had left New Orleans. A fine sailing ship, she had already made a few food hauls and was supposed to continue privateering for three months; I presented myself and was accepted as aspiring volunteer.[26]

Many less well-off refugees, including Daubert, took the path traveled by Lemonnier-Delafosse as they attempted to rebuild their lives after having escaped the flames and swords of the revolution next door. Unfortunately for Daubert, however, his own experience was somewhat less favorable than that of Lemonnier-Delafosse.[27]

In December of 1805, Mr. Daubert received a summons from the St. Domingue delegation at Baracoa, Cuba, to appear in response to a judgment that had been made against him in October. This delegation had been set up to guarantee that the French government—which still took an economic interest in the exiled St. Domingue refugees—received its due from marine seizures.[28] Apparently, Mr. Daubert had been part of a group of privateers that had intercepted two American vessels—the *Minerve* and the *Marie*—and brought them to Baracoa.[29] Although they profited from the seizure, their satisfaction was short-lived as there was some disagreement or misunderstanding about what portion of the catch was due to the French government. The judgment rendered by the Baracoa delegation demanded a larger share of the payment than what was delivered.[30]

Nearly two years later on September 30, 1807, Mrs. Daubert—who was now described as a widow—was named in a letter which affirmed that a Mr. Thebodières had the right to receive money from her related to this same marine seizure made years earlier by her husband.[31] Here she was asked to remit to Mr. Thebodières proceeds stemming from the sale of the ships and cargoes of the *Minerve* and *Marie*. In separate and lighter handwriting below that which gave Mr. Thebodières the power to receive the funds from the widow Daubert was a note in the former's own hand declaring that, on behalf of the St. Domingue government at Baracoa, he had received some of the funds owed by the widow Daubert. The matter was not fully settled, however, because less than a month later she received another, more urgent letter demanding further payment related to the sale of the *Marie* and the *Minerve*.[32] In fact, it would not be until April 21, 1808, that the widow Daubert would make the final payment related to this years-long case—and this after having received a strongly worded letter in February of 1808 giving her no later than July 1 to render to the government of St. Domingue at Baracoa what it was due.[33] The April 21 letter noted final payment of 837 gourdes and 77 cents and this was added to the amount she had already paid toward the outstanding debt. It is signed by Mr. Thebodières, who followed the matter to its conclusion. Thus ended the nearly three-year saga related to the two captured ships. Unfortunately for the widow Daubert, however, her peace of mind would shortly be upended again by political storms brewing across the ocean.

In 1808, following the fall of the Spanish Bourbons, Napoleon seated his brother on the Spanish throne. Spain's American territories, however, remained loyal to Ferdinand VII. These events put the French-allied refugees from St. Domingue in quite a difficult position. Initially, they were protected by Cuban officials who welcomed the economic boost the refugees had brought to eastern Cuba. But the situation deteriorated when

Spain suffered further defeats in campaigns from 1808 to 1809. Officials in Cuba were pressed by irate public opinion to take a sterner approach to the French refugees. Fires began to break out on the refugees' properties, and it became clear that in order to guarantee life and safety they must flee yet again. Even a politically well-connected refugee experienced frightful intimidation. He wrote:

> We have been threatened for over a year now.... French belongings are confiscated, sold, and pillaged. Mine were not touched because I was in the king's service, but I have nonetheless been pillaged; even my coffee has been taken this year. In town, I was respected and nothing was done to me.... During the revolution [of 1809–1810] I was denounced for holding some of your money and for not denouncing that fact myself and putting the money in the royal treasury. I always maintained that you were in Spain serving in the army and General Don Juan Errera, my friend, furnished me with the papers necessary to get me out of this embarrassing situation and I was able to save your money.[34]

The writer who penned this letter, the Marquis Duquesne, was in a privileged position for he had sworn his loyalty to Spain and was working for that government when hostilities broke out. But this was not the case for the vast majority of St. Domingue refugees who were harassed and intimidated into fleeing yet again. Many fled with little more than the shirts on their backs and were forced to sell quickly, and at a loss, the lands they had poured so much time and money into. Seeking a place to go in a hurry, many headed for Louisiana, which had a French heritage and was relatively close to Cuba compared to other possible ports of refuge.

When they arrived in Louisiana, many were destitute or nearly so. Because of the extreme tensions surrounding their departure from Cuba, many were forced to leave even their slaves behind. Such was the case of a refugee who penned an update in 1811 explaining his change in circumstances:

> If I waited so long in letting you know my current whereabouts, it was only in the hope of being able to impart to you more favorable information about my situation. But everything has conspired against that wish, particularly as this might just be the most wretched country known to man. That's all I needed, to be thrown upon such a marshy land after having lost, through my Spanish sequestration, the dependents [slaves] who had remained faithful to me. Your Negro Anne and her nephew Amédée were, most unfortunately, among that group. I was allowed [to leave with] only two slaves who, because they spoke

English, worked aboard the American ship which, in view of its advanced age and poor condition, miraculously transported me here. No matter what I did or how much I spent trying to get them to accompany me.[35]

This letter introduces the question of what happened to the slaves who accompanied their owners to Cuba and then Louisiana. What was their situation, and what impact would they have on racial and cultural relations in Louisiana? The story of Justine de Carle—a white woman from St. Domingue—and her slaves provides a glimpse into the situation of the enslaved.

Madame de Carle lost her husband Simon Navarre in 1799 while he was on some business in Jamaica. She then became known as the widow Navarre. Later in 1803, as the revolution in St. Domingue waged on toward victory for the revolutionaries, Justine took her children and slaves to Cuba, where they, like the Dauberts, settled and attempted to recover from the ravages of war.[36] When the refugees were pushed out of Cuba because of the war with Spain, she transferred her children and slaves to New Orleans.[37] This was no doubt a difficult move for Justine—both emotionally and logistically. She had lost her husband during the revolution in St. Domingue; fled to Cuba with her children and slaves a few years later in 1803; and began to rebuild her life as a planter in Cuba.[38] Now in 1810 she was being forced to flee again. Though the second exile must have been difficult, Justine had financial resources in the form of several slaves whose labor helped her to reestablish herself financially. Although she had led the life of a planter in St. Domingue and Cuba, there is no evidence that she continued this work in New Orleans. Instead, she used the strategy of renting out her several slaves to various other people in order to establish a flow of income to support herself and her household.[39]

In her work on the lives of the refugees in New Orleans, Dessens explains that this practice of leasing slaves was quite common in Louisiana.[40] But the St. Domingue refugees also imported a less formal way of gaining income from slaves who worked for others. In St. Domingue, it had been common among many owners to simply allow slaves to seek work where they could, so long as they returned a certain amount of money to their masters. The importation of this looser practice to Louisiana allowed for slightly greater freedom for urban New Orleans slaves than had previously been the case. The practice would also, no doubt, have been frowned upon by the Anglo-Americans who were in favor of a stricter slave management system than Creoles from either Louisiana or St. Domingue.

Justine followed the Louisiana custom of organizing specific leasing arrangements for her slaves. In a letter dated September 20, 1810, she gives a Mr. Guillotte the authority to oversee the care and rental of her slaves while she is away on business.[41] In the course of that letter she makes note of her property in Cuba, saying that:

> I leave to Mr. Guillotte different papers, titles and documents; among them my titles of ownership of my plantation of Cuba, with the prayer that in case the French would be called back on the island of Cuba to send my children and my negroes on my aforementioned plantation of Cuba.

Among these slaves there was, apparently, one named Françoise for whom she had a particular fondness. There is, in fact, among the St. Domingue refugees and their descendants down to the present day, quite often the story of the loyal slave who helped the family through the Revolution and helped them to survive in exile.[42] Although we can never know for certain how "faithful" such slaves were or how they weighed genuine affection with considered pragmatism, certainly some had gained the confidence of their masters after many years of service.[43]

All indications are that Francoise had gained Justine's confidence to a great degree. Francoise accompanies Justine to Cuba and then to New Orleans, where she makes her way on the coveted road to freedom. In her 1810 letter to Mr. Guillotte, Justine instructs him to "require from Francoise only four piastres a month during two years. At the expiration of this term, I free her unless she can't pay the expense of the ratification." After some time Francoise does finally attain her freedom in 1816.[44]

Francoise's story is unique in that she provides a glimpse into the lives of the enslaved as well as the lives of free people of color into whose ranks she entered in 1816. As a slave, she shared the fate of many other St. Domingue slaves who continued to earn money for their masters wherever they followed them in exile. But as a free woman of color, she was newly eligible to enter into a more protected social status and, potentially, to work for the preservation of the many freedoms this group sought to retain even as the Americans worked to dismantle this third tier of Louisiana's racial structure in favor of the Anglo-American preference for two unambiguous opposing categories—black and white. With her emancipation, Francoise joined forces with the large group of free people of color whose demographic impact and political strength would go on to leave its imprint on Louisiana's racial and cultural life for generations to come.

TRANSFORMING LOUISIANA

This brief synopsis of the refugees' social, cultural, and political life before their flight to Louisiana illustrates the many ways that St. Domingue acted as a training ground for the transformative impact they would have on Louisiana. Their first major contribution was to reinforce the tripartite division by color, class, and status that had existed in Creole Louisiana before the Purchase of 1803. While this three-fold division had existed in Louisiana—and especially in New Orleans—this racial system was in the initial stages of being challenged by the new Anglo-American administration, which sought to discipline what they considered to be unruly racial relations in the Louisiana Territory. The arrival of nearly ten thousand St. Dominguans who brought with them the concept and practice of a tripartite racial system set back the process of Anglo-American racialization by generations. The refugees also exercised a significant cultural impact in that they bolstered French language and culture in the newly Anglo-American territory.

But even as the St. Domingue refugees influenced the structure of race and cultural practice in Louisiana, they were also pressed slowly, but ineluctably, into the mold of Anglo-American racial custom over the course of a long and tumultuous nineteenth century. White refugees would experience a clash of racial interpretations that would leave them defending their whiteness before Anglo-Americans who viewed with suspicion St. Domingue refugees' greater willingness to publicly acknowledge their relationships and liaisons with people of color. Free people of color found that they, in turn, would have to fight valiantly to preserve the freedoms they had worked so hard to have in St. Domingue. Some did this by emphasizing their distinctiveness from enslaved black Americans, whereas others insisted on the essential dignity and equality of all people of African descent. And finally, enslaved blacks were feared and regarded with great suspicion because of their ties to revolutionary St. Domingue. But by the end of the nineteenth century, formerly enslaved persons descended from St. Domingue, formerly enslaved persons descended from Anglo-Americans, and people of color who had long been free were now all equally subject to legalized segregation as "negroes" or blacks. This would usher in a time where St. Domingue refugees and their Creole descendants of color struggled to find their place socially and culturally in a context where they continued to see social and cultural distinctions between themselves and Anglo–African Americans that were not recognized by law or social practice.

The following four chapters chart, in greater detail, the fate of the black and white St. Domingue refugees and their descendants. This examination highlights the effects of the emerging racial palimpsest and reveals patterns of race-based inclusion and exclusion that have shaped the social and cultural terrain of present-day southern Louisiana. In the following chapter we turn to the story of white refugees from St. Domingue who entered unawares into the racial and cultural maelstrom that awaited them in nineteenth-century Louisiana.

CHAPTER 3

༼ঌ

White St. Domingue Refugees and White Creoles in Nineteenth-Century Louisiana

When the St. Domingue refugees trickled into Louisiana between 1791 and 1809, they faced a multifaceted transition as they encountered new social, cultural, and political realities. Those who had fled St. Domingue via Cuba had been, within little more than a decade, under French, Spanish, and then American rule. The dynamics and stakes of this transition were quite different for whites, free people of color, and the enslaved. While white St. Domingue refugees were considered a distinct group when they first arrived in Louisiana, by the 1850s they were largely incorporated into the pre-existing community of white Creoles. Thus, the white refugees' story overlaps in many ways with that of native white Louisiana Creoles who also struggled with the racial and cultural processes of Anglo-Americanization.

This process of incorporation into white Louisiana Creole society was relatively swift and complete and occurred within one generation because of high rates of inter-marriage with white Louisiana Creole families. Although their distinctiveness as a refugee group was short-lived, their cultural impact was long-lasting. They lent their considerable numbers to the reinforcement and longevity of Louisiana's native Franco-phone and Creole culture and its attendant ways of conceptualizing and organizing race. But even as white St. Domingue refugees extended the period of Creole cultural dominance in Louisiana, they also came to share native white Creoles' fate in being negatively associated with a kind of tainted whiteness.

This chapter will examine the ways that white St. Domingue refugees and their Creole descendants struggled mightily to meet the stringent criteria of Anglo-Americans' definition of whiteness. Their eventual acceptance as white was made possible not only by their light skin color but also by their willingness to shift from the racial-structural practices and assumptions of the Latin/Caribbean system to the racial practices of the ascendant Anglo-American system. In the process of making this transition between the logics of contrasting racial systems, they were also forced to sacrifice their ethnic-cultural identification as Creoles. This was necessary because white Creoles' racial practices, which included public social proximity to and even overt intimacy with people of color, could not be separated in the Anglo public imagination from their ethnic-cultural identity as Creoles. Their acceptance as "white," therefore, depended on their acceptance of racial practices which called for much stricter social divisions between whites and nonwhites.

In the first section, we examine how white St. Domingue refugees and white Creoles handled the cultural challenges of the shift to Anglo-American rule. In the sections that follow, we see how they confronted the constraints of the Anglo-American racial system. The chapter concludes by tracing the gradual but definitive decline in white Creole identity by the beginning of the twentieth century.

THE AMERICAN CONTEXT OF ST. DOMINGUE IMMIGRATION

In a letter dated August 11, 1803, Benjamin Morgan wrote to his friend and business associate Chandler Price praising the "glorious news of the cession of the whole of Louisiana to the United States." But while Morgan exulted in the news, he expressed his concern that the proper kinds of people be appointed to office in the newly American territory. He was keenly aware of the social and cultural complexities of the Louisiana territory, so he wrote to Price in Philadelphia to inform him about the local situation, hoping that Price would in turn "communicate it to the proper authorities."[1]

He was particularly concerned about the finesse needed to manage the diverse group of nationalities in the area. He writes:

> We have a mixed population of almost all nations & it will require men of integrity & talents to overcome the prejudices of these people (*sic*.) & reconcile them to the government of freemen. . . . I hope great pains will be taken by the general

government in the appointment of our officers to make *us* relish the change I say *us* I mean *frenchmen* & spaniards—americans will do well enough, let who will preside they know their rights & will have them.[2]

In an enclosure dated August 31, 1803, Morgan provides a list of what he calls the "principal characters" that he considers to be worthy of consideration for official appointment. These he divides into three categories: those born within the limits of the United States, now residing at New Orleans; those born subjects of Great Britain or of the Louisiana colony now residing in the territory; and persons of other nations, mainly French, who speak the English language. Morgan was not alone in his concerns about the extent to which non-American groups would adapt themselves to "free government." This was an ongoing theme in the letters and communications sent by American residents and officials between Louisiana and Washington. President Jefferson addresses a similar question to W. C. C. Claiborne, who was appointed governor of the new territory. In a lengthy list of questions numbering thirty-six in all, Jefferson asks:

> 19th Are the people litigious? What is the nature of most lawsuits? Are they for rights to land, personal Contracts, personal quarrels?
>
> 20th What would be the effect of the introduction of the trial by Jury in Civil and Criminal cases?
>
> 25th By whom are [officers civil or military] appointed? Are any Chosen by the Inhabitants?[3]

In his answer to the nineteenth question, Claiborne replies that the inhabitants are "in general a Mild and Submissive people, not by any means prone to litigation." But the reason for this mildness is, in Claiborne's opinion, the fact that "such is generally the character of Men under Arbitrary Governments." This is just the tip of a larger mountain of judgments about the incapacity of the French and Spanish inhabitants to understand the "superior" ways of their new Anglo-American governors.

To the twentieth question, Claiborne explains that while the people are likely to be open to criminal trial by jury, he has heard that they will be quite opposed to civil trials operating in the same manner. As an explanation of the latter, he notes that he has been told:

> That Men who have long appealed for Justice to great Personages, whom they looked up to as wise and learned, cannot at first, without reluctance, submit to the decrees of Men, no better than themselves.

Despite this initial reluctance, however, Claiborne predicts that "as the people of Louisiana ... become more enlightened, they will no doubt, learn to appreciate fairly, and acknowledge with Gratitude, the superior Excellencies of the System."[4] Two weeks later, in his response to this same question, Daniel Clark replies:

> In a little time when the French can be made to comprehend the nature of a trial by Jury the effect would be of the most satisfactory kind, at present they know nothing about it, & the Americans ought for some time to be the only Jurors with now & then the admission of a Creole by way of explaining to him the nature of the subject.[5]

Here we see Clark use the terms "French" and "Creole," seemingly interchangeably. At this time, while native-born white Creoles would have been the majority of whites in New Orleans, there were some "foreign French" who included those immigrating directly from France and St. Domingue refugees who arrived in New Orleans before the great deluge of 1809.[6] What is key here, however, is that in the eyes of the Anglo-Americans, there was little social or cultural distinction between native white Creoles and the foreign French who also lived in Louisiana. Clark makes clear his assessment that the French and the Creoles are politically inferior and unsophisticated. These concerns are by no means limited to the political and juridical.

The perception of the newly arrived Americans was that local Louisianans of French heritage—having become accustomed to the stultifying rule of the Spanish—languished far behind in learning and other areas of social and cultural achievement.[7] Thus, the Americans saw before them a task of enormous proportions. Many of the leaders of this fledgling US territory were careful, however, in their approach to carrying out this task, realizing the potential for counterproductive resistance. Consider, for instance, recommendations made to Albert Gallatin, the secretary of the treasury, on the question of establishing the government and choosing a governor:

> Much will depend on the choice of a Governor, of a disposition, that may conciliate the French, by respecting & conforming to their fashions—He ought to speak their language, as the medium of an interpreter will render his situation extremely awkward & irksome .... Independent of his Salary the Government House ought to be furnished, & provided with a Steward for the care thereof—The etiquette of a table, adapted to the French style of living, in plate, linen, &ca &ca—is too expensive for an individual to sustain, without other resources than his salary.[8]

It is notable that such attention is paid to what many might consider to be minor aesthetic and culinary preferences. This level of attention reflects American officials' concerns that the transition go as smoothly as possible. As it happened, however, the first governor of the territory and later state of Louisiana was an Anglo-American. Governor Claiborne—only twenty-eight years old when he assumed his duties in Louisiana—did indeed encounter troubles as he sought to govern the territory. Much of this involved the political difficulties of managing the transition from the French and then dealing with leftover Spanish bureaucrats. But he also had to attend to the cultural difficulties of being an Anglo-American amidst Creoles.[9] The following excerpt from Claiborne's correspondence with President Jefferson reveals his understanding of Creoles' cultural differences and limitations:

> Our new fellow Citizens are indeed involved in great ignorance; a Gentleman on whose veracity I can depend, assures me, that in the settlement of Pointe Coupee where the Society is esteemed wealthy and polished, that not a third of the free Inhabitants can write their names ... my informant adds, that Mental Ignorance pervades the other parts of the Province in an equal, and he believes in a greater degree.[10]

In the next paragraph he counsels that in order to deal with such a population it will be necessary to tread slowly and carefully because "[s]udden and total reformation is best calculated for enlightened minds" and "the experiment may prove hazardous with Creole ignorance."

Together, these letters and correspondences reveal the extent to which Americans viewed Creoles as politically, socially, and culturally lacking. These perceptions paint a picture of Creoles as inferior "others." In this sense, they began their time in the United States on much the same footing as other European groups who were perceived as lacking in the qualities that make for good Anglo-American citizens.[11] There were exceptions, of course, as white St. Domingue refugees and Creoles did fill many appointed offices in the new American administration. For the most part, however, they inhabited the kind of probationary status of many other European newcomers. Although discussion was not framed by questions of race and whiteness in the early nineteenth century, French-identified immigrants' cultural differences from white Anglo-Americans meant that they were in the position of having to prove themselves in their new country. As the century wore on, moreover, questions about their social difference and racial purity would further emphasize their ambivalent position and raise the stakes of their struggle to enter into the mainstream of Anglo-American whiteness.

For their part, the reaction of Creoles to their new American governors was mixed. On the one hand, they looked forward to an enlivened economic environment where it would be possible to make more money. Spanish rulers had carried out a policy of deliberately isolating the Louisiana colony from the territories around it, and especially from the United States. Louisiana ports were not opened to American commerce until 1795. By the time of the cession in 1803, more American goods were coming into New Orleans, but the process was still sedate.[12] As American rule took shape, local Creoles were anxious to be admitted to the full economic privileges of American membership. On January 9, 1804, barely a month after the official transfer of Louisiana from France to the United States had been accomplished, a group of businessmen—the majority with French surnames—wrote to Congress calling on that body to secure for them the economic benefits they expected to accompany American citizenship. They wrote:

> The Memorial of the Undersigned, Merchants of the City of New Orleans in the province of Louisiana, Respectfully Sheweth, That your Memorialists eagerly embrace this occasion to offer their allegiance to the Government of the United States, and to declare their Resolution to support its Constitution, which holds out to them the enjoyment of the equal Rights and Privileges of Citizens. But your Memorialists would be wanting to themselves, and would ill deserve the name of Citizens of the United States, if they refrained from representing to you, the Great National Council, that these Rights and Privileges have not yet been extended to them; and that the Commercial and Agricultural Interests of this Province are greatly impeded thereby.[13]

They go on to explain that they are still subject to Spanish tariffs and duties even on imports from the United States. In addition, because of the transition, they lacked the proper documents for navigation and so had no proper authority to raise the flag of any country. As a result, their businesses languished. The letter combines both urgency and conciliation, and they conclude by emphasizing that they do not wish to "embarrass Government by urging too prematurely the execution of Measures which perhaps are already under Deliberation." They realize, they note, that the transition has been recent, but at the same time they are eager to see "that such arrangements will be made as will place us on the equal footing of Citizens of the United States." In this sense, then, Creoles were quite eager for US citizenship. They looked forward to more efficient and effective government and to an improved economic environment.

Socially and culturally, however, many Creoles were less than excited by the transition. One of the earliest cultural clashes took place just a few weeks after the New Orleans businessmen sent their letter to Congress. The setting of the confrontation was a public ball that took place on January 22. A variety of nationalities were present at the ball, chiefly those of French and English backgrounds. The disagreement that arose had to do with, of all things, the kinds of dances to be played for the attendees. According to an account given by Claiborne and James Wilkinson to the Secretary of State James Madison, some of the French insisted that there be no Contra Danse Anglaise, as this would represent a bias toward the English, their enemies. They thus threatened to deprive the Americans the pleasure of that dance. Claiborne and Wilkinson go on to say that "[s]ome French Officers & troublesome young Men from Bordeaux, were the Aggressors: much Confusion ensued, Swords were drawn." Apparently, they were just on the brink of spilling blood when the authorities intervened and arrested the aggressors.[14]

It is interesting and important to make note of the particular way that Claiborne and Madison make reference to the non-American actors. They describe the disturbance as having taken place "between the American and French Citizens (in which hitherto, the Creoles or Natives of the Province, have taken no Open Part, though we suppose them to favour decidedly the French Interest)." This excerpt reflects the fact that there were at this time, as well as later in the century, both Creole and French residents. The latter had emigrated from France while the former were understood to be native to Louisiana but generally of French heritage and sympathy. Although the differences were noted, for the most part, the two groups were assumed to share perspectives and interests. In his essay on the "foreign" French—those of French ancestry with origins outside of Louisiana—Paul Lachance notes that there was widespread intermarriage between native Louisiana Creoles and this group. He also finds that although differences in education and occupation between the two do suggest somewhat distinct group identities, the foreign French were sufficiently dispersed throughout all economic ranks and played such important complementary roles with the Creoles that they shared many interests.[15] It seems, then, that Claiborne and Wilkinson were right to assume that Creole and French citizens would share views about the events that took place at the ball.

It was just five years after the Creole-American dance skirmish that the largest wave of St. Domingue refugees arrived on the scene in 1809. Initially, the St. Domingue refugees were seen as a distinct group, but within a couple of decades they too were integrated into the Creole and French population that Claiborne and Wilkinson saw as sharing many interests. In the early years, however, the white St. Domingue refugees clung to each other, forging ties of solidarity in order to cope with the serial traumas they had endured. In her comprehensive study of the refugees, Dessens describes their social bonds in the following way:

> There seems to have been an imperious need for these refugees to meet, share their hopes, imagine the future, and devise plans for revenge and for the recovery of what they had lost. This favored the development of strong links between them, the longing for private occasions to meet, and the existence of public places for socializing.[16]

One of their principal meeting places was the Café des Refugiés which was a gathering place for the newcomers.[17] In addition to private gatherings and public social spaces, in the early years the refugees were also largely endogamous.[18] Thus, during the first decade or two of their arrival in Louisiana, the refugees maintained a distinctive community and identity that initially made them distinguishable from native white Creoles and other immigrants who came directly from France.

The insights of Jean Boze, a white St. Domingue refugee and property manager for Henri de St. Gême, provide some interesting insights into the relationship, affinities, and tensions between the St. Domingue refugees, native Louisiana Creoles, and Americans. In his letters to St. Gême—who returned to France, leaving his friend to look after his affairs—we see Boze sometimes distance himself from both Creoles and Americans, but we also see evidence that he ultimately blames the Anglo-Americans for what he sees as the decline of the city.

On May 15, 1830, Boze describes the situation between Creoles and Americans as follows:

> It seems there is opposition ... between the Americans and the Creoles that will always keep them from having a perfect union. These nations are legitimate owners of this wonderful country and can freely ... aspire to ... places of honor. Oh well! These Gumbo filés who have no majority other than in spirit ... are jealous to the point of [detesting Americans] because they would like to have everything and have superiority in everything.[19]

When Boze uses the term "Gumbo filés," he is using it in a derogatory way to refer to Creoles. Gumbo is, of course, a dish popular in New Orleans. Filé is a powder made from sassafrass that is often used as a thickening agent in gumbo. The local nature of the dish is meant to stand in for the local origin of the Creoles, but Boze is not making this linkage in a favorable way. In another letter in 1831, he explains how the tension between Creoles and Americans has manifested itself politically. He writes:

> Those beloved Creoles, partly by intrigue, partly through connections have today succeeded in occupying almost all the honorable Government jobs, as well as the best paying positions ... we regret that they are less strict in their work of collecting taxes.[20]

Here again with his somewhat sarcastic use of the phrase "les aimables Créoles," Boze places some distance between himself and Louisiana Creoles. His observation that the Creoles were trying to keep political power in their own hands is quite accurate. By the 1830s, Creoles were concerned about the increased numbers of Americans in the state and tried to counteract it by holding on to political power. They were initially able to hold onto this power because they were the numerical majority and because many were property owners and thus met the tax roll criteria for suffrage. Many Americans were less well off and thus unable to meet these requirements. Moreover—despite some of the tensions between native Creoles and recent French immigrants—the two shared enough interests to form alliances in order to hold onto political power.

In a similar way, Jean Boze, despite his implicit critique of Creoles, was quite clear in his letters that it was the Americans who were ruining things in Louisiana. In an 1831 letter he writes:

> This land of ours ... does not have today that same tranquility which the inhabitants of your time enjoyed, its population has changed so much since the entry of the Americans who, unfortunately, have been followed by a heap of vagabonds of all nations who exude crime.[21]

While his criticism of Creoles is often oblique, Boze's entries concerning Americans are quite clearly and emphatically negative. During this time period many Francophones, be they Creole, St. Dominguan, or French saw their interests as aligned and worked together to hold on to political power for a few decades after the Purchase in order to stem the influence of Americans. Although they were initially successful, the tide would begin to turn by the mid-1830s.[22]

It is, in fact, the 1830s that are identified by historians as the crucial point when the St. Domingue refugee population began to dissolve decisively into the larger white Louisiana Creole population. Dessens notes that the St. Domingue refugees began to marry exogamously in rather large numbers after their first decade in Louisiana. By the 1830s, the Café des Refugies—an important gathering place and source of support for the refugees—had ceased to exist.[23] Then by the 1850s, Brasseaux and Conrad note that "only eight percent of all refugees remaining in Louisiana had a refugee spouse."[24] Paul LaChance also uses marriage records to support his dating of refugee absorption into the Creole community. He explains that "Marriages in the 1820s and 1830s indicate that over time the preference of Saint-Domingue refugees did shift from the European French to Louisiana Creoles."[25] This was particularly true for white refugees who, as we will see, lost their ethnic distinctiveness quite a bit sooner than did refugees of color.

Part of the reason for the refugees' dissolution into the white Creole population was almost certainly that persons of French heritage—whatever their origins—were becoming overpowered, numerically and politically by the 1830s. By this time, Americans and other non-Creole immigrants were gaining in numbers and economic strength. The most vibrant economic area was the Faubourg St. Mary, which had large numbers of Americans and American businesses. This is where one could find the majority of banks, insurance companies, retail stores, commodity brokers, and so on. Tregle notes:

> So controlling had this presence become even as early as the mid-1820s that newspapers regularly began to use the terms commercial quarter and American section almost interchangeably, generally embracing in these designations the area comprising the First, Sixth, and Seventh wards of the city, extending from Conti to the upper limits of St. Mary.[26]

The Americans took advantage of their growing numbers and wealth to turn the tide decidedly in their favor. In 1836 they were able to use anti-French sentiment in other parts of the state to get legislative approval to divide the city of New Orleans into three separate municipalities. Americans fought hard for this change because though they had managed to do relatively well, they often felt harassed and sabotaged by Creole and French officials who made it difficult for the American section of the city to operate smoothly. Tregle explains:

> It soon became clear ... that what some called the "bosom of the city" meant vindictively to keep from the American quarter an equitable share of street paving, gas lighting, and other major improvements, no matter how substantial its contribution to city tax revenues.[27]

On the map in Figure 3.1, the area at the far right is the Faubourg Marigny (Third Municipality), where many new immigrants, including a large portion of those from St. Domingue, settled; the area in the center is the old city or French Quarter (First Municipality); and the area on the left is the American Quarter, also known as the Faubourg St. Mary (Second Municipality).[28]

The line separating the First and Second Municipalities is Canal Street. In popular New Orleans lore, Canal Street is still recalled as the physical and symbolic line in the sand historically drawn between Creoles and Americans. As Tregle points out in his work, however, the line was not quite so hard and fast as it is generally remembered to be. Well before the division of the city, plenty of Americans lived in what came to be called the First Municipality, and American business interests were established well within this area beginning at Rue Conti.[29]

It is the case, however, that once the three municipalities were legally established, the effect was to intensify the differences on either side of Canal Street. The American sector took off economically, leaving the First and Third Municipalities to languish. Income from taxes plummeted in those areas, and services as well as quality of life deteriorated. Dominguez describes the situation as follows:

> The "American sector" had notably better transportation facilities, well-kept wharves, a superior public school system, fire engines, market houses that made $70,000 a year (amounting to half the interest on the city debt), and a beautiful municipal hall.[30]

To make matters worse, the 1830s and 1840s were marked by even higher numbers of Irish, German, and Anglo-American immigrants. All of this pointed to the imminent demise of Creole and Francophone cultural hegemony.

As difficult as these cultural changes were for white Creoles in Louisiana, the ascendance of Anglo-American hegemony would have even more powerful and painful repercussions in the realm of race. This is because, for Anglo-Americans, being Creole signaled the likelihood of racial mixture. Put another way, Anglos were unable to disentangle Creoles' ethnic-cultural identification as Creole from the group's racial-structural practices. Within Creoles' more Latin/Caribbean approach to race, lines of cross-racial sociability and intimacy were less strictly drawn. While Creoles saw no conflict between these practices and their own whiteness, Anglos could only see the taint of racial mixture that made them incompletely white.

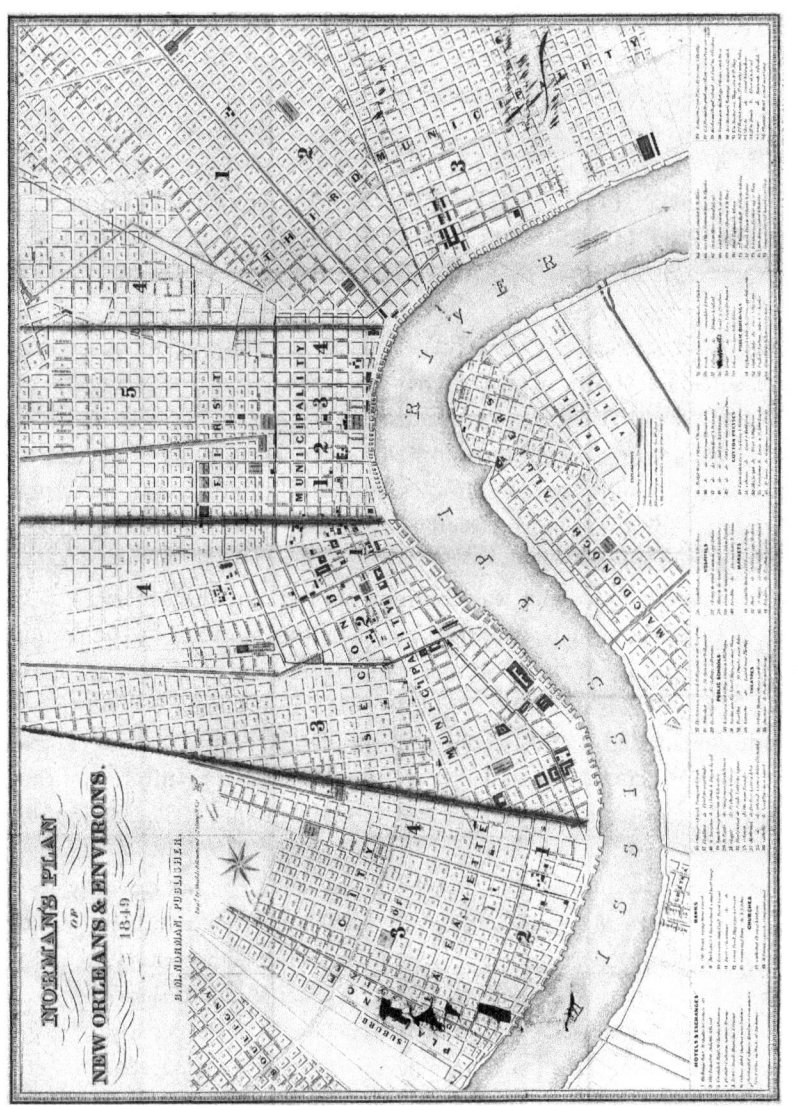

Figure 3.1 Three municipalities: The schism of New Orleans.

The social struggles embedded in the Civil War and the period following it focused a magnifying glass on the uncertain racial status of white Creoles. This war, which placed issues of race and status at the center of national dialogue, forced white Creoles to make a decisive separation from what Anglo-Americans perceived as racial ambiguity. The following section takes us to late nineteenth-century Louisiana with its aggressive insistence on white racial purity leading to the ascendance of the new racial regime known as Jim Crow.

CONSOLIDATING WHITENESS IN NINETEENTH-CENTURY LOUISIANA: THE INELUCTABLE ASCENDANCE OF THE ANGLO-AMERICAN RACIAL SYSTEM

As the Anglo-Americans consolidated their cultural hegemony over the Creoles, Anglo-American approaches to race also gained strength and ushered in an increasingly stark and strict separation between white and black. Whites in St. Domingue and white Creoles in early Louisiana had long had a different approach to race and racial mixture than had Anglo-Americans—differences which left them open to the accusation of being racially mixed themselves.

Whereas racial mixture was common throughout the Americas, white visitors to St. Domingue remarked on what they found to be the scandalously *public* nature of the relationships between white men and women of color. The relationships were so public that white men were said to have become enthralled to the sexual charms of mixed-race women of color. John Garrigus cites Moreau de St. Méry's views as representative of these negative reactions to the public nature of racial mixing in St. Domingue:

> The sexual power of free women of colour over white men was especially disturbing because of the public nature of that power. White men lived openly with their black and brown mistresses and acknowledged their mixed race children. Though born in Martinique, Moreau de Saint Méry was shocked by St. Domingue's *mûlatresses*. "One is not protected by the public decency ... that preserves morality [even] in [Europe's] capitals ... Publicity, I repeat, is one of the sweetest pleasures [of Saint-Domingue's *mûlatresses*]."[31]

In some cases, such relationships were consolidated according to patterned, semiformal arrangements. Some single white men in St. Domingue were, for instance, in the habit of taking on a mixed-race *ménagère*—a woman who ostensibly kept house for him, but who often was his sexual partner and the mother of his children. These *ménagères* were generally protected by contracts that spelled out what kinds of goods and resources they had a right to as a result of the services they provided to the men who engaged them. Another less formal kind of partnership was that of *plaçage*, where white men were known to create semipublic relationships with mixed-race women of color.[32] This public racial mixing had some analogues in pre-Purchase Louisiana as well, where *plaçage* was also a recognized form of relationship.[33]

When they arrived in Louisiana, white St. Domingue refugees reinforced white Creoles' perspectives on race and racial mixing. Nathalie Dessens describes this process in her chapter on the social impact of the refugees where she reflects on the ways white refugees lived out an approach to race and racial mixture that caught the attention of Anglo-Americans. She explains:

> the ties between the whites and free people of color were stronger in Saint-Domingue than in Louisiana. In Saint-Domingue, there was no residential segregation, and when the refugees reached New Orleans, they all flocked into the same areas of New Orleans, without any racial distinction, principally to what is now known as the French Quarter and to the Faubourgs Trémé and Marigny.[34]

In addition, white refugees were quite insistent on recognizing their mixed-race offspring. Dessens notes: "The Books of Wills of New Orleans show the pains they took to ensure that their children, legitimate and illegitimate, would inherit their property."[35] In sketching out their different approach to race, Dessens concludes that while the St. Domingue refugees and native white Louisianans had similar approaches to race and racial mixture, the refugees' rootedness in Caribbean racial practices "reinforced resistance to contamination by the Anglo-Saxon perception of races."[36] This resistance to the Anglo-American racial system held true until the Civil War years in the United States. Until that time, it was understood that the term "Creole" could refer to people of any race who were native to Louisiana before the Purchase or who were descended from this population. By the 1850s and 1860s, St. Domingue refugees and their descendants would also be counted in this larger "Creole" category given their cultural background and their shared non-Anglo social practices with regard to race. In his essay on the social skirmishes between Creoles and Americans, Tregle notes that white Creoles in antebellum New Orleans "perceived no danger from common acceptance of blacks and whites under the creole rubric, no risk that such definitional partnership might diminish the social status or prerogative of the dominant class."[37] Although white Creoles were not initially concerned about sharing the descriptor "Creole" with black and mixed-race persons, they had long been aware that outsiders had a troubling tendency to lump all Creoles together as potentially mixed race. Their sanguine response during the antebellum period was to make fun of this tendency while also clarifying that being a Creole was not synonymous with being mixed race.[38]

The situation became more grave, however, as Anglo-Americans poured into Louisiana during the period of Reconstruction following the Civil War. This was a time when white Louisianans—confronted by military rule designed to ensure racial equity—were defensive of their way of life and fearful that Northern influence would lead to black takeover of the reins of power in the state. Tregle explains:

> White fear of blacks mounted at the same time that the second invasion of "Yankee buzzards" brought new hordes into the city and state with less than accurate preconceptions as to the community's always complicated racial nuances. Those earlier northern identifications of "creole" with "mixed blood" and "mulatto" now took on infinitely greater significance as newcomers repeatedly demonstrated their continuing misunderstanding of the terms, to the ever growing consternation of the older community.[39]

In considering the precarious situation of white Creoles, Tregle puts it clearly when he writes: "the creoles added to the common white man's rejection of the black this additional spur to hatred: they might be confused with blacks."[40]

In *White by Definition*, Virginia Dominguez affirms the grave racial status of white Creoles in 1870s, Reconstruction-era Louisiana. She, like Tregle, highlights the fact that preserving the term "Creole" for both whites and blacks became very problematic for white Creoles. In commenting on this time period, Dominguez explains:

> Northern newcomers to the city and other non-Creoles began to insinuate rather openly and insistently that all Creoles had at least "a touch of the tar-brush.".... Although white Creoles did not exactly *look* colored, rumors spread that they had skeletons in their closets. Why, otherwise, would they continue to identify themselves as members of the same social group or category as thousands of colored people?[41]

What white Creoles were up against was the Anglo-American racial system's insistence on biological "purity" in its definition of whiteness. The long record of mixed-race practices and racially integrated living among white St. Dominguans and white Louisiana Creoles represented the racial-structural dimension of Creole social life, and it compromised Anglo-Americans' views of their racial integrity, placing all of them under a cloud of racial suspicion. The cauldron containing white Creoles heated up significantly as local outrage mounted over the politics of Reconstruction. The toxic situation gave birth to a virulent movement for white power in Louisiana which took the form of a popular movement that organized itself under the banner of the White League. This movement would require that white Creoles definitively put to rest ongoing suspicions about their racial purity.

In April of 1874, *The Opelousas Journal* published an article under the title "White vs. Black—The Coming Issue." The author, E. T. Lewis, laid out his case concerning the need for a White League given the unity of blacks amid the lamentable division of whites. Lewis provides a long list of grievances to support his argument for a White League. He writes:

> Who rules the State? Who has robbed us of millions? Who taxes us? Who has ruined our public schools.... Who has shut the doors of courts of justice against the distressed taxpayer who seeks relief against iniquitous taxation.... Who has made the Legislative and Executive departments of the government a shame? Who has outraged public virtue and prostitutes power and position to the base purposes of rings and stock jobbers.... Let the black man answer for these evils lie at his door.[42]

As he says quite clearly, Lewis lays the blame for every kind of public dysfunction and injustice at the feet of the black population of Louisiana. Given this analysis of the problem, there was only one solution. For Lewis it was clear that:

> The white banner alone can unite us. On the question of race against race there can be no doubt as to where the white man stands and none as to where the black man stands.... [We are] conscious that the real contest is for the permanent ascendancy of the one over the other.[43]

After laying out his argument, Lewis invites the white readers of St. Landry parish to a meeting that will unite them under the banner of the White League.

In the same edition of the paper, the editor, J. W. Jackson, responds to Lewis's call with a counterargument that lays out his concerns. Jackson argues that there had been previous attempts to pit white against black, and that these had come to no good. In direct contradiction of Lewis, Jackson cites a reduction rather than an increase in taxes. He goes on to note that the white people of St. Landry have not fared ill because of black people. Instead, he explains:

> The active inauguration of the issue proposed by this gentleman would disorganize our agricultural labor; and the material salvation of the country depends on *that*, not on the "white versus black" issue. The country white people . . . who make good crops, with the assistance of the blacks, can well afford to make no such issue, but let the politicians fight it out among themselves.[44]

Lewis took this response quite badly and very personally. At the White League meeting, he made a personal attack against Jackson, disparaging him and his point of view.[45]

It was, no doubt, the lack of love between Jackson and Lewis that caused Lewis to change the venue of his political rallying from *The Opelousas Journal* to another paper: *The Opelousas Courrier*. The May 2 edition of this paper published a very favorable review of Lewis's White League meeting.[46] On May 9, Lewis published a large piece in the *Courrier* thanking its leadership for endorsing his movement. By May 25, the *Courrier*'s editorial page was entirely taken over by the White Leaguers.[47]

Although acceptance of the White League agenda was not uniform among Louisiana whites, there was enough energy and organization behind the movement to make clear the high stakes of whiteness in Reconstruction Louisiana. These stark racial politics were keenly felt by white Creoles. Some responded in the French-speaking press by rallying their consociates to put aside petty cultural distinctions between Creoles and Americans in order to unite around "pure" whiteness. The French language paper *Le Carillon* reached out to white Creoles by proclaiming:

> The time has come to indicate what the sons of Louisiana want—that one must be either WHITE or BLACK, that each person must decide for himself. There are two races here: one superior, the other inferior. . . . Their separation is *absolutely* necessary. SO let us separate ourselves as of today into two distinct parties—the White Party and the Black Party. Positions will be made clear—between white Louisiana and black Louisiana, *Le Carillon* displays the white's flag, with the profound conviction that only within its folds can Louisiana be saved.[48]

This declaration reflected the convictions of the White League and the League idea spread rapidly. White Leaguers set out to literally take over the city of New Orleans. On September 14, 1874, between three and four hundred of them fought five hundred metropolitan policemen—many of whom were black. The conflict erupted into shooting which lasted fifteen minutes and resulted in the deaths of eleven policemen and twenty-one White Leaguers. The latter dubbed the struggle the "Battle for White Supremacy." On the next day, White Leaguers took over the statehouse and the Metropolitan Police Station in the Cabildo. The governor was returned to power a week later, but the events signaled a significant rise in racial polarization.[49]

The politics of the White League created a situation where white Creoles were increasingly obliged to defend their whiteness. The response of at least one reader to an 1873 piece published in *Le Carillon* provides an example of how sensitive some were to the need to protect the idea of Creole whiteness. This piece suggested that Arab people were mulattos and garnered the following response from an incensed reader:

> What should our fellow Spanish citizens, who are descended to a large extent from Arabs, think of that assertion? The Arabs are white, essentially white, just tanned by exposure to light and to the sun, as are all whites who live out in the open in hot countries. They are a pure people, without mixtures. They're a well-marked type that has preserved itself without change throughout the centuries.[50]

This reader's note highlights the great sensitivity Creoles had to the slightest suggestion that they might not be fully white.

We see similar concerns in a different piece published in *The New Orleans Bulletin* in 1875. Here the author, Alexander Dimitry, responds to one P. S. Moran, who had written to request that the term "Creole" be defined.[51] Dimitry obliges with a comprehensive argument which holds that Creoles are only, and purely, white. He cites the definition of Creole from Spanish and French dictionaries which define "creole" as the progeny of Spanish or French persons born in the Americas. He goes on to say that the term has later been misapplied to slaves, animals, and all manner of produce. This, he explains, is a corruption of the original meaning. Dimitry's painstaking response is similar to many others that occur in the late nineteenth and early twentieth century as white Creoles become more and more embattled in their quest to lay claim to the pure whiteness required of the Anglo-American binary system. The incendiary insinuations at the root of these white Creole defenses would ignite into an inferno of Creole opposition with the 1880 publication of George Washington Cable's book *The Grandissimes*.[52]

Cable was a New Orleans native of Anglo-American background. He was well known across the country for fiction and nonfiction essays. His great passion, however, was social critique, which he pursued in all of his writing, including his novels. He felt the treatment of people of color in Louisiana to be particularly disgraceful and dealt with these issues creatively and passionately. *The Grandissimes* began as a serial carried by newspapers across the country. In 1880 the individual pieces were assembled into a book and found a very receptive national audience.

In the book, Cable takes on Creole New Orleans by creating a complicated family called the Grandissimes. The family and its relationships are presented in such a way that it is quite difficult to know just what is going on racially. He has, for instance, a section entitled "Family Tree"—but the reader, at least this reader, emerges more confused after reading it than before. It is not until halfway through the novel that it becomes clear that there are actually *two* Honoré de Grandissimes and that one is white and the other is of color. Before that time, the reader believes she is reading about the same man. Cable deliberately confuses the situation because he wants to make the quite contentious point that the bloodlines of Creoles are often complicated and mixed. As it turns out, the two Honorés share the same father but different mothers.

The reaction of the English-speaking press—in New Orleans and across the country—was generally quite enthusiastic. The *New Orleans Item* called the book "certainly the most remarkable work of fiction ever created in the South" and lauded Cable's powers of description and his contribution to understanding and preserving Louisiana's cultural heritage. The reader notes, however, that the city's Creoles will likely view the book differently:

> We doubt whether this book, in spite of its delicate merit, will become a favorite with residents of the Creole city ... its paintings are not always flattering to native eyes;—its evocation of dead memories will not be found pleasing.[53]

The prediction that Creole readers would not appreciate the book was well founded. Indeed, the French press excoriated the book and Cable himself. In an 1885 column which announced a conference that would critically examine Cable's work, Placide Canonge described the author as "a minor writer, but one whose audacious pretentions—audaciously mediocre—are great ... saw there was money to be made by attacking the Creoles at the core."[54] When he refers to Cable's pretensions being "great," he uses the term "grandissimes," a mocking reference to the title of Cable's book. He then goes on to declare that Cable has no real knowledge of Creoles and thus no authority to write about them. He explains:

> There's not one of us who remembers having met him at a salon. This population of color which he describes with such aplomb ... he knows not the least thing

about them.... Moreover this analyst who makes himself out to be knowledgeable about a society for which French was the usual language during the time he writes about, does not understand even a word of French.[55]

He concludes by noting that a conference on *The Grandissimes* will take place on March 22 at 2 p.m. at L'Union Française with Charles Gayarré as keynote speaker.

Gayarré was a logical choice for conference speaker because he had spent much of his life defending the cultural integrity and pure whiteness of Creoles. Born in 1805, just after the Louisiana Purchase, he had impeccable Creole credentials. He was the grandson of Jean Etienne Boré, a Creole and the first mayor of New Orleans under the Americans in 1803.[56] Gayarré came to maturity during what was arguably the most tumultuous time of political and cultural change in Louisiana. He was active in politics during the period from 1836 to 1852 when New Orleans was divided into three municipalities. Later on he channeled his passion into the realm of culture, serving as president of the Louisiana History Association from 1860 to 1888. Gayarré had quite a lot to say about Cable's book. In addition to the L'Union Française talk, he delivered a lecture at Tulane University in April 1885, which he entitled "The Creoles of History and the Creoles of Romance." He spent the first part of the talk parsing in fine detail the collective genealogy of the Creoles. His argument was that Creoles were, by definition, white. People of color never had been and never would be "Creoles." He explains:

> Without going into a learned etymological investigation about it, I will content myself with stating that, according to the definitions given by the dictionaries of the French and Spanish Academies, which, as to language, are as of much final authority as the Supreme Court of the United States in matters of law, *creole* means the issue of European parents in Spanish or French colonies.... Therefore to be a *criollo* was to possess a sort of title of honor—a title which could only be the birthright of the superior white race.[57]

He then goes on to explain that over time the term "creole" developed from a noun into an adjective used to describe everything from plants and animals to slaves. Thus, one would refer to creole slaves to distinguish them from slaves born in Africa. The slave himself would never, however, have been called "a Creole"; only the adjective form of the word would apply to him.

There is quite clear evidence, however, that Gayarré is wrong in his assertion that the noun form of "Creole" had never been applied to people of color. In her work, Dominguez addresses this issue directly, noting that when the first legislature of Louisiana passed an act creating a militia composed of men of color, the act specified that the men "be chosen from among the Creoles, and from among such as shall have paid a State tax." Although white Creoles objected to the creation of a colored militia, there was no objection to the men's designation as "Creoles." Dominguez also points out that in his many letters to St. Gême, Jean Boze refers freely to people of color as Creoles. In a letter dated February 1831, he made reference to the death of Madame Vueve Pierre Canué, "ancienne creole louisianaise et de couleur." She is described here principally as a Louisiana Creole and only secondarily as a person of color.[58]

It was not, in fact, until the heightening of racial tensions during and after the Civil War that the campaign to redefine Creoles as "pure white" took off. The stakes were particularly high with the failure of Reconstruction and the advent of "Redemption" across the South. This new period saw the rise of Jim Crow segregation and thus truly required that anyone who claimed to be white be free of any insinuation of color. By writing *The Grandissimes* and thus declaring to a national audience that Louisiana Creoles were a racially ambiguous people, Cable placed white Creoles in an untenable position.

A decade after the Grandissimes controversy, another skirmish emerged over a Creole burlesque show that stopped in Louisiana as part of its national tour. The show was put on by the Creole Burlesque Company, founded by Sam T. Jack. Mr. Jack was a well-known showman who was the creator of many entertainment ventures. The Creole Burlesque was among his most popular, gaining great attention across the country. In an interview where he is questioned about the company, Jack provides a dramatic summary of all he went through to get the Creole Burlesque group together. He reports that he gathered "fair beauties," which included not only Creoles but also Cubans and others from tropical Caribbean lands. In a particularly dramatic comment, Jack explains:

> Do you know, I spent weeks down in those places searching for material. They are so jealous of the fair natives down there that it is almost worth a man's life to carry one of them away. I was accompanied by trusted agents and we were watched with undisguised suspicion. We were repeatedly prostrated with fevers, being unaccustomed to the climate, and the natives felt so unfriendly toward us that we had to make a little hospital of our own. I wonder to this day how we escaped alive.[59]

It is difficult to know how much Jack's wild descriptions accord with reality. Given his flair for showmanship, it is not unreasonable to suppose that he significantly embellishes the adventures and misadventures he experienced in his quest to form the company. What is clear, however, is that Jack studiously exoticizes the idea of the Creole belle and carries his "material" back to the United States, where he profits greatly from it. His description is all the more provocative for his intimation that he either forced or lured women away from their countries to follow him back to the United States.

Although the show was well received across the country, it met great opposition when it got to Louisiana. The St. Landry Clarion was aghast at this "company of negro half-breeds, who have the brazen effrontery to style themselves "Creole beauties." This the writer sees as a direct insult to Louisiana's Creole women who are most emphatically *not* mixed race. The affront was so keenly felt that a meeting of Lake Charles residents was organized at which an indignant resolution was adopted. The resolution reads, in part:

> Resolved, that the citizens of Lake Charles do publicly and solemnly protest against the wanton insult openly heaped on the fair name of Lousiana's daughters by a certain wandering troupe of negro female half-breeds who are advertising themselves as "The Creole Beauties" constituting Sam T. Jack's La Belle Creole company.... We urgently request all fair-minded citizens ... to resolutely turn their backs upon this slanderous show.[60]

The revolt against the show was so heated that the Creoles' protest was heard and remarked across the country just a few days after the publication of the resolution.

On October 25, the *New York Sun* commented on the disastrous Louisiana reception of the show. The *New York Sun* editorial writer leads off by explaining that the "controversy over the origin, derivation, and significance of the word creole began years ago and has been in progress ever since."[61] The author explains the racial root of the rancor against the Creole burlesque show and then goes on to explain that "Creoles are full-blooded white persons without any admixture whatever of negro or Indian ancestry, and they pride themselves particularly upon this fact." The response of the *Lafayette Advertiser*, which reprints the *Sun* article a few days later, takes issue even with the *Sun's* sympathetic coverage, declaring that the *Sun* "commits a most egregious blunder in saying there is now or has been in the last half century any controversy as to the significance of the word creole.... a Chicago mulatress is one thing and a Louisiana Creole quite another."[62] There was, therefore, no need at all to go into an educational lecture to explain what creole means. The racial controversies stoked by *The Grandissimes* and the Creole Burlesque show are examples of mounting slights against Creoles' claims of "pure" whiteness, and they made it clear that white Creoles must be diligent in their attempts to exit their ambiguous status and enter safely and securely into the privileges and protections of US-style whiteness.

White Creoles ultimately made their successful entrée into American whiteness by distancing themselves from Creole identification. Tregle writes that by the time of Gayarré's death in 1895 the tide had turned definitively so that white Creoles were more or less absorbed into the general white American category. This incorporation, however, came at the high price of the loss of white Creole identity. Tregle argues, in fact, that the transition into American identity was so complete that "[creole language and customs] . . . would never again be more than a nostalgic remnant in the midst of an American city."[63] He goes on to conclude his essay with a sober glimpse into Gayarré's funeral service:

> The coffin came finally to the vestibule of the cathedral, resting there at the focus of all those monuments to the Latin heritage which he had so passionately defended. As the mournful cadences of the dead march poured forth, the great doors were thrown open to an interior ablaze with gleaming candles. Inside, the church was empty.[64]

This dramatic conclusion makes Tregle's point that by the end of the nineteenth century, white Creole identity had lost much of its social and cultural significance.

In his work, *Imagining the Creole City*, Rien Fertel's findings echo Tregle's declaration of the demise of white Creole identity in the late nineteenth century. With his documentation of the rise and decline of a white Creole literary culture, Fertel shows that Creole literary production reached its height in the 1840s, and then experienced its nadir in the 1890s with the death of literary giants like Charles Gayarré, Adrienne Rouquette, Plaçide Canonge, Alcée Fortier, and others.[65] The decline of a vigorous, white Creole world of letters did not, however, spell the end of white Creole literary production. Instead, Fertel argues, the late nineteenth and early twentieth centuries gave rise to a new era of Creole writing that was oriented toward capturing and preserving the past.

This new preservationist Creole literature is a good example of what historian Pierre Nora calls *lieux de mémoire*—or memory sites. Nora explains that *lieux de mémoire* "originate with the sense that there is no spontaneous memory, that we must deliberately create archives, maintain anniversaries, organize celebrations, pronounce eulogies, and notarize bills because such activities no longer occur naturally."[66] We might add to this list the creation of literature—fiction and nonfiction—that has as an express purpose helping members of a group remember or celebrate who they are.

Key among the authors of this era is Grace King, who made a five-decade-long career of immortalizing white Creole social and cultural life in her short stories, novels, memoirs, and historical works.[67] King begins her magnum opus, *Creole Families of New Orleans*, with an introduction whose language closely mirrors Nora's description of *lieux de mémoire*. While Nora writes of the ways memory sites emerge just as memory is disappearing, King's introduction to *Creole Families* records her intent to "follow the *traces* [the founding families] impressed upon the soil two hundred years ago" and the ways "traditions are still carrying a *pale reflection* of coloring and wavering outline of them." Finally, from her perch in the early twentieth century, King sees these Creole traditions as "little stories ... still to be met hanging on a withering memory like shriveled berries on a tree that the next blast will rend from their twigs and scatter to the ground."[68] This last, in particular, resonates clearly with Nora's declaration that *lieux de mémoire* consist of the memories of social minorities which, "without commemorative vigilance, history would soon sweep ... away."[69] King's reference to "traces," "pale reflections," and "withering memory" illustrate her acknowledgment that the glory days of Creole society have passed. Her work is to preserve these faltering memories for future generations of Creole descendants.

This period of white Creole transition and *dénouement* also saw the rise of local-color poems, stories, and novels by Kate Chopin, Mollie Moore Davis, Sidonie de la Houssaye, and others who used these genres to explore and memorialize the Creole past.[70] In the popular press, similar themes were examined by Henry Castellanos's series of columns in the *Times-Democrat* from 1892 to 1895. These columns were devoted overwhelmingly to the heydays of white Creole life before the 1860s—the decade that witnessed the Civil War and the decisive unraveling of the fabric of white Creoles' cultural life and social institutions. The Castellanos columns boast titles such as "Olden Times"; "Reminiscences of New Orleans"; "'Jackson' Square"; "Public Balls"; "Diversity of Customs and Language"; "The Market"; "New Orleans Fifty Years Ago"; and "Facts Worth Remembering."[71]

One of the most consummate writers and chroniclers of this era was Edward Laroque Tinker, a scholar and philanthropist who was born in New York and who married a New Orleanian. Tinker spent much of his professional career producing scholarship and other kinds of writing that were focused on Louisiana and New Orleans in particular. In 1928 he wrote a novel called *Toucoutou*, which used fiction to chronicle the real-life story of a young woman whose mother unsuccessfully tried to pass her off as white.

The novel is based on the story of Anastasie Desarzant, and her failure to pass as white was taken up as a moral and cautionary tale with the lesson that "truth will win out." This novel and its writer nicely demonstrate the existential crisis arising during the transition from settled white Creole identity in the early nineteenth century to the embattled group fighting to retain its social place and cultural significance by the end of the same century.[72]

In a two-page discussion which bears the heading N. B.—*nota bene*, or "take note"—Tinker goes into a detailed discussion of who the Creoles are. He describes them as follows:

> Most of the good dictionaries in both French and English agree that this word, [Creole], derives from the Spanish "Criollo," which in turn comes from the word "Criar," to create, to be born, and that Creole means the issue of European parents in Spanish or French colonies; and of course the fact that the parents must be of European descent necessarily implies that they must be entirely white.[73]

This definition of Creoles as "pure white" demonstrates the superordinate position and strength of the Anglo-American racial system over that of the Creoles. It is a system dominated by "black" and "white" where whiteness requires the complete absence of racial mixture in the lineage. More than that, however, the Anglo system is one where even close associations with people of African descent cast doubt on the purity of an individual's and an entire family's claim to whiteness. Such an understanding contrasts greatly with their initial openness to living more racially integrated social lives in St. Domingue and early nineteenth-century Louisiana. Try as they might, white Creoles were unsuccessful in their attempts to shed the racial-structural legacy of public cross-racial relationships while hanging onto their ethnic-cultural identification as Creole. Creole identity remained hopelessly entangled in the public imagination with black lineage, and most white Creoles gave up the fight and relinquished the descriptor "creole" to people of color.

The incentives for white Creoles to blend into Anglo-American whiteness were as clear as the stakes involved. Either cling to a Creole identity that has become muddied in the US imagination with blackness, and suffer the social consequences, or drop the identification in order to make a clear break from this sullied social status. The story of white Creoles' tumultuous but final transition into Anglo-American whiteness follows quite closely the trajectory assumed in classic assimilation theory that is based on the experience of other light-skinned European immigrants. What this case reveals, however, is that nineteenth century immigrants from across the Americas who came from a different racial system characterized by widespread inter-racial relationships, had to make a conscious shift from a Latin/Caribbean way of understanding whiteness and managing cross-racial relationships to one in line with Anglo-American standards. This racial component complicates the assimilation narrative generally applied to light-skinned Europeans.

In the following chapter, moreover, we examine the highly racialized reception of free people of color among the St. Domingue refugees. Their story represents one of those "less-told historiographies" Saenz and Douglas make reference to in their call for the abandonment of European-centered analytical tools.[74] Afro-Creoles' struggles with and resistance to the Anglo-American racial system across the nineteenth century will demonstrate their very different integration experience as immigrants of color. The following chapter follows this group across the nineteenth century as they grapple with the ascendance of the Anglo-American system while also holding onto the greater flexibility of Louisiana's foundational Latin/Caribbean racial system. Their incentive to hold onto the tenets of the Latin/Caribbean system contrasts greatly with white Creoles' willingness to abandon that system and blend seamlessly into Anglo-American whiteness.

CHAPTER 4

St. Domingue Refugees and Creoles of Color

[Upon] what footing will the free quadroon mulatto and black poeple stand; will they be entitled to the rights of citizens or not. [T]hey are a numerous class in this city say 1/3 or 1/4 of the population many very respectable and under this government enjoy their rights in common with other subjects—It is worth consideration of government they may be made good citizens or formidable abettors of the black poeple say slaves if they should ever be troublesome.
—Benjamin Morgan to Chandler Price, *August 7, 1803, New Orleans*

In Chapter 3 we considered how white St. Domingue refugees blended into the white Louisiana Creole population within little more than a generation and were forced over the course of a somewhat harrowing nineteenth century to grapple with Anglo-American cultural and racial norms that conflicted with their own. Morgan's statement at the opening of this chapter provides a glimpse into the related but quite different struggles that free refugees of African descent faced as they sought to make their way in the rapidly consolidating Anglo-American system.[1] As was the case with white St. Domingue refugees, those of color were largely integrated into the local Louisiana Creole community within a generation.[2] In their case, however, ethnic-cultural Creole identification would last longer than it did for whites because the racial-structural dimension of Creole categorization provided a third rung in the racial hierarchy which provided a kind of buffer from the indignities of Jim Crow segregation. Entering into the realm of Anglo-American blackness carried very different consequences for refugees of color than the benefits acquired by white refugees and their descendants who entered into Anglo-American whiteness.

We last heard from Benjamin Morgan in Chapter 3, where he was delivering another of his reports to Mr. Price concerning what the Americans could expect to find as they took up the reins to govern the newly American territory. He puts his finger here on the hot-button issue of the time—how to deal with that class of free people of color so unusual and so threatening to the Anglo-Americans. Here, Morgan takes a pragmatic approach: give them their rights and they may be of use in helping the white Americans keep down the possibility of slave revolt. Indeed, the threat of slave revolt was living and active for Morgan and other Americans. Even as he penned his letter to Price, the revolutionaries in St. Domingue were sealing their victory over the French and would soon expel them from the newly independent country of Haiti. Placating the free people of color could possibly, then, help the Anglo-Americans to avoid the fate of St. Domingue.

But the politics involved in merging two different racial systems were more complex than Morgan allowed for in his recommendation. There was a pervasive sense that this in-between group was dangerous and potentially explosive. So great was the concern that Anglo-American observers expressed real misgivings about white Creoles' willingness to consort with this ambiguous, in-between class. Consider, for instance, James Brown's update on security issues in the territory, where he communicates his dismay upon learning that some native white Louisiana Creoles and a few white St. Domingue refugees had been recruited into the militia. Their great flaw, apparently, was that "[t]hese miscreants frequent at all hours of the night, if my information is correct, the tabarets or little Tipling houses and drink with free negroes or slaves, who appear to be their principal associates."[3]

For Anglo-Americans, it was difficult to imagine a social context within which it would be acceptable for a white person to associate so liberally with a person of color on terms that would even remotely suggest equality. For Brown, therefore, drinking together with mixed-race people was an unpardonable social sin that raised questions about the integrity of the white Creoles and St. Domingue refugees. There was, moreover, little space in the Anglo-American social imagination for acknowledging or accepting a group of people of African descent who enjoyed the kind of power and high social status that many St. Domingue refugees of color were accustomed to. The following section contrasts this Anglo-American view of free people of color with the perspective of those familiar with a Latin/Caribbean racial system.

FREE PEOPLE OF COLOR IN TRANSITION FROM FRENCH, TO SPANISH, TO AMERICAN LOUISIANA

Although the French and the Spanish had different approaches to thinking about and organizing race, there were key similarities between the two systems that contrast greatly with the Anglo-American system imported into Louisiana by the United States. First, in both French St. Domingue and Spanish Louisiana, there was a distinct, socially recognized space for free persons of color, many of whom were mixed race. They were not simply people of color who happened to be free, but, as their numbers grew, they were seen as belonging to a distinct social group with whom whites cultivated many different kinds of social and business relationships. Second, there was greater social acceptance for publicly recognizing mixed-raced relationships. This made for a climate where white men had greater freedom to publicly acknowledged children born of unions with women of African descent. As we saw in Chapter 3, this was the kind of behavior that led to trouble for white Creoles in their quest to be accepted as fully white.

In Chapter 1, we saw that while there were also communities of free people of color in other US cities, the racial system in those areas remained, for the most part, a two-tiered system where the major division was between black and white with little social or institutional space for persons who were mixed race and free. In contrast, when we consider Chapter 2's discussion of free people of color in colonial St. Domingue, we recall that many were persons of some wealth and status in the community. There were theater seats reserved specifically for free people of color, and many owned slaves and plantations in their own right.

Even free people of color who were not wealthy could enjoy relatively high status and associate openly with whites in St. Domingue. As an example, Emily Clark writes of the little-discussed social role of the *ménagère*—a mixed-race woman who was engaged as a housekeeper for a single man. In many cases, the *ménagère* became a life partner of the man who employed her. Although this may seem on the surface to be nothing more than mixed-race cohabitation, the practice was more formalized than the idea of cohabitation allows. Clark explains that *ménagères* generally had formal contracts with their employers that outlined the services they would provide and the compensation they would receive. She provides the example of Hélène Piquery, who was engaged as *ménagère* to François Siriery in 1778. Hélène was responsible for "administering the budget necessary to keep the household running smoothly, managing the shopping, overseeing the preparation of meals, and supervising cleaning and laundry." In Port-au-Prince, Marie-Louise à Traité had a contract which explained that "in addition to a salary of 2,400 livres she would receive lodging, meals, laundry service, and medical care if she fell ill." In many of these arrangements, the *ménagère* would receive substantial compensation at the end of her term that went beyond what was called for in the contract. Some received pieces of property, valuable household goods, and/or money to support children who had been born to the union.[4]

Clark contrasts the situation of the *ménagères* with the more often-invoked figure of the *placée*. This latter is best known as a young woman of mixed race who is "placed" with an older white man who keeps her as a mistress. Here, there was no contract and the *placée* was at the mercy of the man who kept her. The vulnerability of this situation becomes clear in the case of Michele Louise Tonnelier, who was a *ménagère* in St. Domingue and accompanied her employer first to Cuba and then to New Orleans as they fled the Revolution. Tonnelier brought suit against her employer, Jean Baptiste Maurin in 1812, claiming that she was due property that was hers as a result of her position as his *ménagère*. In explaining what happened with the suit, Clark makes clear the social and legal contrasts between St. Domingue and New Orleans concerning free people of color. She writes:

> [Marie Louise] was not a dependent without resources when she arrived with Maurin in New Orleans, but part of a team, her slaves serving as a source of income for the household. But severed from the society that had recognized the place of the *ménagère* and without friends or protectors, her bid for agency failed.... Marie Louis Tonnelier came to New Orleans a *ménagère*, but like so many other unmarried refugee women and their descendants, she is remembered as a *placée*.[5]

Thus, despite the fact that Marie Louise owned her own slaves and had contributed to the household, she was seen in the Anglo-American racial system of Louisiana to be a dependent black woman with no claim to the property she had helped Maurin to acquire. This transition from *ménagère* to *placée* is very significant, for it represents the larger reality that Marie Louise and others like her faced as they moved from a situation where there was a well-respected social and legal space for free people of color to one where this space was barely tolerated and was in the process of being whittled away as Creole Louisiana became more American. We also see a great contrast between Spanish colonial approaches to free people of color and that of the Anglo-Americans when we consider the situation of free people of color in Spanish Louisiana during the pre-Purchase years. As we saw in Chapter 1, it was during the Spanish period, from 1763 to 1803, that the population of free people of color in the Louisiana colony was greatly multiplied. The Spanish system of *coartacion* contributed to this growth and to the degree of economic strength and social respectability enjoyed by this growing population of free people of color.

Thus, by the beginning of the nineteenth century when the Anglo-Americans took over Louisiana, there was a large and well-established community of free persons of color in New Orleans. This was, of course, greatly increased by the 1809 influx of St. Domingue refugees who also carried with them an implicit understanding of the distinct social place and roles of free people of color. Anglo-Americans, however, were not prepared to receive this population favorably. In the Anglo-American imagination there was, quite literally, no way to think of free people of color as a significant, respected segment of the population with rights that should be respected and with whom white Americans could and even should freely interact as social partners—intimate or otherwise.

This is not, of course, to say that free colored populations did not exist in other US cities, or that liaisons between white men and free women of color did not occur. Certainly both the population and the relationships were in evidence in cities such as Philadelphia, Charleston, and elsewhere. As Emily Clark makes clear in her work, however, what did *not* exist was a social imagination that included space for the presence and social roles of this population. This lack of social imagination is why, despite the existence of sometimes significant free colored populations in many parts of the country, the existence of mixed-race persons and communities has almost always been exoticized as something peculiar to New Orleans. Although Clark's focus here is on the figure of the quadroon, her argument speaks to a larger refusal of the Anglo-American imagination to allot space and agency to free persons of color in the mainstream US experience. By doing so, this refusal literally and figuratively reinforces a binary racial system where one must be either clearly white or black, privileged or oppressed.

Once the Americans arrived on the scene, it quickly became apparent that the rules of the game would change in life-altering ways for free people of color. As James Brown's letter from the previous section reveals, concerns about the territory's security were paramount and drove many of the new proscriptions that Anglo-Americans would impose on free people of color. Consider, for instance, Claiborne's initial response to President Jefferson's question regarding whether or not there was a militia in the Territory. Claiborne explained that there was a militia and that it included "mulattoes."[6] He nevertheless exhorted the President to beware of this mixed-race group, and he went further to suggest that it might be best to arm the white inhabitants of Orleans because "The negroes in the Island of Orleans are very numerous, and the number of free mulattoes is also considerable;—on the change of Government . . . these people may be disposed to be riotous."[7] This fear of riot or uprising was driven, in part, by the revolution in St. Domingue which was still being waged at the time of Claiborne's writing. In his communication with the secretary of war, James Wilkinson echoes Claiborne's concerns about an uprising and makes direct reference to the revolution in St. Domingue:

> The People of Colour are all armed, and it is my Opinion a single envious artful bold incendiary, by rousing their fears & exciting their Hopes, might produce those Horrible Scenes of Bloodshed & rapine, which have been so frequently noticed in St. Domingo.[8]

The areas of emphasis in this excerpt, noted with capitals, communicate the major narrative about free people of color shared by Wilkinson and other white Anglo-Americans. "People of Colour" are noted here as their own distinctive group, separate from slaves. Though he does not specifically refer to them as free persons, it seems reasonable to assume he is referencing free people since it would not be the case that enslaved blacks would be "all armed." Next, he makes reference to the "Hopes" of this group. Hopes, no doubt, to have rights and privileges equal to those of whites. These were certainly not hopes that Anglo-Americans were prepared to make a reality. They were, moreover, "Hopes" that the people of color might be willing to pursue violently to the point of reproducing in Louisiana the "Horrible Scenes of Bloodshed" witnessed in St. Domingue.

For their part, free people of color lost little time in petitioning Claiborne to respect the military role they had long played in the region. In January of 1804, a group of fifty-five free men of color write and sign a letter imploring the governor to put their military talents and experience to use. They begin by making clear their allegiance to the United States, going so far as to say that they "feel a lively Joy that the Sovereignty of the Country is at length united with that of the American Republic." They then go on to describe their military service to the previous government and to affirm that they "shall serve [the Americans] with fidelity and Zeal."[9]

By 1806, Claiborne's early concerns seem to have abated somewhat so that, rather than seeing the free people of color as a certain threat, he takes a more sympathetic stance in favor of their bearing arms in service to the country. In expressing his views to the secretary of state, he explains:

> With respect to the Mulatto Corps in this City . . . I am indeed at a loss to know what policy is best to pursue . . . late Legislative Council thought it prudent to

take no notice of the Mulatto Corps in the general Militia Law;—this neglect has soured them considerably with the American Government, and it is questionable how far they would, in the hour of danger, prove faithful to the American Standard ... while proper exertions shall be made to conciliate the good will of all, I have little doubt but that those among them who possess property and a fair reputation, will, in any event, prove faithful to their allegiance.[10]

Claiborne's position here is quite different than it was when he penned his letter in September 1803 where he was concerned about the "riotous" nature of this same population. By now he has a more nuanced understanding of the complexities of race in New Orleans, and while he still expresses some ambivalence about how "faithful to the American Standard" they will be, this ambivalence is overcome by his sense that they can be trusted. It would not be until The War of 1812, however, when war broke out with the British, that legislators would finally grant the request of free men of color to have their own corps.[11]

Besides the defeat of the militia legislation, there were other ways in which the year 1806 was an unfortunate one for free people of color. This year marked the enactment of a new set of Black Codes to regulate slavery. While the free people of color would not be directly affected by these codes, they were affected by the addition of a provision at the end of that document that directly affected them. This provision admonished that "free people of colour ought never to insult or strike white people, nor presume to conceive themselves equal to the white; but on the contrary that they ought to yield to them in every occasion, and never speak or answer to them but with respect, under the penalty of imprisonment."[12] Further legal restrictions followed swiftly on the heels of the 1806 codes. Legal changes in 1812 and 1816 restricted access to public accommodations for free people of color and included the segregation of theaters and public exhibitions. Then in the 1820s ombinus lines were either segregated or entirely excluded people of color.[13]

Despite the obstacles and prejudices against them, however, free people of color managed to flourish and established themselves as a distinct group within antebellum Louisiana. They established schools, businesses, and social and cultural organizations that bolstered their unique identity. They were particularly active in the literary realm where they created a vibrant and cultured black and French literary public sphere. This literary sphere was at once a place for individual expression, and a space for the complex working out of Afro-Creole identity and politics. Chief among the tasks of this community was to somehow reconcile the Latinized racial system within which they were formed with the increasingly oppressive Anglo-American racial system that gained steady ground beginning in the 1830s. We consider these struggles in the following section through an examination of the poetry and prose of Creoles of color active in this French literary public sphere. Some of the most prominent actors in this sphere were the descendants of St. Domingue refugees whose inheritance of a legacy of social and political struggle in St. Domingue stood them in good stead as they worked assiduously to defend their social, civil, and political rights.

NAVIGATING COMPLEX RACIAL TERRAIN: AFRO-CREOLES' FRENCH LITERARY TRADITION

Many of the Creoles of color of Louisiana were highly educated, cultured, and tied to the literary sphere of France both intellectually and socially. It was this community that created the first African American anthology of poetry which was entitled *Les Cenelles*—The Holly Berries. This history-making volume, which was published in 1845, has only rarely been celebrated in US literature, but when it has been the subject of scholarly review, it has spawned great debate about the proper way to locate these Francophone writers within the larger black American tradition. Underlying this debate are quite different assumptions about race, culture, and blackness. The Anglo-American approach reads the *Les Cenelles* authors as clearly "black" and thus united to all others of African descent in the United States while the Latin/Caribbean approach takes a more nuanced position, interpreting the writers as people of color who inhabit a social and cultural sphere distinct from those of Anglo-African descent.

In line with these contrasting interpretations, *Les Cenelles* is alternately seen as the beginning of a unitary black literary tradition in the United States or instead as a counter or outlier to this tradition. In the foreword to the centennial republication of the volume, Edward Coleman describes at length the unique social and cultural position of the free people of color and contrasts this population with the majority of enslaved blacks. He describes their situation as follows:

> The French heritage of this group, its racial make-up and its unique position in the life of slave-holding Louisiana and the United States make them outstanding. Neither Louisiana nor the nation offered them the advantages of American culture. These writers turned, therefore, to sources outside of Louisiana for inspiration, training and models of form and style.[14]

Here when Coleman writes "outstanding," he means this in the most literal sense of the term—the Creole authors stood outside of the social and literary context of the United States. By his reading of their lives, Coleman sees these authors as standing outside of American culture and tradition.

Nearly fifty years later, Henry Louis Gates takes a different perspective when addressing the significance of *Les Cenelles* for the African American literary tradition. In his work *Loose Canons*, Gates undertakes the project of revealing and defending the presence of a long-standing African American literary canon. Gates understands *Les Cenelles* to be "the first attempt to define a black canon," and he reads Armand Lanusse's introduction to the volume as "a defense of poetry as an enterprise for black people." Although Gates does acknowledge that the *Les Cenelles* authors did not, for the most part, address issues of slavery and racist oppression as other African American authors did, he sees their insistence on intellectual excellence and their ability to operate on the same level as French writers as evidence that the volume presents an "apolitical art being put to uses most political."[15]

Gates contrasts the apolitical approach of *Les Cenelles* with that of William G. Allen's 1849 production of another black American anthology. Allen's attempt at canon formation featured the work of Phyllis Wheatley and George Moses Horton. In contrast to Lanusse and the other *Les Cenelles* poets, Allen was quite explicit in his efforts to defend the integrity and humanity of black writers. He asked: "Who now will say that the African is incapable of attaining to intellectual or moral greatness?" Gates rounds out this comparison of Lanusse and Allen by noting that there has been a long-standing debate about whether black literature is that which explicitly addresses racial issues or, rather, consists of any literature written by black people. Gates defends the idea that the creation of literature by blacks is, in and of itself, a political act that fits clearly into the black literary tradition. Thus, rather than placing *Les Cenelles* outside of this tradition, Gates instead reads the volume as a politically less overt part of that larger tradition.[16]

In contrast to Gates's reading of the volume, Thomas Haddox, continuing the discussion into the twenty-first century, understands *Les Cenelles* to sit quite outside of the mainstream black tradition of the United States. He begins by quoting from the volume's introduction where Lanusse writes that poetry has the power to "avancer le progrès des lumières parmi nous"—"advance the progress of the gifted among us."[17] Haddox questions who this "nous" is referring to. Within the social context of Lanusse and the poets included in his volume, Haddox sees this "nous" as standing emphatically outside of the mainstream African American tradition, which has taken slavery and racial oppression as its key themes. Here, Haddox argues that Gates's positioning of *Les Cenelles* ignores the cultural conditions that separated the *gens de couleurs libres* from the vast majority of the African diaspora. Haddox goes even further to write that the poets belonged to a group of persons "whose record of solidarity with African Americans and resistance to slavery were less than exemplary during the ante-bellum period."[18]

Coleman, Gates, and Haddox take contrasting stands in their interpretation of *Les Cenelles* and the Creoles of color who produced it. Their varied interpretations stem from the different kinds of racial frameworks they use to make sense of the volume. Gates reads *Les Cenelles* from within the Anglo-American racial system with its binary racial categories—the authors are not white and they are of African descent, so they are clearly "black"—while Coleman and Haddox are more insistent about the influence and applicability of the triracial, Latinized system which formed the *Les Cenelles* authors.

In keeping with the argument developed throughout *American Routes*, I would argue that Lanusse and his coauthors are better understood as inhabiting complex social landscapes that are in the process of shifting like tectonic plates. This shifting is the result of one layer of the racial palimpsest—the Anglo layer—pushing aside the Latin layer, which sinks gradually and grudgingly beneath it. By the 1840s, Creole cultural influence was beginning to decline while Anglo-American cultural and racial systems were in their ascent. Recall that New Orleans was split into three municipalities in 1836, an act that thrust the Americans into a superior economic and political position. At the same time, however, the Latinized racial system of the Creoles, with its finer grained categories and relative fluidity, had not yet lost its grip over the way Creoles of color imagined themselves in relation to others.

When we read *Les Cenelles* through the lenses of the racial palimpsest concept, we see the poets' work in a different light. The authors do not, as of 1845, see themselves as mainstream black Americans, but they are forced to deal with the reality of living in a world where they are being ever more firmly pressed into Anglo-American social categories. Their poetry, with its invocation of French luminaries, is their declaration of excellence and humanity against a system that would deny them both. Under these circumstances, we must understand their work as having been produced within the context of simultaneous and shifting racial systems.

A generation later, R. L. Desdunes—a descendant of St. Domingue refugees—would catch the subtlety and complexity of their tenuous position in his commentary on the poems of *Les Cenelles*. Although he notes that there is no critique of slavery in the volume, he does see a subtle critique of the racial oppression under which the poets lived. The volume is bookended by two striking poems written by P. Dalcour—"Chant d'Amour" at the beginning and "Heure de Désenchantement" at the end, which Desdunes sees as an allegorical statement against the oppression under which the writers lived.[19]

In "Chant d'Amour," Dalcour writes of a lover chasing an ephemeral beloved. In the evening he senses the scent of his beloved and is glad, but then it is revealed as a mirage that flees before him. In response, the lover says:

Reviens o douce reverie	Come back sweet dream
Ombre decevante et cherie	Deceiving and dear shadow
Reviens une dernier fois	Come back again
Helas! Quand ma bouche l'apelle	Alas! When I call her
Je n'entend que l'echo fidele	I hear only a steady echo
Qui reponde au loins a ma voix	That returns my own voice back to me

Desdunes reads this poem as a metaphorical longing for the humanity and justice that Creoles of color struggled for against the racial prejudice of white Louisianans.[20]

Desdunes's interpretation of the political intent of these bookends is particularly compelling when we read "Chant d'Amour," the first poem of the volume, together with Dalcour's poem "Heure de désenchantment," which ends the volume. Here again the poet chases a phantom:

Ainsi l'homme toujours poursuit une chimère	Thus man is always chasing a phantom
Et la possession ne peut le satisfaire ...	And catching it does not satisfy him ...
Ce qu'il aime aujourd'hui sera brisé demain,	What he loves today will be destroyed tomorrow,
Son esprit toujours flotte, inconstant, incertain.	His spirit is always floating, inconstant, uncertain.

The same poet, having started in "Chant d'Amour" full of hope, chasing a beloved, ends the volume still chasing a phantom, but this time he is tired and bitter, even cynical. The full measure of Dalcour's disenchantment comes across in the penultimate stanza, where he laments:

La vertu! la vertu! Ce mot vain, mais sonore	Virtue! Virtue! That vain, but beautiful sounding word,
Que chacun ici-bas diversement décore,	That each one here below dresses up in his own way,
N'est qu'un manteau qui sert à des vices honteux	It's nothing but a cloak, in the service of shameful vices,
Car le plus hypocrite est le plus vertueux!	So that the most hypocritical person is the most virtuous!

The disenchantment described here goes well beyond mere disappointment that things did not turn out as the writer hoped.[21] Instead, Dalcour declares that what is good and right is actively and consistently debased, whereas what is wrong is elevated and praised. This is the bitter note on which *Les Cenelles* ends.

Despite these evocative book-ended poems, one must search hard to find any kind of clear social critique in the volume.[22] A generation later, however, in the 1860s, Creoles of color—many of them descended of St. Domingue refugees—organize radical newspapers that call insistently and explicitly for civil and political rights for all people of African descent.

WAGING THE NINETEENTH-CENTURY CIVIL RIGHTS MOVEMENT IN THE UNITED STATES THROUGH A BLACK FRENCH LITERARY PUBLIC SPHERE

The Afro-Creoles' struggle became most intense during the Civil War years when there was much to be gained or lost as the entire country prepared for a massive restructuring of the status quo. It was during the War that Dr. Louis Charles Roudanez—a very prominent son of St. Domingue refugees of color—established the newspaper *L'Union*. Within the pages of this paper we see unfold the struggle for equal rights in the new United States which will emerge from the War.

For our purposes, there are two key themes of interest in this paper and its successor paper, *La Tribune de la Nouvelle Orleans*. First, the language and content of both papers emphasize the distinctiveness of the free people of color compared to Anglo-American blacks who were, for the most part, enslaved. The articles illustrate that this group of prominent Creoles of color was immersed in a French Atlantic public sphere that included Louisiana, parts of the Caribbean, and France. These were their areas of reference, and the papers' contents demonstrate that as of the mid-nineteenth century, Afro-Creole language and culture were still going strong and still quite distinctive. The second key point is that the free people of color organizing and writing the paper were working through how to position themselves with regard to enslaved Anglo-American blacks who would soon experience emancipation. In doing so, they were also setting the foundation for how Afro-Creoles would position themselves within the Anglo-American racial system that was firmly and swiftly becoming dominant.

The first edition of *L'Union* hit the streets of New Orleans on September 27, 1862. There on the first page the publishers announce that with this paper they inaugurate a new era in the destiny of the South. They frame their mission on the promises of the Declaration of Independence, which they promise to publish in a forthcoming edition. With this action, they stand in a long line of the excluded and oppressed in US history who have turned to this document, holding it forward as a promissory note demanding equality and liberty for all.[23]

The first page of this inaugural edition also highlights the publishers' ties to the French Atlantic political and literary world. This edition, as well as all future editions of *L'Union*, are written entirely in French.[24] Here they publish an exchange between Eugène Hertelou, a writer based in Port-au-Prince, Haiti, and Victor Hugo, the esteemed French writer. In his letter to Victor Hugo, Hertelou expresses his admiration for that author's defense of John Brown and his efforts to liberate the enslaved. Hugo's response declares his sense of brotherhood with black people, whom he declares to be brothers under one God. He goes on further to extol Haiti as a beautiful place of freedom, a torch lighting the way for others.[25]

The editors' decision to publish these letters sets the paper in dialogue with writers and activists in Haiti and France, and future editions of the paper reinforce these connections. The October 1 edition includes a piece entitled "Un mot sur la population de couleur." This piece discusses the ways free people of color have fought for the United States and demands that their rights should be respected and enacted. Just after noting that one of the current literary lights of France is a man of color from New Orleans, the writer notes that although many free people of color could go to Europe, they are devoted to their native soil in Louisiana. Although he says "Europe," the place to which most of the free people of color had social and linguistic ties was France.

On this same page in the next column the editors publish a letter that was originally printed in the Haitian paper *La République*. The letter is from a George W. Wilson, who is described as an "Agent of Ohio." It appears that Wilson visited several parts of Haiti in his capacity as an agent seeking farming opportunities for Ohio residents. He praises the wonderful hospitality he received while in that country and assures the president and others who attended him that he will pass on glowing reports of how fertile the land is and how hospitable the people are. Although there is no explanation for why this letter is reprinted in *L'Union*, it shares the page with another piece that points out other areas of the Francophone world that Americans might migrate to for opportunity. Together these two pieces point to Haiti and France as potential alternatives for Creoles of color who are dissatisfied with the pace of change in the United States, and they also reinforce the ways that this population was tied into a French Atlantic world that would have been alien to Anglo-American blacks, many of whom were illiterate, and the vast majority of whom would have had no facility in the French language.

Given the social and cultural differences between the Creoles of color and enslaved blacks of Louisiana, how did the writers and editors of *L'Union* position themselves with respect to this quite different population? A reorientation in their position is made evident by the decision to make the successor paper *La Tribune de la Nouvelle Orleans* a bilingual paper that was intentional about reaching out to Anglo-American blacks. The first issue of the *Tribune* includes a piece called "Is the Black Code Still in Force?" Here the author declares that the Black Code has practically been repealed first by changes in public sentiment, second by military occupation, and finally by the Emancipation Proclamation. There then follow sample sections of the Black Code, some of which apply to the enslaved and others that apply to free people of color. As an example, a reprint of Section 28 reads:

> Whoever shall, with intent to produce discontent among the free colored population or insubordination among the slaves, write, print, publish or distribute, anything having a tendency to produce discontent among the free colored population or insubordination among the slaves therein, shall on conviction be sentenced to imprisonment at hard labor, or suffer death at the discretion of the court.[26]

This column, with its highlighting of section 28 of the Black Code clearly puts formerly enslaved blacks and free people of color in a similar group of mutually oppressed peoples.

At the same time, however, there was still a consciousness of the special position of the Creoles of color who had a long history of freedom and education. In the July 28, 1864 edition of the *Tribune*, the author announces the end of Louisiana's Constitutional Convention. Although he is pleased that this Convention affirmed the end of slavery, he expresses concern that the voting rights of Creoles of color have not been affirmed. This same theme comes up again on August 4 when the editors respond in disdain to a letter written by William Lloyd Garrison, which argued that it would not make sense for Lincoln to have committed not only to abolishing slavery but also to awarding the vote to blacks. The *Tribune*'s response was swift and severe. The column reads:

> We don't argue with President Lincoln's constitutional power to make citizens of the men of our race whose chains have just been broken by military force; but, although we are of the same race as these unfortunate sons of Africa who have suffered until now under cruel and brutalizing slavery, one cannot, without being unjust confuse these newly emancipated with our intelligent population which, by its industry and education, has made itself as useful as any other class of citizens to our society and country.[27]

This response makes clear that while the writers sympathize with the newly emancipated, they clearly see themselves as distinct from them and more deserving of the immediate right to vote given their greater education and civic experience.

Although this statement of the "intelligence" of the Creole compared to formerly enslaved blacks is evidence of a certain level of bias toward their own group, the *Tribune*'s authors do prove themselves, over the course of many and varied political battles, to be staunchly in defense of the civil and political rights of all blacks. This becomes especially clear in their response to a controversial bill that, if passed, would likely have allowed many of them to exercise the right to vote. This bill, called colloquially the "Quadroon Bill," was introduced by Charles Smith at the 1864 Constitutional Convention and proposed that anyone with no more than one-quarter black blood would be declared white in Louisiana.

The *Tribune* provided its response in the November 10 edition. It is interesting to note that the English section made only scant note of Smith's bill. The report in that section is no more than two sentences under the heading of events happening in the Legislature, where it is recorded that Mr. Smith made the proposal but that the motion failed to carry. It is only in the French section that we receive an extended commentary on Smith's bill. This, no doubt, is because the writers were still more oriented toward their French-language readers, as well as because the proposed bill would have applied to some of their number. The French language response is quite clear in its repudiation of the measure. The editors write:

> We have already declared the absurdity of this measure, which can only create a regrettable division at the heart of our population.... We are in a new century of progress and light, the revolution has been achieved for the good of us all, and in this republic where our brothers spilled rivers of precious blood for our common defense, all should be equally recognized as children of the same land ... and not lose sight of the fact that the peace of the country and the security of the future require that the American republic renew itself by firmly and loudly proclaiming the sacred principles of American independence which do not allow for any distinction by race or color.[28]

This response, together with the *Tribune*'s continued advocacy on behalf of both the newly emancipated and those who had long been free, demonstrates that, despite their sense of distinction from the black masses, and their intense desire for the franchise, the editors and writers of the *Tribune* saw themselves as too much in solidarity with the newly emancipated to desert them for political ends.[29]

Throughout the course of the nineteenth century, and well into the twentieth, Creole and Anglo-blacks worked together to defend their civil and political rights, but they also remained aware of underlying differences that sometimes created tensions. In the following section we consider how these differences between Creole and Anglo-blacks have continued to manifest themselves in the twentieth century.

AFRO-CREOLES AND ANGLO-BLACKS BALANCING COOPERATION AND CONFLICT

[T]here are two distinct schools of politics among the Negroes. The Latin Negro differs radically from the Anglo-Saxon in aspiration and method. One hopes, the other doubts. Thus we often perceive that one makes every effort to acquire merits, the other to gain advantages. One aspires to equality, the other to identity. One will forget that he is a Negro in order to think that he is a man; the other will forget that he is a man in order to think that he is a Negro.... One is a philosophical Negro, the other practical.
—"A Few Words to Dr. DuBois with Malice Toward None"

The sharp comparison Desdunes draws here between the "Latin" and "Anglo" Negro is overdrawn in many respects.[30] It also, however, encapsulates the many tensions pressing upon Creoles of color as they sought to adjust to the shifting layers of the racial palimpsest. On the one hand, by the late nineteenth and early twentieth centuries there was still a vibrant, French-speaking Creole of color community. On the other hand, as Reconstruction gave way to the many and varied oppressions of Jim Crow, the restrictions of the Anglo-American racial system whittled away relentlessly at the tripartite system under which Creoles' free colored ancestors had once held a special status. Desdunes's pointed comments signal his frustration with being lumped together rhetorically with Anglo-blacks who had a history so different from his own and from that of the Creole community he knew so well.

Desdunes's excerpted comments are part of a larger response to remarks made by W. E. B. DuBois in a talk he gave in New York City. On February 17, 1907, DuBois made a speech at Carnegie Hall for the Society for Ethical Culture, and in that speech, he discussed the plight of the Negro in the United States. He said, in part:

> We are ignorant. We want knowledge. Ignorant in the sense of being illiterate. We are unacquainted with modern processes of work, unacquainted with the best traditions of family life and methods of democratic government, with the greater ideals of life. Nor is this wholly our own fault. The laws for generations forbade us to learn, and even today, when it is assumed that the negro is receiving too much education, not one child in three is attending the public schools.[31]

Seven days later on February 24, the *New Orleans Item* reprinted parts of the speech. The *Item* summarized the speech as a whole writing that:

> After declaring that the negroes of the South are lacking in book knowledge, in industrial faculty and even unacquainted with the best traditions of family life, he charged that they were left without the protection even of life that the law affords the whites.[32]

Although the *Item* did not report the speech in full, it did capture the essence of what DuBois had said. It is this essence that Rodolphe Lucien Desdunes vehemently repudiated.

Desdunes's objections to DuBois's assumptions about Southern blacks stemmed from the fact that he was part of a distinctive, long-standing tradition of Francophone education and political activism going back to his ancestors' struggles in colonial St. Domingue. And although these social and cultural roots are *different* from the Anglo–African American experience, they are not *separate* from that experience. Indeed, as the following discussion will reveal, this French and Caribbean influence has intimately shaped southern Louisiana's history and present as well as race relations across the country. Had DuBois more fully understood the history and role of the French and Caribbean influence on black Louisiana, he could not so easily have painted the entire black South with the same broad brush. Furthermore, he would have been forced to acknowledge that not only did many Southern blacks have "book knowledge," but that they joined this knowledge to an indisputably deep understanding of the "methods of democratic government" and "the greater ideals of life" to wage the nation's first civil rights movement.

As evidence of this deep understanding and knowledge, we have only to refer to the earlier discussion concerning the role of the radical black newspapers *L'Union* and *La Tribune* in initiating the nation's first, full-fledged civil rights movement in the 1860s. And though the early commitment to broad-based black solidarity was initially uncertain, within just a few years, the Creole activists transformed their ambivalent relationship to Anglo–African Americans into a clear commitment to fight for the rights of all people of African descent. Their determination continued into the 1890s when their challenge to a Louisiana law led to a Supreme Court decision that would have long-lasting repercussions for the entire nation.

The Supreme Court decision at issue here is that of *Plessy v. Ferguson*. Many readers may be taken aback to learn that French-speaking Creoles with St. Domingue/Haiti roots were at the forefront of this most American of court cases. Widespread ignorance of this fact is a result of the triumph of the Anglo-Americanization of the Plessy narrative, which has largely erased from public view the lives and political roles of Creoles of color who were shaped by a very different tradition. Indeed, the Plessy narrative differs quite substantially depending upon whether we place it within an Anglo-American or Latin/Caribbean-American context. Next we engage in a careful comparison and contrast of the narratives that emerge from these different frameworks.

We first consider the typical Anglo-American Plessy narrative by examining summaries of the *Plessy* case produced by credible mainstream sources. The first comes from "Our Documents," a website of the US government that provides access to documents that have shaped US history.

> In 1891, a group of concerned young black men of New Orleans formed the "Citizens' Committee to Test the Constitutionality of the Separate Car Law." . . . With the cooperation of the East Louisiana Railroad, on June 7, 1892, Homer Plessy, a mulatto (7/8 white), seated himself in a white compartment, was challenged by the conductor, and was arrested and charged with violating the state law. In the Criminal District Court for the Parish of Orleans, Tourgée argued

that the law requiring "separate but equal accommodations" was unconstitutional. When Judge John H. Ferguson ruled against him, Plessy applied to the State Supreme Court for a writ of prohibition and certiorari. Although the court upheld the state law, it granted Plessy's petition for a writ of error that would enable him to appeal the case to the Supreme Court.[33]

Here we see no reference whatsoever to the fact that Plessy was a Creole, nor to the fact that the Citizen's Committee was initially called the *Comité des Citoyens* in keeping with the organizers' French background. Instead, we see reference only to "concerned young black men" and to Plessy himself as a "mulatto."

The PBS summary that follows provides a narrative that is a bit more complex than the one offered earlier, but that nevertheless stays firmly within an Anglo-American interpretive framework:

> On June 7, 1892, 30-year-old Homer Plessy was jailed for sitting in the "White" car of the East Louisiana Railroad. Plessy could easily pass for white but under Louisiana law, he was considered black despite his light complexion and therefore required to sit in the "Colored" car. He was a Creole of Color, a term used to refer to black persons in New Orleans who traced some of their ancestors to the French, Spanish, and Caribbean settlers of Louisiana before it became part of the United States. When Louisiana passed the Separate Car Act, legally segregating common carriers in 1892, a black civil rights organization decided to challenge the law in the courts. Plessy deliberately sat in the white section and identified himself as black. He was arrested and the case went all the way to the United States Supreme Court.[34]

Here Plessy is properly described as a Creole, heir to the diverse national and cultural roots listed in the PBS summary. The *Comité des Citoyens*, however, is described simply as "a black civil rights organization." Here again the reader is given no indication of just how French and Caribbean the roots of this group were. These roots were so important to the mounting of the *Plessy* case, that it would not be too much of a stretch to say that both the case and the other civil rights agitation surrounding it would have been unlikely to occur were it *not* for the French and Caribbean roots of the men who created the organization.

To better understand why the French and Caribbean roots are so central to the emergence of the case at this particular time in US history, we turn to an alternative Plessy narrative—a narrative very rarely proffered outside of the relatively narrow confines of academic scholarship on the Creole community of New Orleans. The first narrative grows out of work on the historical role of black immigrants in the United States and was produced by the Schomburg Center for Research in Black Culture:

> After Reconstruction collapsed in 1877, Creole activists fought the restoration of white rule. In 1890 Rodolphe L. Desdunes, a Creole New Orleanian of Haitian descent, joined with other prominent rights advocates to challenge state-imposed segregation. Their legal battle culminated in the 1896 Plessy v. Ferguson Supreme Court decision.... Haitian immigrants and their descendants appeared at the head of virtually every New Orleans civil rights campaign. Their leadership role in the struggle for racial justice offers dramatic evidence of the scope of their influence on Louisiana's history. From Colonel Joseph Savary's militant republicanism to Rodolphe Desdunes's unrelenting attacks on state-enforced segregation, Haitian émigrés and their descendants demanded that the nation fulfill the promise of its founding principles.[35]

Here we see a concerted effort to put Desdunes, Plessy, and their fellow activists into a larger Caribbean and American context. In contrast to the PBS description, which only notes that Plessy was a Creole, the Schomburg narrative notes that the case grew out of the concerted organizing of a community of Creoles, many of whom were of Haitian descent. In line with this approach, the entry concludes by recognizing the crucial role Haitian émigrés and their descendants have played in pushing forward civil rights in US history.

In addition to the Schomburg's offering, other scholars have also been intentional about emphasizing the French and Caribbean roots of the *Plessy* activists. Michel Laguerre's *Diasporic Citizenship: Haitians in Transnational America* is one of the earliest to insist on the pivotal role Haitians have played in the making of US history.[36] In his telling of the *Plessy* case, the actors were Haitian Americans acting to promote civil rights in the United States. Although most of the activists would have thought of themselves as Creoles, and probably not at all as Haitian Americans, Laguerre uses terminology that would be accurate for today where it is common to call the second generation born of Haitian parents "Haitian-American."

Rebecca Scott takes a position more in line with Creole activists' self-identification. Although she does not claim that the activists were "Haitian-Americans," she provides an analysis that insists on the Caribbean roots of the movement. In her framing of the *Plessy* case, she clearly challenges the Anglo-American framework commonly used to make sense of the case. She explains:

> It is common to view the *Plessy* challenge as quixotic and to see the defeat in court as a coda, formalizing the end of a long battle lost. But if we look at Louisiana as

part of a larger Gulf of Mexico, we see that for the *Plessy* activists the claim to rights and standing was part of an ongoing and multi-national struggle. Ramón Pagés, identified in the record as the head of the Spanish cigar workers' union in New Orleans, spoke at a meeting called in 1893 by Louis Martinet and the Committee of Citizens and expressed his support for the campaign by invoking "public rights." The label "Spanish" was New Orleans vernacular for Latin American; Pagés was a Cuban revolutionary in exile. For him the struggle in Cuba was a piece of the struggle for equal rights in Louisiana.[37]

With this reading, Scott clearly places the activists within a larger Caribbean and American context—in her terms "a larger Gulf of Mexico." Pagés is one of many Cubans in New Orleans who supported the cause of Cuban independence and Scott's analysis shows how these Cuban activists were tied into activist Creole circles.[38]

It is important to understand, however, that when she writes of an "ongoing multinational struggle," Scott refers to more than the struggles for Cuban independence and civil rights in Louisiana. Indeed, she reaches back to eighteenth-century colonial St. Domingue, where free people of color agitated for their rights within the colony. Here she cites the signing in 1791 of a "Concordat" between citizens of color and white colonists where those of color insisted that "the progress of a ridiculous form of prejudice" which "violated the rights" of free people of color be put to an end. Though the historical record shows that this Concordat did not result in long-term recognition of the rights of free people of color, it is an early example of the political organization and agitation for rights that many free people of color took part in. Then, once exiles of the Revolution found themselves in Louisiana, Scott notes that "Whatever their positions on slavery and the Haitian Revolution, the men and women of color among the *émigrés* brought a strong tradition of claiming equal rights for themselves."[39] When we view the *Plessy* activists in this light, we see how strongly these men of the *Comité des Citoyens* were shaped by their St. Domingue/Haiti ancestry and social ties.

Given what we have learned about this group, it is not difficult to see why, from Desdunes's standpoint, DuBois was operating according to a limited understanding of black identity and experience in the twentieth century. In fact, up until the great social changes of the 1960s and its effects on black identities, many Creoles drew a strong contrast between themselves and Anglo-blacks. In the following section we consider how many Creoles of color continued to think in terms of an alternative racial system that was more in line with a Latin/Caribbean approach to race well into the mid-twentieth century.

CREOLES OF COLOR IN THE JIM CROW SOUTH: THE PERSISTENCE AND WANING OF A LATIN/CARIBBEAN RACIAL SELF-UNDERSTANDING

After the failure of the *Plessy* case, the outlook for civil and political rights for black people in the South was grim. Whereas initially politically active Creoles of color had fought hard for these rights for all people of African descent, the early twentieth century brought something of a reversal of this movement. Members of the *Comité des Citoyens* were aging and dying, others were becoming discouraged, and the next generation was unable or unwilling to take up the torch.

Desdunes reflects on these changes in *Our People and Our History*. In his chapter on the 1890s mobilization for civil rights, he writes that even though the outcome of the *Plessy* case was difficult, "the committee did not become discouraged." They still had the *Crusader*, a newspaper founded by Louis Martinet that acted as the civil rights organ for its generation. Over time, however, even this failed. Desdunes explains:

> Uncompromising in his ideas, invincible in his perseverance, precise and yet varied in his style, [Martinet] reflected in the columns of his newspaper the hopes of his people in all their strength and integrity. But this paper, however useful and independent it showed itself in expressing its views and in fulfilling commitments, however powerful it seemed to be in the community, was doomed like its predecessors, doomed to fail through lack of support. We can attribute this failure only to discouragement on the part of some and to the poverty of others.[40]

This discouragement took different forms. Many continued to struggle under the weight of racial oppression, doing the best they could under the circumstances. Others—those who had the resource of very light skin, and who despaired of the possibility of leading any kind of satisfactory life as a black person in Louisiana— made the ultimate sacrifice of passing into whiteness.

Desdunes reflects bitterly on the phenomenon of racial passing. He notes that some Creoles of his day "have fallen to such a point of moral weakness that they have disowned and rejected not only their fellow blacks but even their own kin.... They live in a moral depression that seems to represent the last degree of impotence."[41] This moral depression would have long-lasting impacts for many Louisiana families of color. In Chapter 6 we will meet interviewees who only recently discovered that although they were raised as white, their parents and grandparents were listed as "colored" in official documents. One of these is a descendant of Dr. Louis Charles Roudanez, the founder and publisher of *L'Union* and *La Tribune*. This sobering generational change in the Roudanez family, from radical civil rights activists for black solidarity to white Midwesterners separated from their radical black heritage, is a sobering one that emphasizes the depth of the despair and dejection many Creoles of color faced in post-*Plessy* Louisiana.

The virulence of racial oppression, combined with a longstanding commitment to an alternative, triracial conceptual framework, led many Creoles of color to separate themselves socially from African Americans. Part of this separation involved holding firmly to Creole identification. This is in stark contrast to white Creoles, who found the racial costs of Creole identification too high going into the twentieth century.

For people of color, holding on to Creole identity in the early to mid-twentieth century often went hand in hand with keeping clear boundaries between themselves and Anglo-blacks. In this sense, earlier efforts in the mid-nineteenth century to forge alliances among all blacks were forgotten or pushed beneath the surface. Consider, for instance, the perspective of two older Creole women who grew up in New Orleans. Mrs. Mercedes Prograis Barthé explains:

> Well, my childhood days, I came up during Depression. And people at that time worked for a dollar a day. Some people got less than a dollar a day. Some got fifty cents. It all depends on what type of work you did.... Red beans were twenty cents a pound. And that's how people lived, bring up their families. We was poor. But not like the ... [pauses and lowers her voice] ... blacks—they didn't have nothing—maybe not even the ten cents for beans.[42]

Echoing Mrs. Barthé is Mrs. Bernadine Bart Moore, who also grew up during the Depression era:

> It was one family that lived way in the back, about two blocks down the street ... they were black people that we didn't associate with at all. We used to call the lady Miss Jo, and the husband, my father said he was a jailbird ... and he had all these children ... My mother would come and walk those two blocks and she says, "Poor soul doesn't have anything," so she'd take some of her sheets, tear them, towels and whatever she thought she needed, and she brought [Miss Jo's] poor child into the world.[43]

In each of these reflections, we see the women making very clear distinctions between themselves and "blacks." Both Mrs. Barthé and Mrs. Moore describe blacks as being poorer than themselves. In addition, when Mrs.

Barthé lowers her voice in order to say "blacks," she hints at the stigmatized nature of the group with which she does not associate. Mrs. Moore also gestures at the stigmatization of blacks as distinct from her people when she explains that "they were black people that we didn't associate with at all."

The remedy for surviving Jim Crow Louisiana without succumbing to the fate of poorer stigmatized Anglo-blacks was to stay within the confines of a carefully cultivated Creole community. Gaudin provides a glimpse into this protected sphere as she reports on the way Mr. Ferdinand Delery got through the Jim Crow years:

> Mr. Delery defined his little Creole group, the closed circuit in which he came up . . . as a community that acted as a shield to protect those within its boundaries from the negative forces of Jim Crow and white racism. . . . "We went to basically our Creole places and that was it," Mr. Delery simplifies his youth in the Seventh Ward. "We had our own way of living, our own group and all," he said, and referring to segregation, he noted, "We didn't feel that we missed anything, really. . . . We didn't feel that we were segregated."[44]

Mr. Delery is among many older Creoles who grew up within the halls of Creole of color churches, schools, and social clubs. Although this strategy served his generation well, it began to fall out of favor with the generation that came of age during the Civil Rights movement.

For a younger generation of Creoles of color, the exclusivity of Creole communities and institutions was problematic. As injustices perpetrated against all people of African descent were more widely publicized both in the United States and abroad, and as the fight for basic civil rights gained ground, young Creoles of the 1950s and 1960s took note and arrived at new ways of thinking that brought them into closer alignment with an Anglo-American way of thinking about race and African American identity.

Gaudin marks this transition in the pages of the *Xavierite*—a student publication of Xavier University in New Orleans—a black Catholic, and in its early years, largely Creole university. She notes that the 1970 edition of the *Xavierite* listed new programs like Afro-American Studies and a new organization called Brothers and Sisters of the Afro-American Student Union. The introductory pages of the 1970 edition show the students' reappraisal of themselves as black:

> Within these pages are the boundaries of your mind. . . . Within this book evolved a sense of self-mastery or an autonomy which led our (the staff's) initiative in its final production. The change in Blacks' traditional thinking of themselves and

toward their brothers encouraged us to choose this theme: The Experience of a Communiversity; Blackness Exhibited. Within these pages, fellow Xavierites, is a reflection of you.... Now as we approach the reality of Blackness in its fullest and most effective sense, the word relate [sic] assumes a new connotation—relate to MY world, relate to MY people, relate to ME.... To whom do we owe the privilege of voicing at last this long-smothered identity?[45]

These opening words amount to a kind of manifesto, a declaration of a new way of being in the world. Where their parents and grandparents were steadfast in protecting the boundaries of Creole community and identity, this 1970s generation of Creoles of color was redefining itself as black.

These selections from the *Xavierite* articulate a new day among Creoles of color growing up during and after the Civil Rights movement and usher in a period where the Anglo-American racial system became dominant nearly one hundred years after it did for white St. Domingue refugees and their Creole descendants. But in contrast to the case of white Creoles who distanced themselves both from racial-structural and ethnic-cultural Creole identification, Anglo-American dominance did not fully eclipse the salience of Afro-Creole identity and social institutions. The reason for this, in part, is that Creoles of color were, if anything, advantaged by the racial-structural dimension of Creole identity for it placed them as separate from and higher than Anglo-blacks in Louisiana's racial hierarchy—this was the legacy of Louisiana's foundational Latin/Caribbean system, which had a tripartite rather than a binary logic.

Although Jim Crow segregation made all blacks formally equal in their stigmatized status, in everyday life among many Creoles like those whom Gaudin cites earlier, there was a clear sense of separation from Anglo-black Americans. Moreover, many Creoles of color were descended from free people of color who had a structural advantage over Anglo-blacks and generally were more advantaged both socially—in their closer proximity to whites—and economically. These racial-structural advantages made holding on to the ethnic-cultural dimension of Creole identity an asset rather than the liability it was for white Creoles.[46] On the other hand, the solidification of Anglo dominance did make the assertion of Afro-Creole identity more problematic and contentious as the politics of the 1960s pressured all people of African descent to see themselves as equally "black." The nearly one-hundred-year gap between white Creoles' embrace of Anglo whiteness and Afro-Creoles' tentative acceptance of Anglo blackness foreshadows what we will see in the racial practices and identification choices of contemporary immigrants of color from Latin America and the Caribbean. Many of these immigrants are neither quickly nor simplistically embracing the logic of the Anglo-American racial system.

Chapters 5 and 6 bring the comparison of white and black descendants of St. Domingue refugees and their Creole descendants into the twenty-first century. What we will see is that, although the influence of the Latin/Caribbean system has been greatly reduced in Louisiana, it continues to leak through the cracks of the dominant Anglo-American layer. The continued, though muted, influence of the submerged Latin/Caribbean layer of Louisiana's racial palimpsest suggests that in areas of the United States that are presently experiencing the effects of a racial palimpsest, the foundational Anglo-American layer is likely to continue to exert some force for generations to come.

CHAPTER 5

Twenty-First Century Remnants of a White Creole Past

I was studying all these folk tales and they would talk about Creoles. I knew it wasn't Anglo or anything that was here after the United States. My family has intermarried for the last one thousand years. When I told my daddy I was going to marry an Anglo, he fell over backwards in his chair. This was 1988.
—Norman Marmillion, *interviewee, 2013*

[My grandfather] worked at the bank here in town and I would hear him speaking French there. A lot of the old people would come in and they didn't want to do business in English like Les Américains.
—Angelique Bergeron, *interviewee, 2013*

Norman and Angelique are unusual among the study respondents in that, although they are white, they publicly identify as Creoles and have a clear and palpable connection to their families' Creole heritage. Chapter 3 described the racial angst white Creoles faced and traced the death of white Louisianans' public identification as Creoles. That discussion also charted a gradual decline in white Creole social institutions and cultural practices. Grace King captured this decline metaphorically when she referred to "traces" of the Creole past that are as fragile as "shriveled berries on a tree," waiting to be shaken to the ground by the next wind. For most white Creoles, the twentieth century was that wind. By the time this study began in 2005, there were very few self- and publicly identified white Creoles. This shift occurred because the ethnic-cultural meaning of Creole that white Louisianans struggled to hold on to could not be successfully separated from the racial-structural meaning that Anglo-Americans ascribed to it.

At the same time, however, the effacement of ethnic-cultural Creole identification among white Louisianans was neither monolithic nor complete. Some young and middle-aged respondents still recall parents or grandparents who spoke French; some grew up with self-consciously Creole family rituals in terms of the food they ate and the ways they celebrated holidays; others—especially those from elite backgrounds—were initiated at a very young age into their families' illustrious histories as Creoles in early New Orleans. These are some of the rare cases where self-conscious Creole identification has persisted among white Louisianans.

It is also true, however, that relatively few of the study respondents grew up with any of these connections to their family's Creole past. Of the original nineteen interviews with whites descended from St. Domingue ancestors, only nine grew up with any kind of family practice that was explicitly linked to Creole or French heritage. Therefore, to obtain a larger number of white participants with a Creole background, it was necessary to select a group of self-identified white Creoles with whom I could carry out oral histories.[1]

Seven oral histories were conducted with white participants who identified as Creoles or who grew up with a palpable understanding of their Creole heritage. Each oral history covered the individual's entire life course, included detailed discussion of family and community practices, and included respondents' studied reflection on what it has meant for them to identify as Creole given the racial-structural connotations that have attended this identity for so long. When these oral histories are added to the original nineteen interviews, the result is twenty-six portraits of white Louisianans with Creole ancestry.

Added to these interviews is an analysis of *Times-Picayune* newspaper references to "Creoles" over the past thirty years. This analysis reveals the nearly total effacement of white Creoles from the public imagination. Taken together, the interviewees' stories and the newspaper data help us to better understand white Creoles' struggles to cope with the pressures and unfavorable racial assumptions of the Anglo-American system.

In the first section, we take a look at members of white Creole families who were able to resist full Anglo-Americanization. These are respondents whose families have successfully held on to ethnic-cultural Creole identification. These respondents tended either to come from less populated areas outside of New Orleans where the population was more homogeneously Creole, or to have been born into elite New Orleans families where there was great incentive to hold on to proud family histories. Even within this group, however, we will see that lingering racial-structural understandings of what it means to be Creole have continued to cast a pall over their embrace of their Creole heritage.

The stories of those who have maintained a Creole identity are then contrasted in the second section with those of interviewees who only recently discovered their Creole heritage through family history research.[2] It is in telling the stories of the embattled survivors juxtaposed with those of the fully assimilated that we can most clearly see how remnants of a Latin/Caribbean approach to race have battled with the Anglo-American insistence on white racial purity and the tendency toward racial segregation. This struggle has resulted in the near evisceration of white Creole identification across the twentieth and into the twenty-first century.

The final section presents data from the *Times-Picayune* newspaper analysis. This analysis shows quite clearly that the idea of the "white Creole" as a social identity relevant to and existing in the late twentieth and early twenty-first centuries has been obliterated. References to contemporary Creole persons are made exclusively to persons of color, while historical references are nearly all made to white Creoles. In this sense, the major newspaper of the area both reflects and reinforces the general population's understanding that white Creoles have ceased to exist.

MAINTAINING CREOLE IDENTITY AGAINST THE TIDE OF ANGLO-AMERICANIZATION

I'm a product of a mixed marriage. My father is a white Anglo-Saxon Protestant and my mother is a true Creole. I mean, both of her parents come from true French and New Orleans Louisiana families. And so, I've spent a lot of time with my maternal grandparents growing up.... I always had this sense of family from them.... I'm a twelfth generation New Orleanian, through my grandfather, obviously well before the St. Domingue relatives came over.... They're true Creoles.

—John Ellis, interviewee, 2006

Here John Ellis is clearly articulating an ethnic-cultural Creole identity. His story, and others described in this section, communicate the experience of the relatively small portion of white Louisianans who came through the twentieth century with their Creole identification intact. Whereas the stories in this section will emphasize the preservation of an ethnic-cultural Creole identification among whites, the next section will show how the racial-structural dimension continues to hang like a pall over white Louisianans who are brave enough to publicly assert an ethnic-cultural Creole identity.

Many white respondents whose families persevered in their Creole identification inherited a narrative about the differences between Creole and American ways of doing things. The distinction remains alive in stories handed down across generations, as well as in everyday observances about what makes southern Louisiana culture unique. This Creole/American distinction is exemplified in John Ellis's quote. His story also, however, reinforces the study findings that the descendants of the most elite Creole families were among those most likely to resist the full pressure of Anglo-Americanization.

John comes from a very old and distinguished Louisiana Creole family. He is a direct descendant of James Pitot, the St. Domingue *émigré* who became the first mayor of New Orleans after it had been incorporated under the Americans.[3] He is a proud New Orleans native with intense ties to the city's history and culture. This comes from being steeped in the family's St. Domingue oral history through which he learned of his ancestors' desperate flight from the revolution in St. Domingue and James Pitot's rise to power in the city. He grew up not far from the Pitot House, one of the nineteenth-century mayor's former residences which is now a small museum open to the public. The oral history, the physical reminder of the Pitot House, and the influence of his maternal relatives who held onto French language and Creole culture shaped John's sense of himself. It is quite interesting to note, in fact, that he describes himself as a product of a "mixed" marriage. Often, in a US context, we would take his reference to "mixed" as one that is racial in nature. This, however, is quite far afield from what he actually means. What we see in his quote at the beginning of this section is that "mixed" refers to a union between Creole and Anglo-American. Both parents were white, but what distinguished them was their ethnic background.

Other interviewees also made note of mixed marriages. Renee Natell works as a plantation tour guide and so is always steeped in Louisiana history.[4] She describes her family as follows:

> I have two sides of the family. My father's side of the family are what I call the Creoles. My mother's side are the Americans. I can see the difference, knowing the history now, I know when my father's family comes to America, he comes from Louisiana actually, and then I know when my mother's side came.

This clear distinction between Creole and American branches of the family is also reflected in Norman Marmillion's quote at the beginning of the chapter, where he described his father's near fainting spell when he decided to marry an American. Dialogue from later on in the Marmillion interview further communicates the significance of the distinction and helps to convey the ways these cultural distinctions played out in his home and the homes of others from similarly mixed marriages.

> A.P.: Do you see ... separations between people who are white Creole and people who are Anglo who are white?
>
> N.M.: It's called Anglo and Creole. My wife is Anglo, right? When I get home she doesn't cook. I have to cook—I'm Creole. My family members who married Anglo wives understand.
>
> A.P.: Now what words would they use when they would say that?
>
> N.M.: Actually, the word is American.
>
> A.P.: Even today?
>
> N.M.: Yes.

It is instructive here to note that Marmillion clarifies that the proper term to describe the cultural background of the non-Creole wives is "American." Lest there be any confusion, Marmillion was born and raised in the United States as were generations of his family before him. And yet he draws a contrast between his "American" wife and himself.

The Creole/American distinction was also communicated through family stories. A common story was one having to do with Canal Street being the division between Americans and Creoles in the nineteenth century—particularly after the division of the city into three municipalities in 1836. Jerry Gandolfo provides an example of what he used to hear from his grandmother.[5]

> J.G.: My grandmother was very Creole. To the extent that for example one did not cross Canal Street, the downtown part of Canal St ... this part of Canal St was where the Americans lived. The Americans were a foreign people. They had to explain to me why it was when I went to school I had to say the pledge of allegiance. But she said you know it's like a benign occupation.
>
> A.P. What year is this? Fifties and sixties?
>
> J.G.: Probably, let's see I'm born in '52. My grandmother died in '72. My grandmother was born in 1887. She spoke English as a primary language. She also did a little of the French patois. Very often little clichés and stuff like that. Had a lot of the old French habits. I know when I went to her house to dinner and stuff like that, no matter how old we were we always had to drink red French table wine. Which when you are a kid tastes like battery acid. It's bad. That was her. She was very strict in the old French Creole habits.

As we saw in Chapter 3, the Canal Street division is, in many ways, a product of myth. Certainly Creoles and Americans did cross Canal Street and did do business with each other. The street remains, however, a powerful symbolic marker that Louisianans with Creole heritage use to describe to themselves who they are and what forces have shaped their history.

Alice Dantro and Loretta Clark also inherited the notion that Creoles and Americans were fundamentally different. Alice grew up with stories about her St. Domingue ancestors and their transition to New Orleans. When I asked her who told her these stories, she explained:

> Mother and grandmother until I was twelve, and she would always say "a la Criolla la bonne sang" . . . good blood, she loved that. [My grandmother] always referred to anyone outside of New Orleans as "the Americans."[6]

Alice's experience is similar to Loretta's in that they both grew up with older relatives who were shaped by the distinction between Creoles and Americans. Here Loretta describes a time in her life when as a young wife and mother, she was moving back to New Orleans after having been gone for some time:

> I was so thrilled. I was coming back home. When we got home though, Tante D and Tante Vaughan would still talk about "Ces Americaines." That was just their mindset. I guess my children were nine, three, and twelve when we moved back home and [one] came to me with eyes as big as saucers and he said, "Mama, aren't Tante D and Tante Vaughan Americans?" and I said "Yes, why?" and he said, "Why do they say , 'ces Americaines?'" And I said, "Honey they've never been to France." But that was the way they thought. I didn't realize how different New Orleans was until I moved away because I was talking one day about the neutral ground [and] somebody said, "What's the neutral ground?" and I said, "You know that division between the streets." And they said, "Oh that's a median." I had never heard the word *median*. It was a neutral ground. I thought that was the name. I didn't realize how unique that was. And the same way with *banquette* . . . I played hopscotch on the *banquette*. I didn't know there was another word. I thought a sidewalk was a *banquette*. I had to go somewhere else to appreciate it, let's put it that way.[7]

Loretta Clark was in her mid-eighties when we had this discussion, so her aunts would certainly have been born in the nineteenth century, and they were so deeply influenced by a sense of the palpable difference between Creoles and Americans that they passed on their stories to the following generations.

Another example of the Creole/American distinction living on in the twentieth and twenty-first century comes from Marcel Saussy.[8] In the following interview excerpt, she is describing her maternal grandmother's perspective on New Orleanians of French descent:

> M.S.: [My grandmother] was a funny woman—she just would put the French down—oh, downtown French people, and yet her second husband, who was this—oh, he was the most wonderful man in my life, my grandfather.... This beautiful, handsome elegant [man] ... speaking French ... [I always wanted] to speak French and he was the one, when I was very little, who would teach me words.
>
> A.P.: Okay, and then when she would talk about those French downtown people ... what would she mean?
>
> M.S.: She just meant that I guess that would go back to the enmity between the French and the—she was of the uptown, British background—the Anglo uptown background as opposed to the Creole. She, I think, it was just inbred. But then there was her daughter married to an adorable Frenchman and there was her second husband, this beautiful, elegant Frenchman. I'm trying to remember if she actually called them frogs. She might have. I mean, she was not Catholic. You know? And there—Catholics weren't always well liked in this town in spite of the fact that there were probably more of them than anything. And you could just tell that being around her. Funny woman, very outspoken.

Marcel's grandmother was born in the nineteenth century, and thus she was much closer to the time period when Creole society and culture were more robust and exercised more significant control over the forming of social relationships.

My respondents' memories of their grandparents' or older aunts' recounting of the distinctions between Creoles and Americans belong to a different world. While my respondents heard these stories, they did not own these distinctions as strongly as their older relatives did. Nevertheless, growing up with these stories helped to communicate the family's Creole heritage and became part of the way respondents understood themselves and their history.

White respondents who grew up with an understanding of their Creole heritage also frequently reported hearing French spoken when they were growing up. Growing up one or two generations removed from a relative whose primary language was French played a very important role in respondents' understanding of themselves as French and Creole in heritage. At the same time, however, what we will hear in their stories is that this French language fluency ended with the generation born in the nineteenth century.

Norman Marmillion explains the point at which the French language was lost in his family:

> A.P.: Now you had mentioned at one point that French was spoken in your family. As of which generation was the last—
>
> N.M.: My grandparents. All of them. They were fully fluent. Two types of French—the Cajun and the river Creole. My mom's side is Bayou Lafourche Cajun. I could hear the difference as a child.
>
> A.P.: So your parents didn't speak any French at all?
>
> N.M.: No, they were both born in 1917 and that's when if you spoke French you were beaten in school.
>
> A.P.: But yet you grew up hearing some French spoken.
>
> N.M.: When I went to my grandparents' house, absolutely. Everybody that I work with in Vacherie are all that.... People come into the gift shop and start talking French.
>
> A.P.: So when you went to your grandparents' house, did you understand the French?
>
> N.M.: No. I never heard my mother or father speak a word of French.
>
> A.P.: Did they understand French?
>
> N.M.: Oh yes.
>
> A.P.: So your parents could understand, but they just couldn't speak?
>
> N.M.: They never spoke a word of French.

In this dialogue, Norman hints at the fluctuating social and legal status of the French language in Louisiana. The late nineteenth century was the turning point away from acknowledging and accommodating French speakers and toward English dominance. Although the state constitutions of 1846 and 1852 required that all laws be written in English and French, this requirement was dropped in the constitution of 1864. The law went even further, however, to prescribe that all instruction in public schools be done in English.

Fifteen years would go by before the law was reversed so that instruction in French was again allowed in public schools—but the 1879 law applied only to primary schools. Nineteen years later, secondary education in French was allowed by the 1898 and 1913 constitutions. Just eight years later, however, in 1921, public school instruction was again limited to English. This provision would last for at least two more generations until the state decided belatedly in 1974 that people had a right to "preserve, foster, and promote their respective historic, linguistic, and cultural origins."[9]

Norman's parents fell right in the middle of the state's tussle over language rights. It was during their generation that the decisive blow was struck that would obliterate most of the French language in Louisiana. One respondent after another described a similar story of grandparents who were the last to speak French as a primary language. In Marcel's family social obstacles got in the way of maintaining the French language.

> My grandparents only spoke French until they went to school.... And then my father—in my father's generation, his older brother and sister learned it. They didn't use it that much, but they learned it when they were children. And then my father came along [and he] is quite a rebel. He just wasn't going to have anything [to do with it]. Plus it also coincided—there was that period of time here it was frowned upon to speak [French].... There's a long period between when he was a kid and the war, but, you know, they just moved away from it. They rebelled against it, didn't want to learn it.

The twentieth century was very much the century of the triumph of Anglo-American culture in Louisiana. For many white Louisianans born in the twentieth century, being "American" was prized above keeping the older habits and cultural practices of their French Creole ancestors.

Dorothy Carter also remembers relatives of her grandparents' generation speaking French:

> D.C.: My maiden name was Gonzales, but everybody spoke French.
> A.P.: When you say "everybody," who does that include?
> DOROTHY: My aunts and uncles.
> A.P: Okay, did your father speak French?
> D.C.: Mmm hmm. And Spanish. Because he learned that in school. He grew up speaking French, but he learned Spanish in school.
> A.P.: And how about your mother? Did she speak any French?
> D.C.: No, but her mother did ... that grandparent generation, they were all speaking French.

Dorothy's experience is similar to Marcel's in that both had fathers who learned French as children, but the language was strongest among their grandparents.[10] Among other respondents, Angelique Bergeron recalls that "my grandfather spoke Creole [and] my great-grandmother on the other side spoke French," while Julie Livaudais recalls her father knowing French but not using it much at home.[11]

French language loss was also accompanied by a decline in white Creoles' social and cultural institutions. The interview with Marcel Saussy was particularly valuable because she is one of the few respondents who is familiar with several older Creole cultural organizations that are now in decline. She remembers, for instance, when the *Athénée Louisianais* was still active.

This organization was established in 1876 to keep French language and literature vibrant in the city. In his 1904 publication, *A History of Louisiana*, Alcée Fortier noted that at that time, "The contemporary French literature of Louisiana [was] contained almost exclusively in the publications (Comptes Rendus) of the *Athénée Louisianais*."[12]

Marcel has also been an active participant of *Les Causeries de Lundi*, a group that is still active, but irrevocably changed. The group started out meeting on Mondays at 2 p.m. and used to consist only of women who met to speak French. Now, as numbers have dwindled, the time has been changed to noon in order to try to accommodate working men and women who might be interested in the club.

Even with these changes, however, *Les Causeries* is quite different in feeling and structure than it was decades ago when Marcel first started attending. The changes come across in her recounting of the one-hundred-year anniversary of the group.

> It [used to be] smaller, and in people's houses. We would maybe have tea girls—little girls who came and passed the food. I remember that. Because last year when we had our hundredth anniversary we had a tea for the hundredth anniversary and we had tea girls for old times' sake. We also had Sarah Jane McMahon come sing for us. And we had it at that house on First Street in the Garden District. The one where Jefferson Davis supposedly died, on the corner of Camp and First. We had tea girls, because my grandmother was one of them. People would take turns being the hostess and getting the food. We meet at Longue Vue Gardens now, which is a beautiful place to meet. Then we have a small lunch out underneath the awning. And we always have a program in French.

Marcel raises a number of interesting points here. First, her grandmother used to be a tea girl for the group. This points to how long the tradition of *Les Causeries* has been going on in her family. Next, the group used to have a very intimate social feel that marked it as a social group ideal for incubating French language and Creole culture. This contrasts greatly with the situation today which is less intimate, and less focused on strengthening social bonds within an ethnic community. She explains: "So much of what the *Causeries* is, is dying out. I don't even think of half the people in there as Creoles anymore. [It's a] lot of people that just want to speak French from out of town." Thus, the group has moved away from incubating Creole culture to becoming something of a French club open to anyone.

Although French language loss has been swift and steady across the twentieth century, there are still—as Grace King might say—"traces" of the language among Creoles who use occasional French words or phrases as a flourish on English conversation. The following dialogue with Norman Marmillion describes what this looks like:

> N.M.: When I go in to a restaurant, I usually have to say something in French, and it means a much warmer welcome—I'm one of you.
> A.P.: But are these people who could sustain a conversation in French?
> N.M.: No, not at all. But they know all these little words. Some of them do. The French, the way I see it, has lasted among the very rich, the very poor, and the very isolated.
> A.P.: So say you're gong into this restaurant, and they don't actually speak French but they know these few words—can you give me some of the few words?
> N.M.: Bonjour, ça va, comment ça va, just simple words. But they don't speak French.

Marcel makes a similar observation when she talks about hearing bits of French during Christmas gatherings with her father's family.

> A.P.: So you said at Christmas your father's family—his generation—would still be speaking French?
> M.S.: Just a little bit. "Joyeux Noël," "comment ça va." *Mère* spoke French—she really spoke French but it's the only time I really remember them speaking French.
> A.P.: *Mère* is your maternal grandmother?
> M.S.: *Mère* is my father's stepmother.

These small flourishes are all that is left of what used to be widespread literacy and fluency in French. The state's legal history concerning limitations on the use of French as a language of instruction coincides with respondents' memories to confirm that the last generation to operate fluently in French as a primary language was that generation born in the nineteenth century—the grandparents of my mainly middle-aged respondents.

But despite the slow dying out of the language, white Louisianans whose families resisted full Anglo-Americanization did manage to pass on a sense of French and Creole heritage to my respondents, and some of these respondents continue to actively pass that heritage on to their children. This preservation of Creole identification was most intentional among the descendants of elite families. John Ellis, descendant of James Pitot, is a prime example of these descendants. The Creole aspect of Ellis's upbringing has clearly won out over the American influence, and the process continues on in the new generation as Ellis seeks to impart this heritage to his children. When asked if he sees any continued influence of the St. Domingue migration on New Orleans today, he says:

> I think there's still quite a lot of influence. This may be affected by the fact that I'm a Creole, I consider myself a Creole. I'm Roman Catholic and I'm French, and I named my daughter French names. So I think if you look at that, plus how I ate growing up, it was a very Creole diet: beans and rice and shrimp and seafood and gumbos. Cuisine and religion to me are the very last strongholds of a culture. When you arrive in a new world, these are the last things that die.

Here John clearly states his identification as French and Creole and confirms his desire to keep this identification going for another generation.

Julie Livaudais was also raised with a clear awareness of her family's distinguished past. She, like John, grew up with physical markers in the city that memorialize the role the Livaudaises played in establishing the city of New Orleans. In the following excerpt, she discusses her initiation into the family's history:

> [My grandfather] instilled in us a pride of having a French heritage. More by talking about what the Livaudaises did in New Orleans, taking us to Commander's Palace to see the plaque on the side of the restaurant that talks about the Livaudais plantation and that sort of thing.... It's easy to miss, but [you see it] when you come down the ramp, when you leave the restaurant. Well, you know the Livaudais plantation was the Garden District and it says that "This restaurant is situated on the site of the Livaudais plantation." There's a little bitty street somewhere at the end of the Garden District that goes to the river that's called Livaudais Street—he took us to see that. He just wanted us to know that the family had a long history here.

Having grown up with this understanding of the family's history, Julie continues the tradition with her own children.

> A.P.: When it came to your own kids and raising them, did you think consciously at all about passing on their French Creole heritage?
>
> J.L.: They know about [it] .... my son is especially interested in the Livaudaises. They know that the family is prominent in New Orleans. They know what they came from ... they've seen the plaque at Commander's Palace ... my husband has done research on the earliest real estate records for New Orleans and there are Livaudaises registered on the earliest records. And so they like that history about it, and they've read a little bit. So yeah, you definitely pass that on to them so they know who they are and why they're going

to get certain questions. We had dinner last night with our son, who lives here, and he said, "Mom, you're pretty famous, huh, everybody knows you." I'm like, "I don't think everyone knows me." And he said, "No, I mean a lot of people know who you are." When you've been around a long time, what can I tell you?

It certainly is the case that the Livaudaises have been around for a long time. As Julie noted, a significant portion of the Garden District of New Orleans was, in fact, carved out of the old Livaudais plantation. In these kinds of elite families, a consciousness of the family's French and Creole heritage is likely to be passed down for generations to come because the families played such a well-documented role in building the city.

Another area where Creole traditions are continued among white Louisianans—particularly among the elite—includes the social rituals surrounding the Carnival season. When asked about whether or not she was passing on a sense of Creole identity to her children, Dorothy had this to say:

You know the carnival traditions are there, they've been part of an organization since they were three and five, and there's the children's carnival club, which mimics the adult groups and has a little formal ball and everything. So they both had to learn how to dance with a boy or a girl at age 10 or 11 and how to curtsy and how to bow, and the proper way to hold a girl's hand. So those little formal behaviors are kind of descended through some of that French Creole heritage and continuing that. They know they can't wear jeans on Christmas. They know they can't wear jeans to mass on Christmas or Easter, or other big holidays like that. They know the purpose of Mardi Gras, which I guess is one of the bigger outward signs of the French influence of life.

Julie Livaudais also points to the continuation of rituals surrounding the Carnival season as an important site for the continuation of Creole traditions within white Louisiana families. In her case, she got a historical lesson about the importance of these traditions when she was a young woman in college rebelling against them.

So ... we roll around to junior year—I don't want to be a debutante. My father says, "You're coming home" and he told me which balls I was going to be in. He told me I didn't have to come out at a party, but he said, "You're going to do what we do in this family, and that's the end of that discussion." So I came in. But as I grew up, when we would talk about the debutante year he would tell me, "This is how kids got to know each other and found a spouse." They would grow up, be tutored miles away from each other and come into New Orleans at Christmas for these various parties, and then Carnival. And back in that day you'd be assigned a person to take you to a party. So . . . the young man would receive an invitation and it would say "please escort Ms. So-and-So to the party." And you'd go, and that's the way the families met each other. It's sort of an antiquated custom, but it has roots in need. That's . . . you know, a lot of these Carnival organizations were old Creole families. That's how their children met. Back then, certain families . . . were big in that.

For the uninitiated, it is important to understand that in New Orleans, Carnival involves much more than parades and parties on Mardi Gras day. The preparations are year-long and the social rituals in the form of balls and parties occur throughout the winter and up to Ash Wednesday. What most tourists see on Mardi Gras day, therefore, is simply the top of a much deeper collection of practices and social ties.

It is also interesting to note, however, that although Carnival in New Orleans has French and Creole roots, it was actually the Anglo-Americans who gave it its current form and vigor. In his book *Carnival, American Style*, Kinser explains that from the 1770s through the 1830s the Carnival activities had no clearly organized public structure. Instead, there were a series of disparate private parties and masked balls. By the 1850s, Carnival seemed to be dying out. An article in the Ash Wednesday edition of *L'Abeille* in 1856 puts the nail in the coffin of Mardi Gras with a piece entitled "Funeral Prayer for Carnival":

Goodbye time of parties and pleasures! Goodbye joyous hours where each person clamors for a new amusement! The last of the gay children of this crazy season has died, killed, not by the cruel cold which grips us, but by an enemy much colder and more inexorable still, by Time, pursuing its unyielding march. Mardi Gras is no more![13]

Perhaps the death of Carnival would have occurred as predicted had it not been for a group of young American men who started the first of what are now known as "krewes" in Louisiana. A Mardi Gras krewe is a group of people who organize festivities for their members throughout the Carnival season and put together themed floats that participate with other krewes on the days designated for public Mardi Gras parades. The krewe structure was actually developed in Mobile—again by Americans—and then transplanted to New Orleans in 1857 when six men, formerly of Mobile, founded the Mistick Krewe of Comus. The founding of this krewe represents the start of the formalized public parading that has since come to characterize the

Mardi Gras season throughout Louisiana. Kinser notes the pervasive influence of Anglo-Americans in Comus:

> The society issued three thousand invitations to the ball following the parade in the Gaiety Theater, and the mayor led the first quadrille. All the elite of "fashion, taste, and beauty"—at least of Anglo-American origin—was present from this burgeoning city of over 150,000 people.... From its inception the Comus society expressed ambitions of grandeur, and was able to call upon ample resources to that end.[14]

Initially, Creoles were put off by the new group. Young contrasts the response of the English and French-language presses, noting that whereas the former were "unstinted in their praise," the latter either ignored them completely or made fun of them.[15]

It did not take long, however, for the Creole elite to see that the Comus society was on to something durable and significant. Although the group was started by Anglo-Americans, it very clearly drew on French and Creole cultural forms and practices. Kinser affirms this when he writes:

> The Anglo-American origin of Comus was ambivalent: it declared American independence from the French way of participating in Carnival, but at the same time it incorporated the Creole practices of masked balls and sumptuous banquets into its parade-centered activity.... The self-evident truth of man's right to relaxation was spelled with a French accent: Carnival, not Twelfth Night, Christmas, or the Fourth of July, became the center of festive life in New Orleans. Comus very soon attracted and admitted prominent Creoles to its membership. Both elites were satisfied.[16]

The tradition continues today among New Orleanians of Creole heritage like Dorothy, Julie, and many others. This is, moreover, a tradition that white Louisianans of French and Creole heritage are likely to continue for generations to come.

Although Creole-inspired traditions are likely to continue, white Louisianans' public and even private self-identification as Creoles is all but dead. This is because white Louisianans who claim Creole heritage continue to face either incredulity from those who assume that a "white Creole" is an oxymoron, or suspicion that they are really people of color trying to pass as white—these are the lingering effects of the racial-structural understanding of "Creole" which continues to creep into and negatively mark white Creoles' attempts to embrace their ethnic-cultural heritage. In the following section, we see how Anglo-American intermingling of the ethnic-cultural and racial-structural meanings of Creole continues to pose difficulties for white Louisianans seeking to lay claim to Creole heritage in the late twentieth and early twenty-first centuries.

THE INCOMPATIBILITY OF WHITENESS AND CREOLE IDENTITY

> So in young adulthood—young adulthood as a French Creole person, [it was] a little bit more of being aware of the term "Creole" had different meanings to different people.... I was more observant of like, kind of what other people were saying and how they were using it. [It became] a little more evident that African American Creole people when you'd hear different conversations, that they thought that they were "the Creoles" ... "Really, you think so? You think you're the only ones?" So [I had] more of like, a confusion.
> —Dorothy Carter, interviewee, 2013

In Dorothy's response we see how she and other white Creoles continue to encounter the lingering racial-structural dimension of Creole identification where being Creole is inseparable from the idea of racial mixture. Here Dorothy is describing a period in the late 1970s to early 1980s. She had just graduated from college and was beginning to make her own way in the world. By this time, the identification of Creoles with blackness was well underway, but she had been raised in a circle of family and friends where whiteness and Creole identity were understood to be compatible. Other interviewees also described instances where they or their family members received a rude awakening to the racial implications of identifying as Creole.

In the following interview excerpt, Marcel Saussy is responding to a question about when she remembers the transition occurring from Creole as potentially or exclusively white to an understanding of Creole that assumes a black or mixed-race background.

> A.P.: So you're pretty sure that by the time you were married in the 60s [white Louisianans] were still thinking of themselves as Creole without racial context. So maybe [the transition occurred] around the 70s.
> M.S.: I think so. Maybe around the 70s. Because I can remember I have a sister-in-law that, she lived away for years and we had an argument—she says, Creole only means people of color. I said no it doesn't. You know, don't take that word away.... But that has happened, we know that.... And her idea— she lived in California a long time, and that's what she thought. She argued oh no, it doesn't mean white people at all. I said of course it does.
> A.P.: Did she grow up in New Orleans?

M.S.: Yeah.

A.P.: And is she from a Creole family?

M.S. They're not a Creole family—they're from Georgia.

This timing around the 1970s also resonates with Dorothy Carter's experience, which was recounted earlier. Dorothy graduated from college in the late 1970s into a world where her identification as both Creole and white was seen as impossible. William Connick had a similar experience of growing up among white Creoles and assuming that whiteness and Creole heritage went together.[17] He explains:

> the little bit of reading I did and things I have heard, the Creoles, I know that is a word that has a lot of different meanings to a lot of different people. We always used, or [when] my mother and my grandmother used it, they considered themselves Creoles in the family, not from any racial point of view but because of the definition that would be children born away from France in the New World or French and Spanish descendants or whatnot. So they always considered themselves Creole. Mostly my mother's side. My grandmother. They would talk about it a little bit like that. And other members of the family always referred to them as having Creole heritage.

This insider's understanding was not, however, shared by those outside of Louisiana who had quite a different understanding of what it meant to be Creole. In the following quote, he shares the story of what happened to a family member who left Louisiana to go up north:

> I had one of my grandmother's sister's maybe ... when she got married ... she married a guy from Baltimore who was up in society I think a little bit, and she always called herself a Creole. Well, they mistook that up there to mean she might have had some Negro blood in her, so I think that caused some prejudice against her.

Mr. Connick was born in 1939 and his maternal grandparents were born in the 1870s. Assuming his grandmother's sister was about the same age, she would likely have been married in the 1890s when she would have been in her twenties. Estimating generously, therefore, the experience up north would have occurred late nineteenth, early twentieth century. As anyone who is familiar with the racial history of the United States would know, this was certainly a difficult time to be suspected of being part black. The incident also, however, underscores the very different underlying assumptions between insiders and outsiders about what it meant to be Creole. It is quite unlikely that Connick's great-aunt would have said anything about being Creole if she had realized the reaction this would elicit. It is these kinds of reactions—from people outside of Louisiana as well from non-Creoles inside the state that led to the gradual but marked distancing of many white Creoles from Creole identification.

The experiences reported here help to explain why, when Virginia Dominguez did her research among white Creoles in the mid-1970s, so few younger white Creoles identified themselves as such. When she interviewed students at a school with a largely white Creole student population, she found that of 111 interviewed, only 12.6 percent identified themselves as Creole. Instead of identifying as Creole, the young people were more likely to describe themselves as "French" or of French heritage.[18]

Dominguez sees this reluctance to self-identify as Creole as being tied to lost struggles over the course of the twentieth century to take the term "Creole" back from its association with blackness. On the one hand, most of the white Creoles she spoke with believed—at least privately—that a true Creole is a white person born in the United States who has French and/or Spanish ancestry. Under this definition, a person of color would not be considered Creole. But despite belief among many white Creoles that this was the proper definition of Creole, they understood that their definition was not shared by others outside of their group. Thus, as Dominguez succinctly explains: "Younger white Creoles see less sense or purpose in denying the existence of colored Creoles and prefer instead to yield the name rather than fight fear of misrepresentation."[19]

Indeed, more than thirty years after Dominguez carried out her work, several respondents for this study cite lingering racial misunderstandings associated with the idea of being white and Creole. For instance, a routine part of each interview session for this study involved asking interviewees to recommend others who would be willing to participate in the research. The following exchange occurred in response to my request that Norman Marmillion refer me to other white Creoles:

A.P.: You mentioned that the _____ [family] see themselves as Creole. Would they say that publicly do you think?
N.M.: They would probably be reluctant—for racial reasons.
A.P.: They're white?
N.M.: Yes.
A.P.: The perception that there might be African descent in their family?
N.M.: That has not changed at all, since after the Civil War.[20]

The Civil War, as we saw in Chapter 3, was indeed the turning point in the struggle white Creoles waged with Anglo-Americans in their efforts to hold on to a beloved cultural identity without, at the same time, giving up the benefits of being white in Anglo-American society.

Jerry Gandolfo, in fact, refers directly to this time period in his discussion of race and Creole identity.

> You've got to remember after the end of Reconstruction is when for the first time the whole black-white thing became really severe. Prior to that time people didn't mind having black relatives and family.... But at that point in the 1880s on it, the black-white thing, got to be severe and before then New Orleans had a three-part society. Black, white, and free people of color and after that it kind of evolved into two.

Jerry's grandmother was unusual, however, in her willingness to hold together the idea of being white but also having some black family members.

> [My grandmother's] also very big on making it a point ... I don't know either by immunization or by explanation or by what purpose it was but always making a point about the *plaçage* system. And the fact that I would run into people with my name, same last name and they would be black and they would be here in New Orleans and other places. That she was not embarrassed by it, she just wanted it to be known from her rather than to run into it, bump into it kind of thing.
>
> Which is interesting because that whole concept at one point was considered OK until George Washington Cable wrote the book *The Grandissimes*, accusing them and then everybody suddenly started denying it. She never denied it. She was almost proud of that. It was like this is our culture. This was how life was. What we did. She made a point of the fact that we spoke English as a practical means but it wasn't our language, that French was our language.

Jerry packs a lot of Creole history, identity, and racial politics into this tiny excerpt. With the *plaçage* system, it was indeed quite possible to have black and white branches of the same family. This is exactly the racial phenomenon that Cable played up in *The Grandissimes*. The difference, however, is that Cable went farther than saying that there were some families where one branch was mixed race and another was white. He pushed the envelope, insinuating that *all* Creoles were actually mixed race but were concealing this mixture. This, no doubt, is the reason that he opens the novel with a masquerade ball and continues throughout the book to play up the theme of masking and concealment around issues of true identity.

The approach that Jerry's grandmother takes toward racial mixture has much more in common with a Latin/Caribbean approach to race than an Anglo-American perspective. According to this alternative Latin/Caribbean logic, having black relatives in the family does not necessarily compromise one's whiteness. But it was precisely this more flexible or relaxed outlook on cross-racial social relations that led Anglo-Americans to ascribe a pejorative racial-structural connotation to being Creole. According to Anglo-American thinking, anyone identifying as Creole was at least potentially, and probably certainly, mixed race.

Alice Dantro's experience of learning about her family's connection to colonial St. Domingue exemplifies the harsh consequences of the Anglo-American racial system where *any* possibility of racial mixture in *any* part of the family is damaging and should be concealed. In response to my question about whether or not she grew up with any family stories about her ancestors fleeing the Haitian Revolution, she replied:

> Oh yes, that's why they came, they were fleeing . . . That was going on at the time. That there was a lot of unrest and now at that time . . . you have to remember I was born in '47 and these stories started coming to me in the '50s and that was at a time when it was not popular, it was not talked about, Haiti was a place that was far away to most people . . . and some of the stories whispered and some half laughed about it and some family members denying it at all. Denying the fact that there was a Haitian connection so to speak as far as the people of color, but you see records don't lie.

Next, I asked her if her mother or grandmother would mention that there were people of color in the family's past. Alice explained:

> That was sort of understood. We sort of understood that and it was kind of something that was really not to be discussed. You understand what I'm saying. Because I remember when I was in the first grade, I told a little boy that I was Creole and he said well you are a _____ and he used the bad word in the first grade and I cried about it. I was embarrassed, but what he meant was that was what he had grown up in his family hearing that Creole meant, and so I couldn't understand because I had been brought up with that term with such a sense of pride knowing who my ancestors were.

In addition to the social disapproval she experienced when she called herself Creole as a young girl, when she was older, she also found that she was discouraged from learning too much about her family's genealogical history.

> I have had friends here in New Orleans in clubs tell me that it is alright to go back so far in your ancestry here but don't go back too far. Meaning if you go back too far, they know that the color line in the blood lines crossed over and over many, many times. And so it would be better to say that you came in the later 1800s, you know what I'm saying. Don't go back too far. Only go back so many generations. And don't go back that many generations in St. Domingue, only go back that far.

Despite the negative social reactions Alice has had, she has persevered in claiming Creole identity. On the questionnaire for this study, she described herself as having "Creole ancestry."

The extreme racial vigilance that Alice describes in these excerpts provides another clear contrast between Latin/Caribbean and Anglo-American understandings of whiteness. Within the logic of the former, whiteness is determined by a combination of appearance and status, whereas according to the latter, whiteness is determined by purity of lineage. The approaches are so different that in Chapter 1 we saw Edward Telles report on white Brazilians' pride in pointing to ancestors of African descent. For Brazilians, this indicates that one is tied into the country's idea of racial democracy, but it does not at all signal that one is nonwhite. In contrast, Alice is discouraged from discovering ancestors of color as far back as late seventeenth-century colonial St. Domingue.

The racial miscues can, at times, result in wryly comical situations. Dorothy describes an encounter at a party where she was quite misunderstood but couldn't determine the best way to *be* understood, given the deep-seated racial assumptions of those around her. To understand the story, one must know that although Dorothy is white, among many native to Louisiana "whiteness" is determined, at least in part, by social context because there are Creoles of African descent who have skin as light as most white people. It is a testament to Dorothy's good humor that she prefaced the account by describing it as a "funny story."

> [My friend] and her husband would throw these great parties and attract the most diverse group of people you've ever met—socially, economically, racially—you just name it, they were there. And all of her husband's family owned restaurants . . . parties didn't start until 10 or 11 o'clock, so of course they had to invite the neighbors 'cause they were going to keep us up anyway. And I was at one of these parties and I was talking to her brother . . . and this

[other] guy ... who was decidedly African American—and her brother, who looked more Hispanic—and then there's me, and the three of us are talking. And this woman comes in and he says, Jane Tureaud is here! Don't you know Jane Tureaud? I said: "No, why would I know Jane?" and he says, "Her father was A. P. Tureaud." And I said, "What did he do?" Now Jane has blond hair, blue eyes, but African American features, right. So I'm like what did her father do? And he says: "I don't know—come here, Jane. Jane, what did your father do?" And she says he was a lawyer. I said, "I don't know why I thought he did something in education." And she says where did you go to school? I said St. Joseph and UNO. [She replies] "Well, he did the litigation that allowed you to go to school." And I'm standing there thinking I'm female, I could have gone anywhere, you know a big dummy. And she repeats herself. And then I realized what she was saying. I said, "I'm white." And she goes, "Oh honey I thought you were Creole. You're not offended are you?" I said no, I'm not—nobody's ever said that to me. And that's the moment that I was so acutely aware. And I was probably about twenty-six—that those people that thought that they were—you know, the Creoles of African descent that thought that they were "the Creoles" and we weren't.

At this point in the story I asked Dorothy if she corrected the woman to explain that she was both white and Creole. She explained:

No, I didn't because actually... the decidedly African American guy goes "I knew she was white." And it was just ... it was, what do you say. And then when I told my mother the story—my mother is so snarky—she says, "I know, she probably thought you were trying to pass" ... And I think I was probably about twenty-six years old. And thinking, wow. There's something I'm not a part of, you know—that what I thought I was always a part of somebody does not see [me] as a part of them.

Note here that Dorothy's self-understanding is that she is both white and "part of them"—Creoles of color. Her identification as part of them has to do with the ethnic-cultural dimension of Creole identity, but since the late nineteenth century, it has been difficult to claim publicly this cultural membership without also being categorized as black. Despite these racial misunderstandings, Dorothy, like Alice, has persevered in her identification as Creole and has passed this identity and culture on to her children. When I asked her about this, she explained that she taught her daughter French from a young age and that she has a sister and brother-in-law who live in France. She raised her daughter from early on with the knowledge that she was French Creole. And yet her daughter has not been spared the cognitive dissonance that goes along with being white and Creole. Dorothy explains that:

> When they were in sixth grade at the Catholic school here, there's a project of doing your family tree. And so, of course, you had multitudes of stuff on the French part of the family and going through all of that, so [my daughter] knew. So here's the documentation that I am French Creole . . . so that's in sixth grade. At eighth grade here is some substitute teacher in some discussion—I have no idea what—and [my daughter] says, "Well, I'm Creole." And the teacher says, "Oh no honey, I don't think so." Now it was a white teacher, but her interpretation was that Creole was the African descent. . . . She was a polite kid. She kept her mouth shut. She really wanted to say, "No, lady, there's more definitions than that."

Angelique, one of the younger respondents who was in her thirties, has also had many misunderstandings and struggles in her attempts to claim Creole identity as a white woman. She grew up in New Roads, Louisiana, a small town in a mainly rural area where both whites and blacks speak Creole and identify as Creole. When she left her small community to go to other parts of the state, however, she got blank looks when she called herself Creole.

> I remember going to a Creole heritage center conference. And I went to the Northwestern area, again I'd go back to Cane River and I'm looking for Creole speakers up there because I had been working with the Creole group here, Les Creoles du Pointe Coupée, and I wanted to hear their Creole French. I wanted to see what they spoke like, did they say this for that or what did they say. And I couldn't find a single Creole speaker, but everybody that I went up to and told I was Creole understood that I was mixed race. And I wasn't trying to say that. I was trying to say that I was Creole, my family's Creole, we're French, and I didn't realize that other people had that other association with it until then, until I was confronted with it . . . I remember [this man] and I talked to him for a long time and he said, "Wow, you're really fair." And he said something about my hair or something and I was like, "Oh, I'm white Creole." He just looked at me funny.

What is truly interesting here is that even though Angelique comes from a small town where there are still white community members who speak Creole—including Angelique herself—and even though the people of color she met in Cane River did *not* speak Creole, she is the one who got the strange looks when she claimed a Creole identity. Speaking Creole was not enough to be "in." There was literally no place in the public imagination so that the man she was speaking to could situate "white" and "Creole" in the same conceptual space. It would seem, then, that white Creoles have been erased from public memory and thus from the social imagination. This eradication from social memory comes across in interviews with descendants of St. Domingue refugees who were *not* heir to any connections to Creole or even French heritage. We consider their stories next.

THE LOSS OF CREOLE MEMORY

Far more common than the previous sections' stories of connectedness to Creole/French ancestry and culture were stories from respondents who only recently discovered these connections through family history research. For some, the discovery was simply a curiosity that did not alter their own deeply Anglo-American sense of themselves and their family's history. For others, the discovery of French and Creole ancestry captured their imagination and led to long-term immersion in research and culture concerning this branch of their family tree.

Among the first group of these respondents—those who remain most connected to their Anglo heritage—is Carol, a descendant of St. Domingue refugees who initially got interested in family history in order to learn more about her English ancestry. Carol explains:

> Eight years ago I became interested in my family genealogies. A friend had invited me to attend D.A.R. meetings. I knew basically a couple of things. My grandmother said—my grandmother had already died—she said that we, the girls in this family are eligible to join D.A.R., and she left an old letter written in 1910 about her family. So I started knowing basically nothing except the people that I knew when they were alive, which was only her, my parents, her generation, my grandparents, and then I heard stories about people that were no longer alive.

Carol did, however, spend time growing up in New Orleans, but she never felt strongly connected to the French influence of the city.

> We were living in Uptown New Orleans, but we weren't of them. We were Baltimore people. And that was always talked about. This furniture is from Baltimore. The house in Baltimore . . . and my mother always drank hot tea. She never did drink hot coffee. We could smell coffee coming off the wharves Uptown, . . . but it would make her ill. They were so, I guess, British Isles, they were eating shortbread and orange marmalade. Even as a child I felt that we were

a bit different from the New Orleans people, but we did New Orleans things too, but we didn't even sound the same. So, if that makes sense.... The oral history in the family among the older people, they would speak of more the [Baltimore] roots of their family.... We weren't as connected to Louisiana as many of the people around us.

In most white American families there are a variety of family lines coming from many European origins. Because of this variety, it is not unusual for one line to be emphasized over the others.[21] Although Carol has documented linkages to St. Domingue and French ancestors, it was her family's connections to the British Isles that dominated.[22]

Richard was also initially drawn to learning about his family history because of his interest in Anglo-American history.[23] In response to a question about what sparked his initial interest in family history, Richard explained:

> I was interested in my ancestors—not that they were St. Dominguan. Because as a young fellow I studied history and I saw where people came over on the Mayflower and I wondered how did I or did we come over on the Mayflower and that's how I started finding out.

Even though interest in his family's potential connections to the Mayflower inaugurated his genealogical research, he actually grew up within a context where his family discussed their connections to France. Richard noted:

> I remember on occasions and family gatherings with the elderly bringing up the subject of where we lived in France.... all of those members of my family, the momma and all of the children went back to France except one.

In Richard's case, the founding narrative of the Anglo-American United States, with its attending stories about the courage of the Mayflower settlers, was in many ways a more powerful draw than the stories of his Louisiana family's connection to France.

Lydia has also been strongly drawn to her family's Anglo-American line, though she has a much stronger connection to that history than does Richard. Like Carol, Lydia is originally from Baltimore, and she has documented St. Domingue ancestry in her family. Her family's connection to St. Domingue has made her appreciate New Orleans in new ways.

> I would say that definitely the fact that I'm living in New Orleans and that there is the Haitian influence and the history of the émigrés coming to New Orleans it's

kind of kept the interest ongoing for me, because you don't have that same interest in Baltimore. The French that went there, I think by the mid-1820s had died out or [disappeared into] the rest of the population. They never kept their culture separate and apart. Whereas I think here the Creoles of color and the French and Spanish have all been very proud of their heritage, and they've kept it up.

Here Lydia draws a clear distinction between the St. Domingue communities of Baltimore and New Orleans. Even though both received large amounts of *émigrés*, Louisiana's preexisting Creole population and the replenishing of French speakers with the St. Domingue refugees helped to nurture French and Creole culture whereas these were more quickly lost in Maryland.

Growing up in the mainly English-influenced Maryland area has decisively shaped Lydia's cultural identification. For although the St. Domingue connection fascinates her, her strongest identification is with her Anglo-American ancestors. When asked about the social organizations she belongs to that relate to family history and culture, she had the following to say about those that were most important to her:

Probably the [Louisiana Mayflower Society], because I'm governor ... that's a totally different origin [from the St. Domingue ancestors]. That's the pilgrims up in Plymouth and again, the history of the Mayflower is a people who left England, lived in Holland, felt they were persecuted for religious reasons, came to the new world, survived the first brutal winter ... and also from a legal statement the Mayflower compact that they signed onboard the ship was the first legal document in America where a group of people came together and decided to govern amongst themselves according to the consent of the people, which is a very important document. I've been to Plymouth Rock.

As governor, Lydia helps to oversee the Society's educational programs, which provide material for schools to provide information about the Pilgrims. She is also responsible for overseeing the production of the annual luncheon carried out during the Thanksgiving season.

When asked which historical or cultural organization was second in importance to her, Lydia explained:

If I were in Maryland, probably it would be the Ark and the Dove because this is the group of people who were descended from the two ships, the Ark and the Dove, who founded Maryland in 1634 in St. Mary's City. And what they're doing for St. Mary's City is what they're doing for Jamestown. They're trying to re-create an historical village—a reproduction of life at that time. So I would say that if I were still living in Maryland, that would be very important to me.

Again, what we see here is an emphasis on the Anglo over the French and St. Domingue dimensions of her family's history. There are good reasons for this emphasis. First, it is clear that Lydia's St. Domingue ancestors married liberally into Maryland's Anglo community. Second, the Anglo branch of the family has elite origins. Quite naturally, the family would have been more likely to preserve and remember the elite origins over less elite origins. Here we see elite Anglo origins working against the vigorous cultivation of French cultural memory.

Denise also tells a story that involves intermarriage between Anglos and Creoles, which results in the eclipse of the latter.[24] She explains:

> Let me tell you my own situation in my family. My mother since I was two years old was dying with TB. She died when I was ten. When I was two, we had to stop being a family and move in with her family. My mother was Protestant. Because this connected to Martin Luther, my daddy had to stop being Catholic, even though he went to mass every Sunday. He didn't go back into the Catholic Church until after he died. But we moved in with my mother's family so that my mother could be taken care of and I could be taken care of. So there was no sitting around the table and discussing anything like would be done in a normal family. So this is why I had to pick up the information from outsiders.

For Denise, the French and Catholic parts of her family history were cut off because of family dynamics beyond her control. Eventually, Denise reconnected with her family's French history. She is descended from the Lamberts of St. Domingue, whose family has extensive archival documents at Tulane University.[25]

Whereas some interviewees emphasized Anglo over French and Creole ancestry, others who unexpectedly stumbled across their connections to St. Domingue ancestry held on to and were deeply influenced by the connections. Augusta Elmwood is a prime example of this. She was fifty-nine at the time of the interview, was born and raised in New Orleans, and described herself as racially white and ethnically a mix of French and German. She had no idea that she had St. Domingue ancestry when she was growing up and did not have family members who emphasized the family's French background. When asked whether or not doing genealogical research had strengthened her racial or ethnic identity, she said:

> A.E.: Yes, definitely. I think it gave me a strong feeling of my Frenchness and of the character of my ancestors. Sometimes I can maybe see, or I see things in me and I don't know where they come from, like sometimes I attribute them to my mother or my father or grandmother and I'll do things and

I'll say things [and] I wonder where I got that from. So sometimes it helps me understand myself better.

A.P.: When you say it has reinforced a feeling of Frenchness, what do you mean?

A. E.: Not necessarily characteristics. I think I feel closer to the French than my German ancestors. And it may be because I have so completely immersed myself in the French. I taught myself French, even though I did study German in high school. I think also the French reciprocate more. The Germans are not as forthcoming with the genealogical information as the French are. I think it may be a little bit skewed by the present-day French people, but I feel more French than German, although on my mother's side I am German and Prussian, Polish.

Here we see a very clear choosing of the French over the German parts of her family history. Although she had no deliberate socialization into her family's French background, she is intentionally reviving the connection to her St. Domingue ancestors. It was mainly Augusta's genealogical fascination that led her to immerse herself in France. Since beginning that work she has travelled to the country several times, she speaks conversational French, and she has founded the St. Domingue Special Interest Group, which helps genealogists from Louisiana find and document their ties to colonial St. Domingue.

Lisa is another whose family has a well-documented connection to St. Domingue that she has only recently discovered. A family register from St. Domingue containing the names of one hundred fifty-eight slaves was included in the Historic New Orleans Collection's "Common Routes" exhibit, which explored the linkages between St. Domingue/Haiti and Louisiana. It was only much later in her life, however, that Lisa began to learn of these connections. Even the French language was not passed down very effectively in her family. She explained that "no matter what you were, for a while you wanted to become very American. So I found out later they didn't want you to speak French . . . but I'm just amazed how much was lost, what they didn't know or didn't speak of." Since her discoveries, Lisa has travelled to France and learned French in order to read historical documents.

Eva Campos was forty-three at the time of the interview and she, like Augusta and Lisa, was born and raised in New Orleans. She described herself as "white and Hispanic" on the questionnaire. She describes her perspective on her ancestry as follows:

I never really gave ancestors much thought other than I guess just normal, but now it makes me feel like, you know it makes me feel like part of the mix. It makes me feel like we are just so integrated especially here. Such a special environment here in New Orleans. And apparently it happened in St. Domingue and it just makes me feel that, I feel more human. I feel more part of the population. It makes me more conscious that we are all just, we are all part of everybody else.

What Eva describes here is a sense that doing genealogy and discovering a family history and ethnic background links her into a larger historical context than she had before she started the research. Eva's experience was somewhat unique among the interviewees in that she also identifies as Hispanic, but there was little indication in her interview that this dimension of her background significantly shaped her identity. For the most part, the narrative provided in her interview portrayed her as mainly white, American, and only lightly—if at all—connected to any particular ethnic identity.

The stories from respondents in this section show how fragile family connections to Creole/French identification and culture can be in an Anglo-dominated context. Over the generations, intermarriage, cultural assimilation, and selective remembrance of certain family lines resulted in either the attenuation or complete loss of French and Creole identity for many of these respondents. Private losses in Creole memory and identity have been accompanied, moreover, by a parallel loss in public memory. This loss has resulted in a social reality where "white" and "Creole" are understood to be identities that cannot overlap in the twenty-first century. We consider this public loss in the concluding section, which offers an analysis of the last twenty-five years of the *Times-Picayune* newspaper's treatment of white Creoles.

THE BANISHMENT OF WHITE CREOLES FROM THE PRESENT

For hundreds of years, newspapers have acted as a social glue that cultivates a sense of belonging to the larger community. Benedict Anderson is well known for demonstrating how the newspaper helped to nurture a nascent sense of national belonging.[26] Similar dynamics occur at the local level, where city papers bring together diverse persons into regular communion with each other as they share in the ritual of daily reading.[27] In New Orleans, the most widely read paper has been the *Times-Picayune*, a paper that has been in circulation since the nineteenth century.

As we have seen in the first section, respondent stories combined with Virginia Dominguez's anthropological work in *White by Definition* indicate that the 1970s were the turning point in the breaking of the slender straw which had held together the overlapping identities of white and Creole in the social imagination. An analysis of the *Times-Picayune* from 1989 to the present shows how complete is the banishment of contemporary white Creole identity from this imagination. When they are mentioned at all, white Creoles are portrayed as having existed only in the past. Conversely, nearly all references to Creoles living in the present are to people of color.

Indeed, the story of how it was possible for me to find white Creoles *at all* in the *Times-Picayune* testifies to how thoroughly this population has been eradicated from the social imagination. An initial search under the term "Creole" from 1989 to 2015 produced 16,873 hits. The vast majority of these articles, however, made reference to food, housing, or some other inanimate object described as "Creole." In an attempt to limit the search to people, I searched under "Creole heritage" and got 193 hits. This brought some progress as now the articles were either about food or about people. The people mentioned, however, were overwhelmingly Creoles of color. Next I tried "French Creole," knowing that white Louisianans with a Creole background are more likely to emphasize their connections to France than to Creole heritage. This produced 328 hits but, surprisingly, most of them dealt with food or architecture—the people had largely disappeared again. Finally, I recalled that when I had seen white Creoles referred to in various kinds of writing over the course of this project, it was often with the qualifier "old" or "distinguished" as in "old Creole family" or "distinguished Creole family." Indeed, this should have been my first instinct, considering that the most referenced book concerning white Creoles is Grace King's *Creole Families of New Orleans*. Once I changed the search to "Creole family," I finally hit upon what I was looking for: most of the articles dealt with people, *and* there was a healthy representation of both white Creoles and Creoles of color among the articles.

The "Creole family" search yielded 162 articles. After discarding repeated items, the final collection of documents included 105 distinct articles. A review of these articles resulted in nine separate codes, which are listed in Table 5.1. When these nine codes were applied to the 105 articles, the result was 173 coded segments.[28]

When we combine all of the segments that are definitely white or most likely white, we have a total of forty-seven segments. When we combine all that are people of color or likely to be people of color, we end up with forty. Thus, when we exclude articles where it is difficult to decipher the race at all, we have an almost equal division between black and white references to Creole families.

Table 5.1 TIMES-PICAYUNE CREOLE FAMILY SEARCH

Code Names	Number of Segments per Code
Educational or cultural event	42
Race not signaled—probably or definitely white	42
Housing	30
Race identified as African descent	17
Race signaled—mixed race	13
Race not signaled—probably or definitely black	10
Race not signaled—unable to decipher	7
Food	7
Race identified as white	5

The following examples provide a sample of the kinds of segments that were coded as "Race not signaled—probably or definitely white":

> THE BLOCK: The 600 block of Reynes Street, on the odd-numbered, or east, side, between Royal Street on the north and Chartres Street on the south. Just across the street is the sole remaining building of the former campus of Holy Cross school (now in Gentilly), *the 1895 landmark* designed by renowned architect James Freret. The former campus occupies much of what *was once the riverfront plantation of the Reynes family, a prominent Creole family* whose patriarch, Joseph (originally Jose) Reynes, completed construction of the Pitot House about 1800.[29]

> At the scheduled time, we arrived at Maison Olivier to be warmly greeted in the garden by Park Ranger Bill Pratt, who gave us a 30-minute tour of the house *built in 1815* by Charles Olivier, a *wealthy Creole* from New Orleans. Starting with a detailed history of the family, Pratt led us through the lower two levels of the house, explaining the construction of the home, a raised Creole cottage, and the lifestyle of *a Creole family living on a sugarcane plantation.* The Oliviers thrived here until the *Civil War,* after which *they departed "in distress."*[30]

> ABOUT THE ARTIST: Marie de Hoa LeBlanc is regarded as "one of the most colorful and prolific of the early Newcomb designers," according to the www.tulane.edu Web site. *Born in 1874* into an *old Creole family* , LeBlanc *became a student at Newcomb College at age 20* along with her sister, Emilie, also a prolific artist. Despite the reticence of many Creole families to encourage higher education for girls, the LeBlanc sisters were allowed to ride the streetcar from their French Quarter home to Newcomb's campus on Washington Avenue to attend classes.[31]

In these segments, the sections of the text that indicated the Creole in question was probably or definitely white are italicized. The first and second make reference to large homes owned by wealthy persons. These are both tourist sites, and when their promotional materials are consulted, none of them mention the owners being people of color. This lack of racial signaling is quite common when whiteness is assumed. If these homes had been owned by Creoles of color, this would be a significant historical selling point that would be mentioned somewhere in promotional material. The second segment is also read as most likely white because, although there were some blacks on the Confederate side, the overwhelming majority of persons were white. Finally, the third example is read as describing a white woman because she attended Tulane's Newcomb College in the late nineteenth century, but Tulane did not admit African Americans until 1963.

All of these segments, and the vast majority of the other forty-two coded as probably or definitely white, made reference to Creoles of the nineteenth century. One notable exception is a segment that refers to Mrs. Mignon Josephine Cressy Faget. This segment, which is taken from her obituary, reads:

> Mrs. Faget, who was born into a Creole family just off Esplanade Avenue, was named for her mother's favorite opera, Ambroise Thomas' "Mignon." She grew up speaking French and attending a small French school before graduating from Girls' High School, now John McDonogh High on Esplanade.

This is the only segment concerning a white Creole that referred to someone who had lived in the late twentieth century. Here, there is no qualifier like "old" or "distinguished," most likely because everyone from New Orleans knows that the Fagets are an old and distinguished family. No qualifier is necessary. At the same time, however, the description of her being born into a Creole family conforms to the general assumption that white Creoles are of the nineteenth century because Mrs. Faget was one hundred and three when she died in 2000 and thus was born at the tail end of the nineteenth century when "white" and "Creole" were still overlapping identities in the public imagination. Other than this reference to Mrs. Faget, however, there were no other white Creoles referenced in the *Times-Picayune* "Creole family" search outside of those who lived in the nineteenth century or earlier.

On the other hand, nearly every reference to Creoles of color referred to persons living at the time the article was written. The following excerpts provide samples of persons who were marked as probably or definitely black in the "Creole family" search.

> "It's a typical New Orleans shotgun," said Luster-Stipe. "I've heard stories from other family members that up to 30 people lived in that house at one time."

We're a Creole family, and they used to do everything in their homes.... My great-great-great-grandmother Mama Jean's funeral was there in the house."... "Uncle Tootie [Montana] was raised in that house," Luster-Stipe said. "He used to start his *Mardi Gras [Indian]* walk passing by that house."[32]

Rocking the Rails: Today, featuring jazz singer *John Boutte* 5–7:30 p.m. at the Covington Trailhead, 419 N. New Hampshire. Boutte was *raised in the 7th Ward*, where most of his Creole family still lives and sings. He played coronet and trumpet in his junior high and high school marching bands but is known as a singer and writer who has performed on stages around the world.[33]

Through her two cookbooks and Allen's "Listen, I Say Like This," a lot of people know *Chase's* basic story: *Born in 1923* into a large Creole family in rural Madisonville. Moved to New Orleans at age 13 to live with relatives and attend high school. In 1946, she married musician Edgar Chase Jr., whose family ran a small, popular restaurant. She raised five children and sewed, then went to work in the restaurant, where her cooking, her generous spirit and her love of her community eventually made her an icon.[34]

But what brought the young filmmaker from St. Louis, and more recently New York's New School for Social Research film program, to the *black Creole culture* of the Deep South? .... " One of the things that attracted me was the uniqueness of the situation for (Louisiana's) black Americans—that there were *free people of color* (there) since the 1700s," she says. "Eve's Bayou" is a multi-generational drama about a prosperous and sophisticated Creole family. The story, *set in Louisiana in 1962*, is told from the perspective of 10-year-old Eve Batiste (Jurnee Smollett). The girl is the descendant of an African-American woman (also named Eve) and Jean Paul Batiste, a Frenchman whose life the woman saves. He, in turn, frees her from slavery and gives her his land.[35]

In these segments, we see that the italicized time periods are in the twentieth century and there is direct reference to Creoles of African descent who are still living at the time the article is written. The first segment references the Mardi Gras Indians—a well-known New Orleans phenomenon where black New Orleanians create elaborate beaded and feathered costumes that pay homage to Native Americans. Through their costuming and marching, the Mardi Gras Indians commemorate and celebrate historical connections between Africans and Indians in early New Orleans. Segment two references the Seventh Ward, an area that is a historic center of Creole of color social life and institutions. Segments two and three mention John Boutte and Leah Chase, respectively, two prominent black New Orleanians whose race is widely known. Finally, even though the final segment makes reference to fictional Creole characters, those characters are contemporary Creoles of color—*Eve's Bayou* is clearly described as a story about Creoles of color set in the 1960s.

Taken together, the contrasting newspaper segments provide a sample of the ways the *Times-Picayune* has dealt with Creoles of different racial backgrounds. White Creoles are portrayed—with the exception of Mrs. Faget—as relics of the nineteenth century or earlier. Many of the articles included refer to museum exhibits or historical talks. In contrast, most of the articles referring to Creoles of color deal with persons who are still living or who lived well into the twentieth century. In sum, then, the loss of white Creole identity discussed in the section immediately preceding this one is reinforced by the erasure of contemporary white Creoles in the *Times-Picayune* "Creole family" search.

As we have seen in this chapter and in Chapter 3, there were many social and legal forces that led to the progressive disappearance of white Creole society. These pressures intensified during the post–Civil War period and continued to increase into the twentieth century. With the exception of those from small towns or rural areas—where the Creole and French languages persevered—and the exception of those from elite families, many white Creoles gradually let go of their Creole identities and blended, for the most part, into the white Anglo-American community. Nineteenth- and early twentieth-century Creoles of color were slower to acquiesce to the Anglo-American racial system, but by the end of Chapter 4 we left young Creoles of color of the 1960s reconsidering their identities and increasingly embracing Anglo-American blackness.

Things began to change again in the second half of the twentieth century, however, as the social and racial context Creoles of color found themselves in was transformed by two new forces. First, an increasing number of immigrants from Latin America and the Caribbean entered the country as US immigration laws changed in their favor. Many of these immigrants struggled with the unfamiliar racial categorizations of the Anglo-American system. Second, as social sanctions against interracial relationships decreased, the result was a growing bi- and multiracial population born in the United States. Both of these changes increased the number of persons who felt that the binary nature of the Anglo-American system was a bad fit with their lived experiences of race. These groups' resistance to the Anglo-American racial system provided social support for Creoles of color, an increasing number of whom began to reidentify as Creole and push back against the Anglo insistence that they fit themselves into black or white racial categories. In Chapter 6 we examine the different paths today's Creoles of color have taken as they attempt to negotiate the changing racial landscape of US cities and regions.

CHAPTER 6

Into the Twenty-First Century

Creoles of Color Finding Their Way

Now I'm very comfortable with the label Creole. In the 60s I was not.... [My mom and dad] were taught that they were Creole and that they were separate and they tended to live apart. They tended to co-marry, co-mingle, or intermarry with others of that culture. And so I didn't like the prejudice that I saw.... if you were dark skinned and you had the French or Spanish surname, then it seemed to be OK with the family that you intermingle because somebody in that family was a known entity.... but if you were not linked and you had dark skin, then that was a problem.... So I was bitter and very confused. So I believed that I had to show my black ethnicity through my dress and my hair and that's when I stopped using permanents and straightening my hair ... I wore an afro there all through graduate school. So I think I went around the block to get across the street. Now I'm comfortable.

—Laura Rouzan, *interviewee, 2006*

Laura's reflections speak nicely to the transitions in Afro-Creole identity that attended nationwide struggles over race and inequality in the 1960s. Her experience also resonates with Wendy Gaudin's analysis of changes in black consciousness and black identity within the Creole community as reflected in the pages of the *Xavierite*, which we reviewed in Chapter 4. Nearly one hundred years after the Anglo-American system largely swallowed up white Louisianans' public identification as Creoles, would the process repeat itself for black Creoles? As the stories considered here will illustrate, the answer continues to be more complicated for Creoles of color than it was for their white counterparts. For this group, both the ethnic-cultural and racial-structural aspects of Creole identification have continued to be embraced by many in the community. In this sense, Afro-Creoles have been much more tenacious than white Creoles in their insistence on the relevance of an alternative self-understanding characteristic of the Latin/Caribbean racial system.

The complicated dynamics of being Creole and black within an Anglo-American racial system have meant that Afro-Creoles have had widely varying experiences with race and identity depending on where they live and what the dynamics are within their own families. Whatever their situation, however, Afro-Creoles living in the United States have had to confront and respond to the racial status quo that characterizes the Anglo-American system. The material presented in this chapter explores their experiences.

The first section lays out the ways many Afro-Creoles have struggled with ambivalence or confusion about how to position themselves within the Anglo-American system as well as in the Creole community. This first section provides greater insight into stories like Laura's so that we can better understand how disorienting it is to grow up being shaped by the assumptions of a subordinated racial system while having to function at the same time within a dominant racial system that follows different rules. The discussion here will lay out the many ways that the Anglo-American and Latin/Caribbean systems continue to clash in the lives of study participants.

The second major section takes up the issue of how participants have decided to respond to this confrontation between racial systems. The results of this study indicate that there have been three dominant responses: (1) identify as both black and Creole; (2) flee to the lighter side of the Anglo border and become white; or (3) challenge or resist the Anglo-American racial system altogether. As we conclude the chapter, we will see how the experience of those who choose the third response—challenging and resisting the Anglo-American racial system—resonates with that of many present-day immigrants of color coming from Latin America and the Caribbean.

DEALING WITH AMBIVALENCE AND CONFUSION

The average person of African descent who was born and raised in the United States over the last one hundred years has harbored few questions concerning racial identification. If she was identifiably of African heritage, she was black—full stop. She may have anything from light, nearly white skin to skin as dark as coffee, but she would still clearly, and usually unproblematically, think of herself as black. Within this blackness, of course, there have always been aesthetic hierarchies shaped by the bias toward whiteness that is endemic to all of the United States and most of the world. Thus, straighter hair is preferred to kinky hair; straight noses to rounded; and light skin to dark. There have always been differences of class and status that shape varied kinds of black lives and cultures. But still, at the end of the day, being black, understanding oneself to be black, and identifying with the struggles of other black people has gone largely unquestioned.[1]

For many Afro-Creoles, however, little concerning race and identity has been straightforward or taken for granted. Having identifiable African heritage has *not* necessarily meant that one's family thinks of itself as "black" or African American. Relationships and identification with non-Creole blacks have *not* always been assumed to be a good thing. Furthermore, the standard issues of colorism experienced in most black communities may go well beyond aesthetics and preferences into questions about the extent to which one is or is not Creole—that is, if one's skin is not sufficiently light, then perhaps one does not belong to the Creole community at all. Such a contention goes to the essence of one's sense of being and belonging.

Whatever the challenges of being black in the United States, Anglo-blacks who are native to the country have had the relative comfort of knowing—even if in a very broad sense—with whom to identify racially. In contrast, the stories that follow will take us to the other side of the looking glass to see how differently this often taken-for-granted reality is experienced by many Creoles of color.

Struggling to Position the Self in an Anglo-American World

Many of the Creoles of color interviewed for this project expressed a sense of feeling racially out of place. This sense of disconnection stems from the fact that their lived experiences put them outside or on the margins of the Anglo-American racial system. As children, they began from an early age to understand that something was different about them.

Terralyn, thirty-four years old at the time of her interview, remembers feeling isolated as a child growing up in Chicago.[2] She explains:

> In general, I remember not being dark enough to play with the black children, not light enough to play with white children ... an isolating feeling. I had white friends and black children would make fun of me. In the black community, because I was high yellow and had long pretty hair and was cute, I got singled out by darker girls.[3]

Terralyn's sense of dislocation did not change until her father came into her life when she was older and helped her to make connections she had not been able to make before.

> I was very shy. Something was missing. I didn't grow up with my biological father, that's where the Creole heritage was.... Then three years ago I found out that I had a Creole background. I found my father. I'm interested because I have something I can trace back. I can't do this with the African part, but this is its own set of cultures. I can trace it back. I have something that I can pass on.[4]

Note here that Terralyn describes being Creole as "its own set of cultures" distinct from her African heritage. Discovering her Creole heritage gives her an identity that is different from being black and that explains why she never fit in fully with any children—black or white.

Allan described growing up in a homogeneous community in Jackson, Mississippi, where there was little diversity. The city was polarized between black and white. Beneath the surface, however, he sensed that the reality was more complicated.

> ALLAN: There were plenty of Creoles, but many don't talk about it. I was so close to traditional Creole communities, some people still have the name or have relatives who live in those communities, or certain events they celebrate around Lent because I'm Catholic. There were Mardi Gras celebrations, Mardi Gras parade in Natches, Mississippi. One of the major krewes is in Jackson, and they had advertisements. I've been to celebrations in and around Baton Rouge and there's a strong interest in Jackson for Creole food. Several older community members are from Creole families and still speak the language fluently and they've taught me.
>
> A.P.: Why do you think people are so reticent to talk about Creole heritage?
>
> ALLAN: Everyone tries so hard to *fit in between black and white*.[5]

Allan pushed through the silence and did some geneaological research. He found that he is descended from Creoles and has met some Creole family members who have welcomed him into their lives. In his own way, he has begun to push against the imposition of a black and white binary that has no room for the messiness of Creoles' complex racial history.

Some of the older women I spoke with, women in their sixties, experienced the cultural difference as young women when they married non-Creoles. Amelie Durant grew up in a solidly Creole cultural context in New Orleans during the period of segregation.[6] She was raised in New Orleans and was sixty-six at the time of the interview. In the following passage she explains how Creoles of color distinguished between Creole and non-Creole people of African descent. The person she is referring to in the beginning of the excerpt is the man who became her husband.

> I remember my aunt asking me if he cooked American or Creole and that's the distinction they made if they talked about other black people . . . that generation the way they distinguished verbally or descriptively, the way they distinguished Creole of color from other colored people was either they were American or they were Creole. . . . I don't think we ever thought of ourselves as African American.

Amelie's sentiments are echoed by Stephanie, who describes the experience of marrying into a non-Creole family as "foreign":

> The family I married into didn't live the way mine did. They weren't the people I grew up with; they were foreign, strange. How they lived, what they ate, and when and how they dressed. They were Catholic and lived in the 8th Ward. I grew up Uptown, farther from the 7th Ward. My father-in-law was in construction; my father was a postal worker and owned a business. My husband's family is not Creole. . . . I just had to make adjustments to how I lived, no loud music. When we were growing up, we liked the music loud; we went to dancing school.[7]

This sense of having married into a "foreign" culture, even though her husband was American, and even though her family has been in the United States for many generations, communicates the intensity and tenacity of the differences between Afro-Creole and Anglo–African American experiences.

Some Creole families responded to the Anglo-American racial system by counseling their children to stay separate from both blacks and whites. Diana was fifty-four at her interview and grew up in California.[8] She describes a childhood visiting Louisiana every summer where she was able to keep in touch with the roots of her Creole heritage. But when she was at home, Diana's mother carefully policed her social relationships.

> The W's were a white family. My mother counseled me to stay separate from both blacks and whites. One day I broke the W's window, and the wife asked me to help her with canning. But then, when she invited me for a barbecue, my mother didn't want me to go. She asked me to stay in my place. It had to do with not being accepted.[9]

When she was still a young girl, Diana's family moved to a very small town in northern California where her mother sent her to public school because the local Catholic school was considered to be too "hippy" in nature. The public school was a culture shock as well as an exercise in negotiating blackness and whiteness. There were no other Creole children.

> Everyone would ask me who I was. I became friends with some of the black girls. I told them I was a Negro, so the blacks seemed more friendly. Some of the white girls were friendly too; we met through extracurricular activities. I had a rainbow coalition of friends. This was okay when it was happening at school. But I had a friend who was supposed to visit me, but the friend's parents didn't want her to go to a Negro family's house.

Diana's description of her friendships with the black girls shows that she positioned herself as friendly yet different from them. When she says, "I told them I was Negro," there's a sense that she said this to befriend them, even though she didn't feel that the label really fit her. On the other hand, there were clear limitations to trying to befriend whites because of the racial prejudices their families harbored.

The duality of the black and white Anglo-American system was further reinforced for Diana when she returned to Louisiana in the summer and saw colored-only bathrooms—something she thought was ancient history. There were ways, however, that her Creole background allowed her to slip between the cracks of expectations for blacks and whites, even in segregated Louisiana.

> Once I got to Louisiana, there were tons of Creoles. They had their own society. The Denatos in Opelousas, their family owned the town.... I walked into a fabric store and there was a white woman who admired the stitching on my clothes. She said I must be a Denato. They have a huge family reunion every three years.

Diana's experiences demonstrate the awkwardness of trying to fit herself into one or the other of the rigid categories of black and white. Although much of the country's racial structure pushed her into the category of blackness, her subjectivities were clearly shaped by her Creole mother's emphasis on separateness and by some of the protective aspects her Creole background afforded her in Jim Crow Louisiana.

Velva Flot also grew up during the Jim Crow era, but unlike Diana she had the advantage of doing so within Creole communities in Louisiana.[10] In the following excerpt she provides an in-depth description of what it was like socially and culturally to grow up in this environment:

> The area where I grew up it was ninety-five percent Creole. The New Orleans neighborhoods were not segregated then. They didn't have that many black

people in the city like they have now. See, nothing was segregated. You had blacks, you had Creoles, and you had white. *It was actually a three-class system.* I mean you've heard that before. And where I was it was ninety percent Creole and we had, I can honestly tell you that the block that I grew up in, they had two white families and one black family, like this was in this whole street, which you know where AP Tureaud is? OK, well it was London Avenue at the time, and we had one black family in our block, that was it. Everybody else was Creole and we had two or three white families. That was our world. This was all we knew and there was a lot of prejudice, oh lord.

I was born in 1940, so we are talking all the way through the 50s, and then people started to move, but mainly the Creoles because they were tired of the segregation, *they ended up being in the middle.* The thing came up with the Black Power and it's like, *I don't really fit in with that and yet you did not fit on the white side.* We had our own thing. We had our own schools, our own shows.

... Like I said, you had like this *three-class system*, the blacks didn't like us at all. I mean they had a whole different view of what we were like and what we thought and what we were about so *we were really caught in the middle.* The blacks didn't want to be bothered with you. The whites didn't want to be bothered with you. [But] it wasn't a major problem growing up because we had such a large community. We were fine. We had that insulation.

It is clear from Velva's description that she and her family did not see themselves as black or white. When she makes reference to segregation and the rise of the Black Power movement, she clearly does not identify. She even makes direct reference to triracial categorization—a expression of the Latin/Caribbean system—that characterized New Orleans for so long, though the term she uses is "the three-class system." This is the system that she felt best characterized her reality when growing up. Thus, despite not fitting into the dominant Anglo-American categories, she was not isolated because she was part of a larger Creole community that had its own vibrant institutions. This is a marked contrast to the palpable sense of isolation that comes across in Diana's description of her childhood in northern California.

But even growing up in a Creole community did not fully insulate a person from race-based prejudices or from the tyranny and hierarchy of color consciousness. Part of the complexity of existing within or between the layers of the racial palimpsest is feeling torn between those layers even within one's own community and, more distressingly, within one's own family. We turn to these experiences in the following section.

Complexities of Color, Status, and Identity Within the Creole Community

The complexity of negotiating contentious issues of color, status, and identity arose quite clearly during my study of the Cajun/Creole list in the spring of 2004. The Cajun/Creole list is a Yahoo group dedicated to the culture and language of people of Cajun or Creole heritage in Louisiana. In practice, however, the focus is on Creoles and, more specifically, Creoles of color. This group was one of my first introductions to Louisiana's Creole of color community and its diaspora located in different parts of the United States. List discussions helped to illuminate the tensions many Creoles of color continually negotiate when it comes to color, race, and conceptions of blackness. I observed online discussion during the spring of 2004 and then conducted a survey of participants to learn more about how they identify racially and culturally. I then invited a subset of survey respondents to engage in an offline oral history interview which asked them to reflect on the development of their racial and cultural identities throughout their lives.

A conversation that took place on the Cajun/Creole list in April 2004 helps to illustrate these complex issues. On April 1, "QN33" writes:

> We're very clear about what Creole culture is. However, we've also never been taught that we were other than African American/Black. We identify with being African Americans whose culture is the Creole culture inclusive of the language, food and traditions. It seems that some of those who have posted messages within the last two weeks define Creole as separate from being Black or another ethnicity. My family and I see ourselves [as] African Americans whose culture is Creole. Just wanted to share my perspective with you and continue the discourse.[11]

Here the writer embraces the ethnic-cultural aspect of Creole identity and rejects a racial-structural approach that would separate her from Anglo-blacks. Indeed, although claiming Creole identity to the exclusion of African American identity is less common after the 1960s, there is still an older generation that grew up in an earlier era whose members hold to different understandings of what it means to be Creole. We see this at work in the following post written in response to "QN33":

> I find that the creole part of MY family does not consider themselves african-american but creole-american. They unfortunately, see themselves ABOVE those

that are black but aren't creole. Even I, only being half creole, get discriminated against. That's why when I plan to go out to Alexandria or New Orleans I rarely spend time with relatives. The reason I joined this list was in hopes of making bonds to be shown around the area by someone other than my family and their down cast eyes. They speak french to my grandmother and talk smack. Then of course, she translates it for me later. Anyway, that's my little whiny session.[12]

This issue of distinctions made even within Afro-Creole families or within different branches of the same family is something that came up in other interviews as well.

In some cases, those who were darker skinned were treated less favorably. We see this in the story of Alexander, one of the Cajun/Creole list participants I interviewed offline.[13] He explained that his father is Cuban and Creole and his mother is African American. His father is light-skinned, his mother is a bit darker, and Alexander is darker than both of them. He grew up with family members making assessments of his color and hair texture compared to non-Creole blacks. One day when his cousin was washing his hair, she noted the texture and said, "You sure do have pretty hair, I forgot you're not regular black." On the other hand, his sister who was several years younger than him, with much lighter skin but kinkier hair, began to notice the differences by the age of four or five. In her attempt to make sense of this, she said: "I must be the Creole one and you must be the black one." Finally, his grandmother would discourage him from drinking coffee because he might become darker. Although the issue of color-based evaluations within black communities is not particular to Afro-Creole families, what is notable here is that color differences are not merely noted; they are used to equate light skin with being Creole and darker skin with being non-Creole and African American.

Christopher, nineteen at the time of the interview, had experiences similar to Alexander's.[14] He described his background as black, Native American, and French. When he would tell his family that he was Creole, they would tell him that he was too black to be Creole. Even though he would object and say that Creole identification has more to do with culture than race, his explanations fell on deaf ears. Like Alexander, he also dealt with challenging, color-conscious family members. In his case, it was his great-grandmother.

This lady was so prejudiced, she did not like dark-skinned people, she would sit us down, she was high yellow, she looked like a white lady. She would tell us that niggers ain't no good; you need to stay away from them. I was bold, I said, "Well, how do you feel about us, I have dark skin." She said, "True, you all are black as tar but that doesn't change the fact that you have my blood in you, so you're Creole." She wouldn't let some of the darker kids come in the house. She may have lived around the time of slavery; she treated others badly because she was treated badly. So if that's what Creole was, I didn't want any part of it. This was my dad's grandmother; she lived to be 117. I know the French influence was really strong with her.

For Christopher, there was more negative than positive reinforcement within his own family about being Creole. Although his great-grandmother acknowledged him as Creole, she also deeply denigrated him because of his color. And when Christopher did finally identify with his Creole heritage, other family members said he couldn't be Creole because his skin was too dark.

Christopher's experience resonates with that of Laura Rouzan who we met at the beginning of this chapter.[15] She too started out feeling ambivalent and then negative about being Creole until she got a better understanding of the history and culture of Creoles in Louisiana. Her better understanding, however, has not insulated her from the negative connotations of the term "Creole," even when she is dealing with others who have the same heritage. In the following excerpt, she describes an interaction at a conference with a friend who keeps an arm's distance from Creole identification:

It's interesting. At that conference a friend of mine, I said to her why don't you join LA Creole. She said: "Now Laura, you know me I can't deal with all this color stuff." And so that's where she's coming from. She's also light skinned. Her whole family is. I mean there are always exceptions. The families run the gamut of color. . . . she was in Nachitoches. She's [knows about] Cane River, the Letoyer descendents of Marie Coin Coin, so she's interested but she does not want to be linked with anything called Creole. And so there are those people and I forget now because I'm so comfortable.

Marie Coin Coin was a well-known free woman of color and business owner who lived in Natchitoches, Louisiana. She rose from humble origins to become an owner of land and slaves. The friend she is talking to knows this history, and she has a great interest in Creole culture, but the negativity surrounding the Creole label continues to be an obstacle to her embracing her own heritage. LA Creole, the organization that Laura makes reference to, is an organization of Creoles of color in New Orleans who support each other in learning about their family histories, and who put on educational events and conferences for the community. Part of their mission is to educate the public about Creole history and identity in order to dispel the kinds of myths and negative associations Laura grew up with and her friend still harbors.

Some of these issues of color and status are regionally defined. Many times over the course of the research for this book, interviewees or informants would explain that color prejudice, and the desire to claim Creole background for status reasons was particular to New Orleans and less prevalent in areas outside of New Orleans. Rhondale Barras articulates this position especially well.[16]

> RHONDALE: Creole in New Orleans is different from Creole in Southwest Louisiana.... I went [to a Creole event] last year and I was excited ... my family speaks Creole, [and I think of] Creole in reference to the way the foods have been cooked, and things like that. That is what it means to me and that's what they were celebrating. It's also a mix of African, Native American, this and that, that's what Creole means in Southwest Louisiana as opposed to when I was in New Orleans and people were like: "Your family's Creole?" And I was like yeah, and when I finally came to grips with what was meant by Creole in New Orleans, I was like, oh no, that's not my family.
> A.P.: What did they mean? What was different?
> RHONDALE: In New Orleans it has a lot more of ... a social status to it than in Southwest Louisiana.... In Southwest Louisiana when people say [Creole], just about every black person in Southwest Louisiana can tell you that they are Creole.... [But] in New Orleans it was very much attached to a social status and a social class of people who, you know, basically up until *Plessy vs. Ferguson* were a separate ethnic group until that time when they were like if you are of African descent you are black there is no ifs, ands, or buts about it. There's no Creole. There is no in the middle. They totally debunked a whole group and social status of people that existed for centuries in New Orleans and that may have existed to a certain extent in Southwest Louisiana, but it never was as structured as it was in New Orleans where you know I'm not white or black, I'm in the middle and I'm a little better than black people and when it comes down to it that's what it is.

Rhondale's purely ethnic-cultural approach to Creole identity was reinforced by experiences I had when interviewing Creoles in the New Roads community of Pointe Coupée Parish. During the time that I was conducting oral histories on Creoles, I was referred to several white persons from New Roads and made the short drive from New Orleans to meet and speak with them. There I found much less reticence about being white and Creole, and issues of race seemed much less salient than those of culture when considering who was Creole. Part of the reason for this may be that there is a greater concentration of Creole speakers there than in New Orleans, and this concrete cultural practice provides a social glue that makes Creole identity more democratic.

The significance of the presence or absence of the Creole language for shaping understandings of Creole identity is reinforced by Rhondale's experience. Later in her interview she explained that in contrast to small towns and rural areas where Creole continues to be spoken—though even there it is starting to fade—the Creole language has fared very badly in the more cosmopolitan city of New Orleans.

> There was a whole culture in and of itself with the whole social status of being a Creole in New Orleans whereas in my family . . . there are so many different shades of people in the family and everybody's Creole *because everybody speaks Creole the language.*

This cultural understanding of Creole identity contrasts sharply with what Alexander and Christopher experienced at the hands of their own families, and what the Cajun/Creole participants discuss earlier.

Respondents' stories in this section set a foundation for understanding the experience of dislocation and ambivalence that so many Afro-Creoles have experienced. These challenges are directly related to the fact that while many were shaped within a Creole community that is characterized by a latent Latin/Caribbean racial system, they must live their lives within a contrasting Anglo-American system. Although the white Creoles examined earlier on resolved the conflict by dropping public Creole identification, Creoles of color were more hesitant to abandon their Creole roots.

As Chapters 3 and 5 have demonstrated, Creole identification increasingly became a social liability for white Creoles. Conversely Afro-Creoles experienced benefits in holding on to their Creole identity, partly because the racial-structural aspect of this identity worked in ways that privileged them and cushioned them from being categorized as "black." Maintaining the racial-structural aspect of Creole identity divided the world into white, Creole, and black—placed in order of descending social status. These benefits gave them a greater incentive to resist the pressures of an Anglo-American system that sought to press them into the mold of Anglo-blackness, at the bottom of a binary system.

As Diana's experience of Jim Crow Louisiana testifies, Creole heritage provided some protection for people of African descent. Wendy Gaudin also found this to be the case in her oral histories with Afro-Creoles who lived under segregation. The Creole community provided a place of some refuge during a difficult period. At the same time, however, this same protective identity required a certain amount of boundary work that made Afro-Creoles distinct from Anglo-blacks and whites and, in the process, kept aspects of the triracial system of eighteenth- and nineteenth-century New Orleans more or less intact.

As a result of the incentives to hold on to Creole identity, and the boundary work necessary to maintain Creole cultures and institutions, young Creoles of color grew up betwixt and between a confusing clash of systems that only gradually became clearer to them as they matured. Once the outlines of the different racial categories and systems became clearer, they were required to make their own choices about how to respond to them. We examine these responses in the following section.

THREE RESPONSES TO THE DEMANDS OF THE ANGLO-AMERICAN RACIAL SYSTEM

The stories examined in Section I helped us to better understand the sense of dislocation and confusion many Afro-Creoles experience as they seek to make sense of being caught between two different approaches to thinking about race. Many of these stories relate the respondents' experiences growing up, or they are shared by relatively young interviewees who are still in the process of making sense of their own racial and ethnic identities.

At some point in their lives, however, Afro-Creoles interviewed for this study came to their own definitive stances about how to position themselves racially and culturally within or outside of the confines of the Anglo-American system. In the subsections that follow we consider the stories of those who took quite different paths: embracing Anglo-blackness; transitioning to Anglo-whiteness; or resisting the Anglo system all together.

Embracing Anglo-Blackness

Among many Anglo–African Americans there is the perception that Creoles of color prefer not to think of themselves as black. As we have seen in Chapter 4 as well as in the present chapter, these perceptions have a foundation in reality as expressed by some members of the Creole community themselves. At the same time, however, it would be inaccurate to say that distancing oneself from blackness defines the Afro-Creole experience. We can go back to our discussion of the nineteenth-century civil rights movement discussed in Chapter 4 to see how wrong it would be to paint the entire Afro-Creole community with such a broad brush. Moreover, as we saw earlier in this section, even Creoles themselves have mixed experiences with Creole identification and issues of color within the Creole community. For these reasons, as well as many other personal reasons, many of the Creoles I spoke with identify themselves as black *and* Creole. By doing this, they embrace the ethnic-cultural dimension of Creole identity but reject the racial-structural aspect of Creole identity which would place them in a separate category from Anglo-black Americans. This identification is often accompanied by an embrace of black consciousness fueled by their experiences with US racism. In this sense they fit squarely into the Anglo-American racial paradigm by combining a black racial identity with a Creole ethnic identification.

Christopher, who we met in the previous section, was raised in a family that clearly reinforced his blackness. In his case, this socialization occurred at the expense of his Creole heritage.

> It's kind of sad because I was raised as traditionally African American, no mentioning of Creole culture. Most of what I know is my own research.... My mother always tried to get me to see that black people need to wake up and realize that a lot of white kids that you play with, a lot of their parents and grandparents were the ones who were spitting on us. Be aware that racism is still here.

Christopher's commitment to blackness and black consciousness was reinforced when he participated in racially engaged theater during his teenage years.

> When I was on set, it was 1966 [for me] and I immediately got into character. For those five hours I had a real hatred for white people. I was sixteen or seventeen, and started reading about how black people were dealing at that time. The way black people were then—I considered it a culture—they stuck together and fought together. I loved to learn about how people lived.

What we see here is a young man grappling mightily with the complexities of race and identity. At the time of the interview—ten years ago at the time of this writing—Christopher forcefully identified with being both black and Creole and saw no contradiction between them, despite messages he had received to the contrary from his family.

Several interviewees spoke of identifying as black in part because it was the most pragmatic thing to do in order to make it through a world organized into the categories of black and white. Allan, who we also met earlier, said that even though he firmly believes that Creoles are best understood as being in between whites and Anglo–blacks, he identifies himself as only black. On the questionnaire he completed for our interview, he self-identified as African American. It is important to note that on the background questionnaire for this study, race and ethnicity were intentionally left open; there were no boxes to check. Respondents were simply asked to write out how they identified in terms of race and ethnicity. This made it possible for them to use whatever terms they felt best described them. Even so, Allan made no mention of his Creole heritage. He explains the reason for distancing himself from the Creole community as follows: "I still identify this way because in Jackson and even in New Orleans, if you say you're Creole, you get this look and you don't know what they're going to say. So I go by the traditional way. And now that I'm working in the political arena, I can't say Creole." For Allan—who also insisted that his name be changed for the purposes of this study, the negative connotations of Creole identification keep him firmly in the category of traditional Anglo-American blackness.

Some respondents took a situational approach to identifying as black and/or Creole. Minette, a Cajun/Creole List interviewee, explained that she would usually just say that she is black, although she might also say Creole to be more specific. Celine also described herself as black on the study questionnaire.[17] When I asked her why she described herself this way, and whether or not she ever used the term Creole, she explained:

> CELINE: I do [sometimes describe myself as Creole].... it sort of depends on who I'm talking to, how much time I have, and why they are asking the question.... My mom's side of the family has always called themselves black and they are the ones that have the [Creole family] ties. I asked my aunt once, or we were just talking about, you know, when we fill out forms, what does she check, she said she'll check black or she'll check other sometimes or sometimes she'll check all that apply. So I started doing that. But if there is a space for other, I'll check that and black because you have to check one of those.
>
> A.P.: Do you write something in the "other"?
>
> CELINE: I'll write Creole.

Thus, it seems that Celine's identification as black comes partly from family socialization and partly from pragmatic considerations about the easiest way to negotiate a world where checking racial boxes is unavoidable.

Other respondents embraced their black heritage vigorously in ways that would have been unlikely fifty or sixty years ago in the Creole community. Rhondale reflected that in her experience it has been "just the last twenty years that people are even comfortable with speaking strongly about their African heritage going back that far." Lolita is a good example of this increased interest in African heritage. An avid genealogist, she has a strong desire to trace her ancestry back to Africa.

> Coming up, I was always told I was Creole. I was told it was a lot of French, but I didn't hear the African part mentioned much. It wasn't a prejudiced environment, but we thought we were in our own little world. . . . When I get back to the African ancestry, I think it's because of that I have a greater appreciation of that ancestry as a result of getting into genealogy. Because that's where that bloodline comes from. I'm still searching for that. That's where the family strength comes from. I think it's something that has been passed on and links all the way back to Africa. I think it's made me stronger and more appreciative of my African identity. That's something many people don't appreciate, or haven't developed that appreciation.

Lolita's response here resonates with what she shared publicly at a genealogy session that was part of a LA Creole conference. There, when she came to the step that helped her to identify an African ancestor, she described the experience as spiritual. This embrace of African heritage would surprise many Anglo–African Americans, many of whom assume that all Creoles of color seek to distance themselves from their black heritage.

Christina and Mark are both in the interesting position of having grown up as white in families that passed for white.[18] Christina knew and kept the secret for most of her life, whereas Mark discovered it only a few years ago. Both, however, have come to identify with blackness in their own way. For Christina, the embrace is somewhat whimsical. She explains:

> I love it when I'm on a dance floor somewhere and someone says: "You're a great dancer." I say, "My black heritage." They look at me and their eyes open up and they think I'm kidding. I like to shock people. People will say I have curly hair, and I'll say it's not curly it's kinky, that's my black heritage . . . but it's not kinky it's curly, but, I just exaggerate, to point out the fact.[19]

Although Christina could hide the fact that she has black ancestry, she chooses to make it public knowledge in light-hearted ways that require that others come to terms with the seriousness of her choice to be transparent about her racial ancestry.

Mark's embrace of blackness has been different. First, even though he is completely white in appearance, with European features, hair, and blue eyes, he has been embraced by blacks who have learned of his recent discovery that his father was black.

> I would say that in terms of my white colleagues the story is more of historical interest and they're amazed just by the history that I'm uncovering. And to my friends and coworkers who are African American, their reaction is more personal and also kind of loving. They're more interested in the fact that they're looking at me and saying things like, welcome! And they mean it. It's more of a personal reaction on the black side and more of a historical reaction on the white side.

Second, Mark is a direct descendant of Louis Charles Roudanez, the man who founded the radical papers *L'Union* and *La Tribune* in the 1860s. And although Mark does not personally identify as black, his ancestor's pioneering civil rights work encourages him to identify with the struggles of black people today. He explains:

> my own personal relationship with people of color has become more heightened. For example, if . . . I'm a teacher working with an African American child or family, my sensitivity to their issues has been heightened because I understand that my family had sensitivity to the same racial issues. So I've always been progressive in terms of my politics and orientation in terms of race, but it takes on a peculiar personal nature now because I understand that my own family fought for civil rights. It makes a real difference.

Mark's embrace of blackness as personally relevant to his life, particularly because of the continued significance of racial inequality, is also mirrored in the lives of Afro-Creoles who *do* identify as black and who are clear about the ways that being black affects one's life chances in the United States. Stephanie has lived in New Jersey since the 1970s and she compared the experience of being black in Louisiana to being black in New Jersey:

> Your kids are treated different here in New Jersey because they are black, worse than Louisiana could ever be. . . . I always had to go to school to introduce her to the next group of teachers so that my children didn't have problems. . . . One teacher called my son a monkey in fifth grade and I went in to tell them his real name.[20]

In addition to issues at school with her children, she also experienced discrimination at work:

> I was passed over a couple of times. I put it in writing that I felt I was being discriminated against because of race. I was working at AT&T, Bell Labs. You have upper management who just don't like black people.

On the study questionnaire, Stephanie described herself as black American (Creole ancestry). When I asked her what led her to describe herself that way, she replied:

> Black American denotes I'm native, not an immigrant.... Some [people] don't accept that they're black; I'm not trying to deny it. When I was a kid there was the one-drop rule. I think black is a state of mind, what you think you are. I prefer and am comfortable with saying that I'm black.

Again, Stephanie's firm identification as both black and Creole would surprise many African Americans who assume that Creoles of color want nothing more than to distance themselves from black Americans.

Barbara Trevigne and Harold Baquet also have a strong awareness of racial inequality and discrimination.[21] In the following comment, Barbara directly addresses some of the ambivalence around issues of race in the Afro-Creole community:

> You know, race does matter. As much we say we're Creole and we want a Creole organization, we want this, that, and the other, and we don't want to be labeled but race does matter. Because the United States is controlled by Anglo white males.... Race does matter ... Because we are governed by white males.

Barbara's frankness, and her insistence on the significance of race, is something that not all Creoles would agree with. It is very much in keeping, however, with the way many Anglo–African Americans think about race.

Harold relates an interesting story that shows what it is like to live on the edge of blackness and whiteness and to embrace blackness. He has light skin and was in his fifties at the time of the interview. When I asked him if he is comfortable speaking about issues of racial passing in his own family, he explained:

> I'm very comfortable. I love telling people that this is what black people look like in New Orleans. And as a consequence, just like you can't tell what black

people look like or gay people look like all the time ... you're exposed to people's inside talk. You know black people have their inside talk, white folks have their inside talk too, and sometimes without them identifying who I am I've been privy to white folks' inside talk. And it can be embarrassing, you know ... I was a scuba instructor and I taught this guy and he took my program, went off on his dives and enjoyed it so much he brings his wife back the following month and she's taking the course. And at the end of the training they're doing their little pool sessions and I'm outside smoking a cigarette with my dive master and the guy, he says out of the clear blue and he's telling me what he does for a living ... he works on the ferry. And he says, "Harold, man they've got some niggers riding that ferry." "I beg your pardon?" I said, and he repeated it. And I said, "Did you know your wife's scuba instructor is a nigger?" And boy you could tell his wheels were spinning. He looks at me and you see his brain explode and he goes "Aw, Harold I'm so sorry." I said, "It's cool, man." I don't know where he was coming from, but I've heard that before. It's something to think about.

Harold's story provides a perfect transition into the next subsection on passing into whiteness. His experience suggests that in some contexts, he could have passed for white. His decision, however, was not to do this, even when it meant making a paying client extremely uncomfortable. Harold's experience highlights the daily indignities of being black in a world characterized by racism. What is unique about his experience, and that of others like him, however, is that he could be taken as white and could use that assumption to his own advantage.

Given the many benefits of white privilege, it is easy to understand why some individuals and families who had light skin would have made the decision to pass either temporarily or permanently as white. Such a choice clearly, however, is attended by grave consequences that sear the soul and create ripple effects across generations. In the following section we examine the dynamics and consequences of the decision to pass for white.

Passing or Being Pushed into Anglo-Whiteness

Afro-Creole respondents in the study had varied connections to racial passing, but most had been touched by the issue in some way. Some engaged in situational passing or heard stories from family members who had done this. Situational passing occurred during the Jim Crow era when persons of color with light skin engaged in brief episodes of becoming white in order to gain access to jobs or other kinds of opportunities. This kind of passing, while it entailed a certain level of sacrifice, was short-lived in duration. Once the situation passed, the person went back to his or her family and community as a person of color. Amelie's mother decided to pass as white in order to gain access to a job as a seamstress.

> My mother passed as white to work as a seamstress.... My mother was a very talented seamstress. She learned to sew when she was nine years old and made her first dress when she was eleven. When she was fourteen, she went to work as a seamstress at a dress shop on St. Charles Avenue. Her older brother at that time was attending Xavier Prep, a black school, and had a car and he would drop her off at her white job on his way to his black school and this was typical.... this is how you went out during the day to make a living, you came back evenings and weekends and you spent time with your family and you went back and forth.

Amelie herself also briefly experimented with passing for white when she was a young girl.

> I always thought [passing] was a big joke. I really thought [so] and the one time I did it, I think most of us didn't take it seriously.... I remember when movie theaters were still segregated ... there was a movie downtown and a friend and I, we were teenagers, and we wanted to see it. So we went and saw it. But another time my mother was going downtown with me and my younger brother. Again it was going to be a day out. You shop, you have lunch. And the movie she had thought we were going to see she found out was showing at a white-only theater so we didn't go. So she decided not to take us to pass for white to see a movie and we went to see another movie instead.

Although the experience was one of whimsy and fun for Amelie as a young girl, there was a good deal at stake in the family's decision to continue to use passing as a life strategy or to forego the strategy all together. At some point, Amelie's parents decided that all passing would stop.

> [My mother] worked as a white person for several years. But once she left that it was thought [of as] her old way of life. Once she left that and she married and then we went to, we grew up in the 7th Ward and my parents decided that we weren't going to be white anymore under any circumstances. My father when he was a young man ... he was taking this young woman to a high school prom and they needed a taxi and I think he couldn't get the black taxis, [they] were all busy, probably because it was prom night. So he called the white taxi. The taxi came to get them and it wasn't until he gave the address of the destination the taxi driver knew that they were colored. And he said, "Well, don't do that again." But again

once they married and started raising a family, as far as I know we were never white again. But this was the way it was.

For Amelie's parents, even situational passing was not worth the personal costs. It is easy to see, however, how situational passing could have been an entrée to permanent passing. We can think of situational passing as testing the waters, as practice to see whether or not the act of being white will be accepted in varied circumstances. And while there are significant personal costs, there are also immediate and substantial benefits.

Harold recounted a different kind of situational passing, a kind of unintentional passing that occurred as his family sought to attend a Catholic mass.

> I remember as a four year old, my big brother, mom and I—we'd leave the house at 4 a.m. for a trip across the country. About 9, 10 a.m. we're in Opelousas and we see a Catholic church. There's a mass, and my brother pulls in and drops me and my mom off. We walk into church and the usher grabs us ... we were looking for the colored section, and they didn't have a colored section in this church. We found a place to sit down. My brother ... he was darker than I am, he's standing in the back and he stayed in the back. The usher was darker than he was. The usher asked him what he was doing. He said, "I'm here with my mother and little brother." He says, "Where are they?" [He explains] how ... his brother and mother were in the church. The usher came back with other ushers and questioned him. His brother pointed out [me and my] mom, and ... one of the ushers told them that they had to leave because the church was white only. They put us out of a Catholic church. My mom wrote the Archbishop.... In Opelousas they directed us to the black church down the street.

It is clear from the way Harold tells the story that his mother had no intention of passing for white. But when they were allowed to sit down, they temporarily become white, although they were not necessarily aware of this fact. If his brother's darker skin had not given the family away, it is interesting to speculate about how the rest of the service and the time following the service would have gone. Would they have realized at some point that others assumed they were white? And if so, would they have corrected them or left them to their assumptions?

The secrets and silences engendered by conforming to Anglo-American notions of whiteness touched even respondents who did not themselves engage in passing of any kind. When entire families or branches of families became white, then those who did not pass found themselves in the awkward position of having to pretend that these family members were unrelated to them. Over time, it was easier to let the relationships drop. Then over generations, the initial connections between white and black branches of the family were forgotten.

Jacob Plique helped a distant white family member to make these long-forgotten connections.[22] The two came into contact because both were doing genealogical research and were trying to find information to fill the gaps in their knowledge. He made email contact with one of these distant family members and explained:

> She had her research on the Internet, which was erroneous, and I helped her get the true story because she didn't know the oral history of the family. It hadn't come down her branch.... She didn't know how the family split up into different branches. I did. That was part of my oral history. I knew that one brother married an Italian girl, another brother married an Irish girl. Two other brothers married black girls and then the Jim Crow laws in the late 1890s made the family divide.

In Jacob's case, the knowledge was received and the recipient seemed to be satisfied with the new information. But not all family members were happy to learn that there was a connection to blackness in their family history.

Harold relates an example of a less than enthusiastic reaction when he attempted to get some distant family members from California to reconnect with their black relatives.

> HAROLD: There was a whole branch—my "white" uncle A. moved to California in the 30s and there's an entire Baquet clan out there with the same [kinds of first] names . . .
>
> A.P.: Now the family in California, are they living as white?
>
> HAROLD: Yeah. I've contacted them and told them they need to come down here—won't nobody know you're black, come on down! They won't know you're black 'till you tell them your name!
>
> A.P.: How did they react to that?
>
> HAROLD: They haven't come down.

California came up in several interviews as a place to which Creoles who wanted to pass for white would go to start their new lives well away from the community members who might compromise their new identities.[23] Christina and Pat—who both grew up as white, and whose stories we will explore in greater detail below—both described family connections to California that involved racial passing. Christina described her family's connection to California in the following way:

> A.P.: You mentioned that your parents would say don't talk about family moving to California. Do you know what that was about?
> CHRISTINA: Of course, what it was always about. You cross the border when you leave New Orleans and go to California.
> A.P.: Cross what kind of border?
> CHRISTINA: The color border.

Pat recalled the geographic transition in her grandfather's family when most of the relatives moved to California.[24]

> My grandfather still had his family living in Pointe Coupée as Creoles.... his siblings all lived together there, then moved to Baton Rouge. Then all but one moved to California, and their children—my mother's first cousins—lived as white. So it's almost like the family made some kind of an agreement. Now we're this, now we're that. And I'm sure it's not unique. All the people of my generation ... none of them were aware of the Creole ancestry.

In some cases, family members stayed in Louisiana and engaged in a kind of shifting identity dance in order to maintain a white identity even with black family members living nearby. Amy describes this occurring in a branch of the family living in Abita Springs.[25]

> AMY: So many of my ancestors, especially in Abita Springs, they want to be white. The ones in Abita that are living today, they really want to be white. Why I don't know, but you have to be who you are. They live in a close community, and they're really not comfortable with who they are.... My grandmother's oldest brother, Uncle B., went to New Orleans and passed as white.
> A.P.: So how was that dealt with in your family?
> AMY: Well, my grandmother let me know what was going on, and whenever he came over here, he was always welcomed. But when he went back to New Orleans, he lived a white life. It's possible that we were actually white. My father was white, Caucasian. Blue eyes and straight hair. My mother's grandmother was white from Pearl River. We have a lot of Caucasian. I don't know exactly who the black ancestor was.
> A.P.: So when you say that it's possible that you were actually white, you mean that maybe it was a white family?
> AMY.: Yes, because I know my grandmother's mother, they were white from ... a little town between Madisonville and Ponchatoula.

What is interesting here is that Amy goes from taking about others in her family who passed as white to noting that her father's family *was* white. She is unclear about who the black ancestor in her family is. This ambiguity in racial background brings to the forefront how permeable racial barriers have been for some Creoles of color. Where, exactly, does one draw the line between passing for white and actually being white? In the case of Amy's family, wherever that line is, there is enough blackness somewhere in her background to make it awkward to be in touch with family that claims to be white only.

> A.P.: Now your other family that you said wanted to be white, how do they respond to you?
> AMY: I really don't associate with them.... It's just that ... the people in Abita didn't know that their fathers had Creole ancestry.
> A.P.: Would they call themselves Creole?
> AMY: I really don't know what they'd call themselves.

When relatives of color do attempt to sustain a dialogue with family members who have passed into whiteness, the dialogue can be fragile and abruptly ended. This happened to Melanie when she attempted to help a distant relative reconnect with her family of color.[26]

> My aunt continued to live as a woman of color while the rest of her family "crossed over." She wanted to marry my great uncle. She married him and she came uptown to live with his family. Her mother and father and brothers and sisters lived downtown. The brothers and sisters married "white" and hid their ancestry, even though they knew what they were. My aunt was never allowed any contact with them, even though she looked very white she would not "pass." Her children weren't allowed to identify with their [other] side [of the family] because they had "crossed over." Recently, [my aunt's] niece's sisters' children sent me an email and wanted to know more about the family. They haven't had any contact with anyone in [this part of the] family in about sixty years ... now they could finally have contact. I put her in contact with one of her direct first cousins. She could have been in touch with all nine of them. They were in touch, were talking about meeting. One day she said she had to end it ... she said her sisters and her brothers out in a little town in Mississippi were disowning her because they don't want her to go there. We had to stop communication altogether, and my relatives were very disappointed. She said she couldn't afford to lose her family, and I reminded her that this was her family too. [Now my aunt] is dead, she has two young sisters still living and they won't even attempt to acknowledge anything about their sister ... even in their 80s. They won't have anything to do with their nieces and nephews.

Eventually, it is quite likely that these nieces and nephews will lose any chance of finding out about their Afro-Creole heritage. Until, perhaps, a family death provides an opportunity to go through old papers that reveal a secret that was generations in the making.

However the secret comes out, racial passing exacts a tremendous toll on individuals and families. Three of my respondents provide particularly poignant examples of this toll. We have met each of them earlier on in the chapter, but we have yet to deeply examine their stories of confronting the untruths of their families' whiteness. Two of them, Pat and Mark, grew up white and only learned as adults that their families had passed into whiteness, while the third, Christina, figured out what had happened fairly early on but kept the secret going as she raised her own children. Their stories demonstrate firsthand the generational effects of crossing the color line in order to conform to Anglo-whiteness.

Christina grew up in a family where the secrets were palpable. One can hear the loneliness and longing in her voice as she describes what is was like to grow up cut off from much of her family:

> I was curious about our history, our family history. Perhaps because I never knew a grandmother. I'm the tenth of ten children. . . . All the big kids were just about gone when I was growing up. In about the fourth grade I heard someone say they had visited their grandmother. I went home and said to my mother: "What is a grandmother?" So, then I wanted to know about grandmothers, and I kept asking questions and I . . . couldn't remember many cousins but the few cousins I knew were grown and had kids and I couldn't see their kids so . . . even though I came from a large family, there weren't family around me, so I kept asking questions about grandmothers and great grandmothers.

Every once in a while, her father would answer some of her questions. When he did so, her mother would jump in saying: "Don't tell that child that," or "She has no business knowing that." Her father would reply: "The child wants to know" or "What can she do with it?"

At one point, Christina succeeded in getting an old family name out of her father. The name she was given was Toussaint. She got excited and asked if this was the Toussaint L'Ouverture of Haiti. Her father protested vociferously, saying there was no relationship to Haiti. When she was older, however, she did indeed make the family connection back to St. Domingue/Haiti.

It is not entirely clear when Christina's family passed over the racial barrier from black to white. But in the course of her research, Christina has found evidence that the family's racial identification fluctuated over the years:

> In 1920 my paternal grandmother, one of his sisters, and one of his brothers, all three are listed as white. 1910, let me see what they say (consults document), they're listed as mulatto in 1910. And my father, siblings and mother are all listed as mulatto in 1910. So they went from black to mulatto to white, what a story. I didn't even realize that.

This kind of fluctuation is not unusual, as the census-taker used his own judgment to determine how to racially categorize people on the census. Different census takers could make varied judgments about a family's race.

By the time she became an adult, Christina knew what the family secret was. She kept it going for another generation by marrying as white and raising her children as white. She explains: "There were years when I just avoided the issue of color and let people believe what they wanted." This is a kind of passive racial passing where instead of announcing one's black ancestry, one simply doesn't mention it and instead lives out the white identity ascribed to them by others.

But over time the secret wore on Christina and cast an uncomfortable pall over her life.

> AP: During the time that you were [passing], did it affect the way you thought about yourself?
> CHRISTINA: Yeah, of course, sure it did.... How on earth could something that great not affect one's thinking, perception of one's self and the world, and the freedom to listen and talk and be with others, it taints everything.... I never liked or felt comfortable not being able to acknowledge who I am ... but I married a guy who did not want me to acknowledge it.

Later on, having lived under the burden of the secret for so long, Christina decided that she could no longer keep up the fiction. Her children took the news in varied ways.

> So, when I was finishing my Ph.D., I called each one of my children and said to him or her: "When I get my degree, uhm I'm going to come out as who I am and stop the charade. I think that it's time; I've had enough therapy. And I just want to be me. I wanted to let you know this, but before I do, I wanted to know your thoughts on the matter." ... I got three different answers. [One] said, "It's all right with me. It's fine, if it makes you happy, I'm with you, it's who I am

too." [Another] said, "Well, I don't know." He went back and forth and back and forth.... And the third [said], "There you go again, always trying to do something to hurt me. You know I have political aspirations and you know that would kill me and you're only doing it to make me hurt." So I didn't [do] a blanket statement, I just acknowledged it whenever it came up, which is what I do now ... sometimes on the dance floor (laughs).

Because of the mixed reaction, Christina felt unable to initiate a totally fresh beginning to her racial identity. Rather than making a proactive statement about her black ancestry, she felt compelled to continue a somewhat passive approach. Now, however, while she does not announce that she is "black," she *does* take opportunities when they come up to mention her black ancestry. We saw this in one of the sections earlier where Christina would use her preferred style of dancing or the curl of her hair as an opening to let people know that she has black ancestry. For Christina, this has been a refreshing step in the right direction.

Whereas Christina grew up with a sense that something was off, and eventually found out that the family had passed for black, Pat and Mark were blindsided by the news as middle-aged adults. For Pat, things began to change around the time of her aunt's death in the 1990s.

> We were at my aunt's funeral, and we realized that we didn't know a lot about her. So that's what got me to look into the family research. That night, they had a wake and ... my older brother went to the library and looked some things up and found a census record that had her grandfather listed on it as colored. We weren't aware of that. My brother called me and I thought it was a mistake. I went to my mom and asked her about it. She did not want to talk about it. I could tell that it was an emotional issue for her; I didn't press. My older brother lost interest, but my younger brother became interested. We went to the courthouse in Pointe Coupeé and found all the documents there.

Although this discovery might have been a difficult one for many families, Pat and her brother were intrigued and continued to pursue the leads.

> We just ate it up. It was an incredible thing. I called my daughter at LSU, and she's the one who truly helped me in the beginning to do the research. We made a plan and we started with one family at a time. It quickly became more. We uncovered my mother's family pretty thoroughly on both sides. My grandparents were both Creoles, and my mother is Creole but my grandparents made a decision that my mother attend a white school—the French Union school, then public school. That said to me "this is their decision for their children."

> Interestingly enough, my father, I don't think he was aware of his past. He was raised as a white person.

Although Pat traces the transition to whiteness with her maternal grandparents' decision about where to send their daughter to school, it appears that this daughter—Pat's mother—knew what was going on. This would explain her sense of discomfort at the wake when Pat and her brother brought up the issue of her grandfather's categorization as "colored." Like Christina earlier, Pat's mother kept the secret going for another generation, raising Pat as white. Pat, in turn, married and raised her own children as white.

Pat's realization much later in life about her family's true racial background has, however, resulted in overwhelmingly positive outcomes. She has been able to reconnect with California family that was living as white and got a positive response. She was put in touch with a young woman who turned out to be the daughter of her mother's first cousin and this resulted in a joyful reunion.

> She brought her mother to Louisiana to see my mom, and she hadn't seen her since 1945 when they left to go to California. I found out that my aunt did correspond with them, but when she died nobody contacted her and told her that. The joy of having ... my mother's cousin ... they're the same age, they'll both be ninety this year ... when Rebecca came, she remembered that her mother (my mother's aunt) had made my mother's wedding dress. I went in the closet and got the dress. That day was wonderful, and [my mother's cousin] and I have become close. She organizes all the family reunions. When we go, my job is to give the family history. We share pictures. I have a picture of my grandfather with his family when he was four years old. It has been a wonderful experience. It's funny because my mom won't talk about the Creole aspect, [but her cousin] in California will talk and talk about it.

In the course of her genealogical research, Pat discovered the story of a free woman of color named Euphemie Lemelle who was nearly re-enslaved by one of her own relatives who sought to put her on the auction block to make money. When considering Euphemie's struggle to retain her freedom in the face of relatives trying to re-enslave her, Pat had this to say:

> When I find out that I'm related to people like Euphemie Lemelle and what she went through ... and some of my other ancestors ... I just see resiliency and tenacity.... I don't think I really thought about those things before I did genealogy—I just kind of accepted that that's the way it was.

This awareness of her mixed-race ancestor's struggles also pushes her to reconsider racial issues she had not given much thought to before.

> I think that because of the age I am, and having grown up in a racially segregated society, [learning about all of this has] made me more sensitive. . . . In my household growing up, I don't remember hearing a lot of negativities about the racial question that was certainly going on at the time. I never heard "those" words . . . or any of the old people in my family speak negatively about people because of their race. So I'm sure now . . . I understand more.

Pat's newfound sensitivity to racial issues and inequalities resonates with Mark Roudané's response in the earlier section where he talks about the newly personal response he has to working with young people from African American backgrounds in his role as a teacher.

As we noted earlier, Mark is descended from civil rights crusader Dr. Louis Charles Roudanez; but he grew up knowing nothing about his family's illustrious past. All of this changed when his father passed away in 2005. He died with a family secret that Mark discovered the following year: his father had been born as Louis Charles Roudanez with a "z" instead of an accent over the "e." As Mark reviewed the binder that held his father's papers, he discovered a secret past that traced back to Dr. Louis Charles Roudanez, who was born in Louisiana in 1823 and later became the esteemed civil rights leader of the 1860s. What was Mark's response to all of this?

> I was stunned. I didn't know what it meant at the time, but I do remember feeling pride in discovering anything about my past because my father never talked about his father. He was never really raised by his father, so to find out anything I was very proud. But also stunned to learn that I came from a Creole past in New Orleans. At that point I understood that my great-great grandfather was mixed race—black and white, Creole and Afro-Creole. So all of a sudden questions came up in my mind—what does that make me? My initial reaction was pride but also a sense of well . . . what am I?

His response has been to think in a more nuanced way about race than he previously had.

> Well, racially I'm white. So I appear to be white, and I was raised white—same for my father. But in understanding that my grandfather was listed on his birth certificate as colored and his father as colored and Louis Charles Roudanez as mixed race, I began to realize that the world isn't just black and white and *that*

there was this Creole middle ground that had existed in Louisiana that I came out of. So basically my grandfather disappeared into the white race, and my family too in the early twentieth century.

With this response, Mark opens the door to challenging the dictates of the Anglo-American racial system which has pushed some Afro-Creoles to position themselves as black and others to re-present themselves as "white." What was missing for Mark and for others who either embraced blackness or fled into whiteness was the "Creole middle ground" Mark refers to. This middle ground is a remnant of the Latin/Caribbean racial system that shaped New Orleans for centuries and that continues to lie beneath the surface of the Anglo-American system. In this chapter's concluding section, we take a look at the ways some Afro-Creoles are resisting the Anglo system and consider the striking similarities between their resistance and that of current immigrants of color from Latin America and the Caribbean.

Challenging and Resisting the Anglo-American Racial Framework

The first two responses to the Anglo-American racial system involve conforming, more or less, to expectations associated with identifying as black or white. For many Afro-Creoles, this involves taking on blackness as a racial identity while retaining Creoleness as an ethnic identity. For others like the families examined in the previous section, it has meant forcing themselves into the category of whiteness at the cost of self and family. Increasingly, however, Afro-Creoles are pushing for a different kind of response, one that allows them to be who they are racially and culturally on their own terms—terms that do not sit easily with the standard Anglo-American framework.

The ill fit of the Anglo framework is well illustrated by an intense conversation that took place at a conference in the fall of 2003. On the Saturday morning of the conference, I made my way to a meeting room in the Radisson Hotel in New Orleans, where I took part in a session of the Creole Studies Conference sponsored by The Louisiana Creole Heritage Center at Northwestern State University and the Deep South Regional Humanities Center at Tulane. As a newcomer to the city, having just moved there in July of that year, I had only a general sense of Creole identity and had come to the conference to learn more. Wendy Gaudin's session, entitled "We Went Where We Belonged: Color and the Impossibility of Segregation in Jim Crow New Orleans" looked intriguing. She presented material about her research with Creoles of color concerning their experience living under Jim Crow. We saw the fruit of her work at the end of Chapter 4 when we learned from her oral history respondents and highlighted excerpts from the Xavierite of the 1960s.

Things became interesting as Gaudin finished her talk and the audience began asking questions. Many of the people in the audience identified themselves as Creole when they spoke, and they raised points that complicated Gaudin's presentation. The points they raised highlighted the uneasy ways Creoles sat between the categories of black and white. One of the first questions came from a Creole woman who asked: Is there a danger of reifying racial categories? What about acknowledging our white privilege? Others in the meeting room followed up on the first question. What united their questions was a desire to talk about long-submerged issues of racism and colorism and to find new ways to understand and express the complexities of Creole identity and experience.

A young woman who identified herself as Creole brought up the point that Hispanics have similar issues with racial and cultural diversity and wondered how they deal with this when they come to the United States. In response to this last question, a middle-aged woman from California retorted that they use the label "Hispanic" to avoid the black/white characterization they would otherwise be forced into.

This linkage to the experience of people of African descent from Latin America and the Caribbean was a theme throughout many of the interviews as well. Many respondents felt that they were hemmed in by the boundaries of the US racial system and tried to find ways to navigate around it in their personal identification and in their approaches to filling out official forms. In one of the previous sections of this chapter, we saw how Celine would pragmatically check "black" on most forms but would occasionally check "other" and write out "Creole." Naurine also found it difficult to navigate official forms that required her to fill in her race.[27] This stems in part from the fact that the Creole social milieu in which she was formed provided conflicting information on who was black and who was white. She explains:

> [W]hen I was younger, you know there was only black or white. Of course, I didn't, if I told you that I didn't really know what race was, would you believe me? ... I was older, in fact my cousins they used to shake their heads because I told them Abe Lincoln was black and she told me, I was too old, I was in high school, she says Naurine he wasn't. She said there have been no black presidents. I said, well, he looked black. See I thought race was like religion. You had to tell them. I was raised in an area where they had white black people who were whiter than white people. I knew white people who were darker and rather than

try to figure it out, you know, and it's not as easy as black and white and to me the variety and complexity, I just think it's very interesting and ... I don't like being put in a box and have to identify with only one anything if I am a part of other things.

What Naurine describes here is very unlike the typical US racial understanding. The default across the United States is still the "one-drop rule" where any kind of discernible African heritage in one's hair, skin, or features makes one black. Within her Creole community, however, the lines were blurred and the logic used for categorizing people did not work according to US norms.

Naydja has also had to contend with confusion among others about what her racial and ethnic background is.[28] She says:

> I guess I realized all of the mixtures inside of me. The French, of course African American, the Creoles whatever that is. And I'm often asked where am I from. So I guess I must look quite mixed or confusing to people and I'm Caribbean looking and I could be from Jamaica or anywhere down in that area of the world ... And I just realized how much ... New Orleans people are mixed up.

Here Naydja speaks of her skin color as confusing to people who struggle to place her race and who conclude that she might be from some part of the Caribbean.

The somewhat fluid sense of racial identification expressed by these respondents takes them outside of the traditional Anglo-American racial framework that dominates most of the United States. They are, in many ways, more in line with the racial systems at work in many Latin American and Caribbean countries, where there is a continuum of racial categories that vary according to color, features, status, and so on.

For some, this sense of physical difference is accompanied by a way of thinking about themselves socially and culturally that brings up explicit linkages with the Caribbean. When Rhondale was in college, she joined the Caribbean Student Society, even though no one in her family has recently migrated from the Caribbean, and indeed no one in living memory has come from the Caribbean. Her family did, however, have an oral history of ancestors coming from an "island," and she later learned that this island was Haiti. This knowledge was enough to spark her interest in becoming part of the Caribbean student group. She explains:

> Everyone would ask me where's your family from, and I'd say Haiti, and they'd be like where and I'd be like I don't know, but I mean I knew there was some

connection, so I was involved in that and I loved participating in everything. It was mostly students of Jamaican descent or from Jamaica actually in that Caribbean Society. I was one of five people with the Haitian connection, most of whom their parents were from Haiti and it was my great-great grandfather who I never met. Nonetheless [I stayed] involved.

Ronald also made note of the connections between southern Louisiana and the Caribbean:

It's being said now that New Orleans . . . could be more of a Caribbean city than an American city. . . . I wonder if the more southern part of Louisiana wasn't always a Caribbean flair. So it wasn't really too much change when you had that migration. The people just leaving from one area of Caribbean influence to another and all they did was reinforced it and made it stronger.

Here Ronald makes a direct reference to the St. Domingue migration to Louisiana in his discussion of how he continues to see a connection between southern Louisiana and the Caribbean.[29]

Amelie provides perhaps the strongest statement of connection to the Caribbean. Although her position is not representative of most Creoles, her statement is illustrative of the many social and cultural connections between the experiences of this community and those of more recent Caribbean immigrants. When we were talking about what it meant for her to grow up Creole in a community of color, she explained: "I don't think we ever thought of ourselves as African American. I told [my friend] that more and more I consider myself more Caribbean than anything. If I am going to put the African, Afro-Caribbean." Amelie's sense of being Caribbean has come much later in life and was not part of her initial social formation. And yet, what she says here resonates with comments from other respondents who reported racial sensibilities that have more in common with Latin American and Caribbean countries than they do with the United States.

These responses echo the experiences of the St. Domingue refugees of color whose entry to the United States, as we saw in Chapter 4, forced Anglo-Americans to grapple with how to place and integrate these in-between newcomers into the Anglo-American system. The Creole Studies Conference participants who compared Creoles to Hispanic newcomers in the United States made a comparison that affirms the basic argument of this book—that Louisiana's early experience with large-scale, multiracial migration from the Caribbean prefigures similar kinds of developments in urban centers across the United States. In the book's conclusion we weave together the major threads of the book and make a final case for the argument that Louisiana's past experience with shifting layers of a racial palimpsest provides a compelling portrait of where race and racial dynamics are going in many US regions today.

CHAPTER 7

Conclusions

Racial Palimpsests and the Transformation of US American Regions

I'm not black and I'm not white; we don't define ourselves that way.... So I would choose "some other race" [on the Census].
—Kathia Mendez, *mixed race, originally from the Dominican Republic*

We have so much mixture.... These other census categories just don't reflect who we are.
—Nelly de la Rosa, *chocolate brown skin, originally from the Dominican Republic*

The disorienting racial experiences described by Afro-Creole respondents in the previous chapter are striking because all of these respondents, along with their ancestors going back many generations, were born and raised in the United States and should be well acquainted with its binary racial logic. Yet, despite having endured generations of assimilative forces, many have still been palpably shaped not only by an ethnic-cultural understanding of their Creoleness but also by a racial-structural sense that they stand outside of the dominant Anglo-American racial system.

Two hundred years after the St. Domingue refugees heavily reinforced Louisiana's Latin/Caribbean system and blended into the larger Creole community, many of their descendants of color are still affected in one way or another by this alternative racial logic. Even if some of them ultimately came to label themselves as black or white, those identities often emerged after confusing periods of childhood and adolescence spent questioning where they fit in the binary US system. Others like Celine, Naurine, and Amelie have pushed more firmly against this binary and insist on standing outside of it. How closely will the experiences of today's immigrants and their descendants of color from Latin America and the Caribbean correspond to that of the St. Domingue refugees and their Creole descendants? We have a hint of the answer in Kathia and Nelly's statements.[1] According to the rules of the Anglo-American racial system that has dominated the United States for more than two hundred years, both Kathia and Nelly are unequivocally black. But this categorization is in conflict with the terms of the racial system within which they were formed in the Dominican Republic. The argument presented in *American Routes* is that much of Kathia and Nelly's integration experience will be shaped by where they live and what the racial landscape is like in those areas.

St. Domingue refugees settled all along the Eastern seaboard, as well as in New Orleans, but it is only in New Orleans and surrounding areas of southeast Louisiana that their ethnic-cultural and racial-structural distinctiveness has survived in the form of present-day Creoles. This survival was possible because, in nearly doubling the population of New Orleans, they significantly slowed down the progress and long-term effects of Anglo-American racialization. Similarly, for today's immigrants, if they live in a city like Miami or Los Angeles—both of which have large numbers of immigrants from Latin America and the Caribbean—they are part of a shifting racial palimpsest where more than one racial system is at work. The presence of this palimpsest will allow them to more effectively hold onto a Latin/Caribbean form of cultural and racial identification than if they live in Salt Lake City or Duluth, where the Anglo-American racial system continues to hold strong, virtually unchallenged.

In this concluding chapter, we consider how the emergence of a racial palimpsest in certain parts of the United States shows evidence of a fundamental change in the dominance of the Anglo-American racial system as more people like Kathia and Nelly become residents. The evidence we will consider suggests that, in a way that is similar to the St. Domingue refugees and their descendants, today's immigrants of color are likely to push against the Anglo-American racial system. But in contrast to the St. Domingue refugees of 1809–1810 who were the last major wave of nineteenth-century Caribbean immigrants to Louisiana, today's immigrants from Latin America and the Caribbean are the beneficiaries of ethnic replenishment where continual flows of new immigrants from these regions help to bolster their alternative racial understandings. We would thus expect that they will be able to more firmly hold onto both their ethnic-cultural and racial-structural identifications than did the St. Domingue refugees and their Creole descendants.[2]

Our discussion in this concluding chapter will also emphasize the fact that, despite greater flexibility and fluidity in the ways people are categorized according to the characteristics of an alternative racial system, the superimposition of a Latin/Caribbean layer over the foundational Anglo system continues to be attended by the stubborn continuity and strength of racism and white supremacy. Thus, the significance of a racial palimpsest lies not in some hope that it will present a less oppressive racial environment as new kinds of flexibility and new forms of identification emerge, but rather its significance lies in the ways our recognition of its presence pushes us to reevaluate and respond to the shifting dynamics of race and racism in areas where a palimpsest is in evidence.

THE SLOW SUBMERSION OF THE ANGLO-AMERICAN RACIAL SYSTEM

The identification choices of Latinos in the United States—both those born in the United States and those who have immigrated to the country—are the subject of intense debate among scholars of immigration and race. The major questions are as follows: How do/will Latinos identify? How will their identification choices affect the short- and long-term racial composition of the United States? For instance, US Census projections put the Latino population at 29 percent by 2060 with the non-Hispanic white population at just 43 percent.[3] But these projections depend on the assumption that light-skinned Latinos and their children will continue to identify as both white *and* Hispanic, rather than white alone. It is possible that some may become white, non-Hispanic across generations. In this case, the Hispanic population would not be as high and the white non-Hispanic population would not be as low as projected. If this occurs, it would support what scholars call the "whitening hypothesis." In this sense, the racial and cultural choices of Latinos have the potential to significantly change the racial composition of the United States or to reinforce what has been a white majority.[4]

Although scholars have contrasting opinions about how Latinos and their children will racially identify over the next decade or two, what is clear is that as of the 2010 census the majority of those who identify themselves as Hispanic are split between identifying as "white" (53 percent) and "some other race" (SOR) (36 percent).[5] Those who identify as "some other race" may be declaring that they see Hispanic/Latino as its own racial category.[6] If this is the case, then Hispanic identity will function much the way Creole identity did in Louisiana—it will be both an ethnic-cultural and a racial-structural identification that will make them neither black nor white. There is much evidence to suggest that this is the direction many people of Hispanic descent are headed.

First, the experience of people like Kathia and Nelly demonstrates the perspective of many persons of Hispanic origin in the United States, especially immigrants shaped according to the logic of a different racial system, who do not see a place for themselves within existing US racial categories. In her book, *Race Migrations*, Wendy Roth engages in an in-depth analysis of the lives of immigrants like Kathia and Nelly in order to understand what sense they make of race after migrating to the United States. She finds that they tend to carry around "racial schemas" that allow them to engage in racial sense-making based both on the racial system in their country of origin and what they find in the United States. In her concluding chapter, she discusses the ways "Hispanic" is coming to be seen as a distinctive racial group.

In "The Whitening Hypothesis Challenged," Jessica Vasquez also provides evidence that many Latinos are not simply fitting themselves into accepted US racial categories.[7] Her work is unique in that she carries out qualitative research of mixed marriages that include one Latino and one white person, and attempts to understand how these couples position themselves and their children racially and culturally. The results of her research challenge the "whitening hypothesis," which holds that an increasing number of Latinos will identify as "white." What she finds instead is that although there is a great deal of variability in how these families identify racially and culturally, the tendency is more toward what she describes as "social browning" than "social whitening."

Of the persons in her study, six "lean white"; thirteen display everyday biculturalism; five engage in selective blending; and ten "lean Latino." Those who "lean white" mainly identify themselves and their family members as white. Everyday biculturals engage in a kind of symbolic ethnicity, acknowledging and identifying with different cultures in a kind of random fashion without a great deal of intentionality.[8] Selective blenders differ from biculturals in that they are very intentional about deciding which cultural practices to cultivate and which to de-emphasize. Finally, those who "lean Latino" decide to make Latino identity the dominant culture of the household. The most common kinds of respondents were the "everyday biculturals"—the symbolic ethnics— and those who "lean Latino." Vasquez concludes by arguing that the whitening thesis is unsupported because:

> Latino and non-Hispanic white inter-marriages do not unilaterally produce social whitening and minority cultural detachment as predicted by much

race-relations theory. Low-commitment, symbolic everyday biculturalism describes most families. At the poles, leaning Latino (social browning) is a more frequent outcome than leaning white (social whitening), inverting the expectations of assimilation theory.[9]

Although the sample size is small, the results are suggestive. With the first group, children may grow up intermingling white and Latino cultures without thinking much about which is dominant in their lives. If they follow in the footsteps of European groups who have become symbolic ethnics, these children and their grandchildren may well blend into the white majority. In the latter group, however, children are more likely to grow up with a solid Latino identity which could translate into a greater likelihood of identifying as Hispanic, "some other race," on the US Census.

Finally, the Census Bureau itself is in the process of reconsidering the way it asks about race. As of the 2010 Census, the race question was asked in the following way: "Is Person 1 of Hispanic, Latino, or Spanish origin?" If the answer to that question was yes, then the follow-up question was: "What is Person 1's race?" The choices provided included white, black, American Indian, Asian Indian, and so on. But because the Census Bureau does not consider "Hispanic" to be a race, that option was not listed in the follow-up race question. In a new test questionnaire developed by the Census Bureau, however, the approach is quite different. Rather than presenting separate Hispanic and race questions, the questionnaire asks: "Which categories describe Person 1?" Notice here that the word "race" is not even used. The choices offered include the following: white (e.g., German, Irish, English); Hispanic, Latino or Spanish Origin (e.g., Mexican, Puerto Rican, Cuban); black or African American (e.g., African American, Jamaican, Haitian); and so on. This group of choices would allow Kathia and Nelly to simply check off "Hispanic" without ever having to engage with the race question. The likelihood that these women and others like them would do this is supported by Golash-Boza and Darity, who conclude the following in their work on Latino identity:

> [Our findings] demonstrate a growing preference for the collective national labels as ethnic classifiers, Latino or Hispanic. . . . This trend is also in line with Duany's finding that the quasi-racial use of the term "Hispanic" has led many Puerto Ricans to move away from the black/white dichotomy in the U.S.[10]

The kind of evidence provided by the studies discussed here supports the idea that many Latinos—both those who are recent immigrants and those who are born in the United States—are actively challenging the relevance and built-in assumptions of the Anglo-American racial system. They are joined in this resistance by non-Latino Americans who are biracial or multiracial and who also do not see themselves reflected in standard enumerations of racial groups.[11]

Because of the relatively large demographic impact of Latinos, and the growth in persons of mixed-race backgrounds, some scholars have argued that the old black/white color line is in the process of being dismantled. Given what we have learned from the St. Domingue-Louisiana case, however, we should be hesitant to come to this conclusion so quickly. Our examination of the St. Domingue refugees of different racial backgrounds, and their Creole descendants two hundred years later, has shown us that a foundational racial system is slow to die—even when it is slowly but firmly eclipsed by a new racial system.

In Louisiana, the foundational system was Latin/Caribbean because of the territory's initial formation under the French and Spanish. Although the Anglo-Americans took over in 1803, it took nearly one hundred years for that system to become dominant among white Creoles and several more decades after that for the Anglo-American understanding of race to shape Afro-Creoles' understandings of themselves—and even then, an appreciable number of Afro-Creoles continued to reject the logic of the Anglo-American system. Now, as the social and political environment has shifted toward greater openness to alternative racial understandings, a growing number of Afro-Creoles are reidentifying as Creole and resisting the US tendency to push them into either "black" or "white" categories. In sum, the persistence of the submerged Latin/Caribbean perspective on race and identity in the Louisiana case should lead us to expect that the Anglo-American racial system with its black/white color line is likely to be with us exerting its influence in one way or another for generations to come.

In line with this expectation, the insights that emerge from the palimpsest approach are quite different from what is predicted in current research and theories about the shifting nature of the US color line. There are three major color-line transition models: white/nonwhite; triracial; and black/nonblack. Despite their differences, the three models share certain fundamental characteristics. First, each of them is proposed as an alternative to the traditional black/white color line that has dominated the United States for much of its history. Second, scholars writing on each approach tend to take the entire country as the unit of analysis—proposing that a new kind of color line is coming to define race relations across the entire nation-state.[12]

Scholars who discuss a white/nonwhite color line speak mainly in support of this approach as applying to many nonwhite groups throughout the twentieth century. Bean, Lee, and Bachmeier, for instance, cite the legal treatment of many Hispanic and Asian groups as evidence that they were seen to be more similar to blacks than to whites. Such instances include the Chinese Exclusion Act; the Japanese internment during World War II; and Virginia's Racial Integrity Act in 1924, which clarified that there were just two salient racial categories: "pure" white and others that were not pure white.[13] These cases provide evidence of a white/nonwhite color line where being anything other than white makes it impossible to enjoy full membership in US society. Although scholars recognize how a white/nonwhite color line has previously structured race relations, it is generally understood that this model is being replaced by one of two alternative models—the triracial or the black/nonblack model.[14]

The triracial model is best known through the work of Eduardo Bonilla-Silva, who characterizes the changes he has observed in the United States as the Latin Americanization of race. Bonilla-Silva's work picks up from the white/nonwhite color-line discussion in that he sees the status of previously denigrated Asian and Hispanic groups now being rehabilitated to the point that they are no longer denigrated. This means that rather than being lumped together as "nonwhite," and therefore inferior, certain subgroups of Asian and Hispanic Americans are increasingly seen as having achieved what he describes as "honorary white" status. In his estimation, we have moved toward a tripartite division that consists of white/honorary white/collective black. A sample membership for each of these categories is outlined in Table 7.1.

Although Bonilla-Silva's triracial concept rings true in the sense that there is certainly a hierarchy of sorts between and within different racial and ethnic groups depending on skin color, class, and degree of assimilation, the scheme does not account at all for how place and the relative proportion and power of different racial/ethnic groups might affect where a person ends up in the racial and cultural hierarchy specific to that place.

For instance, while Bonilla-Silva lumps black Americans and dark-skinned Latinos together, being a medium- to dark-skinned Latino in Miami might easily place one in a fundamentally different and higher category in the racial hierarchy than that allotted to Anglo-black Americans. This would especially be the case if the person in question were medium- to dark-skinned but had a high level of education and sophistication. Such a placement, higher on the hierarchy than Bonilla-Silva would put such a person, is very much in line with the idea that "money whitens"—a common saying in many parts of Latin America and the Caribbean.[15] In such a case, the large presence of immigrants from these regions creates a racial palimpsest where the racial rules of the game are played more often

Table 7.1 BONILLA-SILVA'S TRIRACIAL STRATIFICATION SYSTEM

Whites	• Whites
	• New whites (e.g., Russians, Albanians, etc.)
	• Assimilated white Latinos
Honorary whites	• Light-skinned Latinos
	• Japanese Americans
	• Korean Americans
	• Asian Indians
	• Chinese Americans
	• Most multiracials
Collective black	• Filipinos
	• Vietnamese
	• Dark-skinned Latinos
	• Blacks
	• New West Indian and African immigrants
	• Reservation-bound Native Americans

Source: Adapted from Eduardo Bonilla-Silva, "We Are All Americans! The Latin Americanization of Racial Stratification in the U.S.A.," *Race and Society* 5 (2002): 4.

according to those of recent Latino immigrants than of traditional Anglo-American notions of blackness and whiteness. Such fine distinctions are unlikely to be made in majority white areas of the United States where most residents are native to the country—but these distinctions do not appear within Bonilla-Silva's conceptualization of a triracial system.

The third color-line approach, that of a transition to a black/nonblack ordering, has been most thoroughly researched and conceptualized by Jennifer Lee and Frank Bean. In their recent book, *The Diversity Paradox*, as well as in a plethora of articles on the same topic, Lee and Bean have argued strongly against competing color-line models and for what they call "black exceptionalism." After examining data that show increasingly high rates of intermarriage between whites and Asians and whites and Latinos as well as increased rates of multiracial identification, Lee and Bean conclude that we are experiencing a collapse of previous racial boundaries for all groups except black Americans. This black exceptionalism leads them to see the emergence of a black/nonblack color line where—for all intents and purposes—racial boundaries are rapidly disappearing for everyone who is not black in the United States.

Although the idea that a black/nonblack color line is emerging may be compelling to some extent, this approach also bears some significant weaknesses. Lee and Bean, in fact, are the first to acknowledge the limitations of their approach. Whereas they generally hold to their argument that all groups except blacks are experiencing permeability across previous racial barriers, they note that the "Latinos" they studied were from California and included mainly Mexican immigrants and Mexican Americans who have little or no African ancestry. They then note that a similar study focused on Puerto Rican and Dominican persons in New York might find that more Latinos fall on the black side of the color line. This would certainly complicate the argument that Latinos as a whole have triumphed over previously obstinate racial barriers. But even if we allowed for the idea that "black exceptionalism" applies to anyone with dark skin who has African ancestry, this conclusion would still provide an oversimplification of racial and ethnic dynamics. Here the example provided about a medium- to dark-skinned Latino ranking socially above a black American in certain places is again helpful for demonstrating the ways that place and the particular layering of systems in the racial palimpsest of a given place matter socially and politically.

In sum, while the color-line model approach to thinking about race, immigration, and social change is on the right track in terms of thinking about the ascendance or decline of different racial systems, studies in this area bear significant weaknesses. The first of these weaknesses is a kind of either/or thinking about color lines, and the second is a tendency to generalize to the national level. When authors working within this approach consider whether or not color-line A is being replaced by color-line B, they either explicitly or implicitly assume that one color-line model is present at a time and do not consider the possibility that there might be two overlapping color-line systems working at the same time in the same place. Secondly, there is an assumption that the black-white color line has dominated every part of the United States with equal strength. Having made this assumption, they pursue the question of whether or not this old system is being replaced by a new system that will also extend equally across the United States. There is little or no recognition that different cities and regions experienced the black/white color line differently depending on their histories. This does not mean that the black/white color line did not exert influence everywhere in the United States, but it does mean that it may have exerted less influence in some regions than in others—as was the case in southern Louisiana.

Each of the weaknesses of the color-line approach is addressed by the racial palimpsest concept. First, the very idea of a racial palimpsest acknowledges the co-presence of different racial systems. Rather, then, than seeking to determine whether we have a black/white line *or* a black/nonblack line, the palimpsest approach encourages us to see the dynamic interaction of multiple approaches to race as characterized by the logics of different racial systems. Similarly, rather than explicitly or implicitly assuming that one new color line is beginning to govern the entire country, the palimpsest approach is attuned to the ways that place, and geographic proximity or nonproximity to parts of Latin America and the Caribbean, may make it possible for the same person to be differently categorized depending on where she is located and what the relative strength of different racial systems is in that particular place. Built into the racial palimpsest approach, then, is an understanding that palimpsests are created through histories of migratory flows back and forth across US borders. Thus, because of its closer proximity to the Caribbean, southern Louisiana has a very different racial terrain than do areas like Minnesota or Washington State in the north of the country.

In fact, the palimpsest approach is supported by many scholars writing about immigration, Hispanics, race, and identity. In their article "Latino Immigrants and the U.S. Racial Order," Frank and her coauthors actively consider the possibility of three potential racial outcomes given the growth of the Latino population.[16] First, these newcomers may be categorized according to traditional US racial rules where the black/white line dominates; second, the US boundary system may expand to extend whiteness to them; and third, the racial boundary system may change to include Latino as a new racial category. As they weigh these possibilities with their research, they find that the racial system in the country of origin for immigrant Latinos plays a role in how they identify in the United States. They describe this as "the long arm of influence wielded by [the] racial categorization system prevalent in immigrants' origin countries."[17] They see this "long arm" as predicting immigrant racial identification in contrast to what would be expected under the US system given their skin tone. In keeping with insights from the racial palimpsest approach, however, they also find that individuals' racial understandings are influenced by racial practices in the specific US region of that person's residence. They write:

> [Our] findings confirm that local-level interpretations of the U.S. categorization scheme influence Latino immigrants and how they self-identify. Latinos in the Southwest, where a Latino identity may be more salient, are more likely than those in the South to opt out of traditional options.[18]

Thus, while the racial system in the country of origin is a factor in identification, the relative strength of an Anglo-American or Latin/Caribbean racial system in a US region also plays a strong role in determining self-identification. The Southwest, with its centuries-long ties to Latin America, is more characterized by a Latin/Caribbean racial system than is the US South, and this makes it more likely for immigrant Latinos in this area to resist the Anglo-American system of racial categorization. The large Hispanic community in the Southwest also provides an environment where Latino immigrants' bodies are more likely to be "read" as Hispanic because this classificatory practice is common in that area. Such practices highlight the importance of paying close attention to the ways immigrant bodies are perceived and labeled and to the role this perception and labeling plays in their racial classification and identification.[19]

Several other authors also emphasize the importance of place in shaping the ways Latinos identify. In "Shades of Belonging," Sonya Tafoya analyzes focus group data and finds that changing place of residence can impact identification. One Cuban-origin respondent, after declaring that Hispanics are accepted in Miami, New York, and California, explains: "If I apply somewhere else [for a job], Tennessee, and the application says are you 'Hispanic' or 'White'? I put white because I want to at least have an interview."[20] This kind of response is certainly in line with older research on situational ethnicity and, in this sense, is not new. It becomes significant, however, when whole areas of the country encourage one kind of racial identification and other areas encourage a different kind. This finding supports the argument that a racial palimpsest is emerging in certain parts of the country and further supports the argument that the racial system is undergoing significant changes in certain US population centers.

John Logan's work supports this point while also providing further nuance concerning the issue of Hispanic identity and place of residence. He emphasizes the need to disaggregate "Hispanics" into three groups: white Hispanics, black Hispanics, and Hispanic Hispanics. The last group consists of those who choose "some other race" on the Census and then write in "Hispanic" or "Latino" as a description of their race. He notes that Miami has the largest percentage of white Hispanics, New York has the largest concentration of black Hispanics, and California the highest proportion of Hispanic Hispanics. There has been a large amount of growth in this third category and that growth provides further evidence that an increasing number of Hispanics are rejecting the black/white poles of the Anglo-American racial system. Logan concludes by writing:

> Though Hispanics are undoubtedly aware of the black-white color line in American society, ... this report offers evidence that they increasingly reject these racial categories and assert a distinct Hispanic ethnic identity. It makes

sense that such a development would draw more heavily on immigrants and *find more resonance in parts of the country where there is a more substantial Hispanic presence.* The recent rapid growth of a Hispanic population that is not fully integrated into the mainstream economy offers conditions that support such a cultural turn and suggests that it will deepen in coming years.[21]

This concluding statement contains much that affirms the racial palimpsest concept. First, Logan notes that the black-white color line is still present and active—the logic of the foundational Anglo-American racial system continues as strong as ever in much of the country. But next, he notes that an increasing number of Hispanics are refusing to live according to this logic and that their place of residence matters for their ability to carry through on this rejection of the system as they live their everyday lives. Finally, he expects that this trend will deepen in years to come.

All of this supports what we would expect given the findings of the St. Domingue-Louisiana migration case study. As a new racial system becomes ascendant and introduces a different racial logic than previously existed, new forms of identification emerge as people reclassify themselves according to its logic. In the case of the St. Domingue immigrants and their Creole descendants, this meant that after a brief window of time where their numbers reinforced Louisiana's foundational Latin/Caribbean racial system, they were eventually pressured to conform to new racial rules as Anglo-Americans increased in number and fortified their political and economic dominance. This conformism was absolutely crucial for white descendants who found themselves at a disadvantage when they identified as "Creole" rather than as simply "white," Anglo-American style.

In contrast, today's Hispanic immigrants are the newcomers who come bearing a new racial logic and their alternative racial perspective is bolstered by continuing flows of immigrants from the same region. In areas where they have significant numbers, they are able to operate according to a Latin/Caribbean racial system that is not necessarily available in other parts of the country. But their example also benefits non-Hispanics who feel out of sorts with the Anglo-American racial system. As we saw in the previous chapter, many Louisiana Creoles of color see the case of Hispanic resistance to black/white polarization as supportive of their own experience and way of thinking. Beyond this, even biracial and multiracial persons who are neither Creole nor Hispanic can benefit from the more flexible approach to race that immigrants are bringing as they help to superimpose a Latin/Caribbean approach to race over the long-enduring Anglo-American system.

In sum, then, the palimpsest approach that has emerged from the study of the St. Domingue-Louisiana migration case has significance for the ways we think about race and immigration. The palimpsest concept encourages us to move away from thinking about the ways a specific "color line" categorizes people, and toward understanding how color, phenotype, and status may be differently configured within varied, overlapping racial systems. Related to this is the issue of how individuals negotiate the logics of different racial systems operating within the same geographic space.

The palimpsest approach also makes it clear that we cannot easily dismiss the social and political significance of an area's foundational racial layer. Thus, rather than declaring the black/white color line to be dying or dead, we would instead expect this Anglo-American racial logic to continue to endure for generations, even as a new, Latinized racial system exerts increased influence in some parts of the United States. This persistence of a region's foundational racial layer is supported by the Louisiana case where the remnants of the preexisting Latinized racial system continue to exert social influence even as the Anglo-American system has become firmly entrenched. We must be clear, however, that increased flexibility in the rules of racial categorization does not necessarily spell the advent of a more racially tolerant or just society. In some ways, in fact, the ascendance of a Latin/Caribbean racial system in several parts of the country may serve to make murkier the roots of racial inequality and thus muddy our understandings of how to uproot them. Consider, for instance, the fact that Latin American elites have used the ideology of *mestizaje* to occlude the significance of race and racism in perpetuating inequality. The Brazilian idea of "racial democracy" is a prime example of this approach. In contrast, while the Anglo-American system has been stark in its categorizations of black and white, this very starkness has made clear where to aim in the attempt to work toward racial justice. More flexible, less clearly marked approaches to racial categorization may make it seem on the surface that race is becoming less significant in the shaping of everyday life chances. Such a conclusion would, however, be in error, as white supremacy—in all its guises—continues to disadvantage people of color whatever racial system is in place.

In this sense, there is much at stake in the ways we make sense of transformations in the US racial system and the weakening of a black/white color line in some parts of the country. For this reason, discussion in the final two sections will consider how the racial palimpsest approach to thinking about immigration, race, and racial transformation can help us to move toward forms of research and practice that equip us to see and address the stubborn persistence of racism and white supremacy.

THE RESILIENT AND WILY WAYS OF EUROCENTRISM AND WHITE SUPREMACY: ON THE NEED TO RACIALIZE THE STUDY OF IMMIGRANTS

Eurocentrism, the placing of Europe and its cultures at the center of social reality, and white supremacy, the valuing of whiteness as the height of what is considered to be good and best, are remarkably resilient, even amid scholarly efforts to effect their demise. Much research and writing on immigration and race continue to be strongly influenced by assimilation theory, the roots of which are literally Eurocentric—in the sense that the theory was based upon the experience of European immigrants to the United States.

The Eurocentric origins of assimilation theory have always made it an awkward fit for studying the integration experiences of people of color. The classic assimilation literature arose in the context of nineteenth- and early twentieth-century immigration to the United States from Europe. Key questions included the following: How well will different kinds of European immigrants assimilate to US culture? What kinds of interventions, if any, might help such immigrants to assimilate as quickly as possible? At the root of this classic literature were concerns about making newcomers into Americans.[22] As the face of immigration changed in the mid-twentieth century following changes in the law which made it possible for the first time for large numbers of people of color to immigrate to the United States, scholars realized that the older approach to analyzing assimilation had to be modified in order to make sense of the new experiences of people of color.

In response, a new concept called "segmented assimilation" arose to fill the gap.[23] Where classic assimilation theory had assumed that all immigrants would eventually become part of the mainstream middle class, segmented assimilation suggests three different paths. While one of those paths includes assimilation to the mainstream, a second possibility is that immigrants of color may hold on to key aspects of their own cultures even as they operate smoothly within US social and cultural contexts. This clinging to the culture of the country of origin can, in many cases, scholars argue, provide resources and networks that protect new immigrants and their second generation from falling into the third path of downward assimilation. Downward assimilation occurs when immigrants effectively assimilate to the margins of US society rather than to the mainstream. An example here would be the son of Jamaican parents who identifies with the lower income African Americans in his school or neighborhood.

Segmented assimilation has been the literature's answer to how to deal with the problem of race. The early assimilation theorists whose framework was developed to deal with European immigrants dealt almost exclusively with *cultural* difference and, for the most part, completely ignored issues of race.[24] This early intellectual colorblindness continues to handicap the ability of assimilation theory to make sense of the experience of newer immigrants of color. Although current work within this paradigm does shed useful light on issues like the pace of English language acquisition, factors contributing to economic or school success, and so on, the approach is inherently conservative, and places the onus on the newcomer to blend into the mainstream—even when this same mainstream rejects her out of hand. There is nothing in the founding of the assimilation framework— and very little in its various new incarnations—that provides a built-in understanding of racism and racialized receptions of newcomers of color.

In contrast, the racial palimpsest concept was forged in the foundry of racial inequality. At its core is a careful and comparative consideration of how different racial systems across the Americas work to variously privilege or disadvantage persons of different colors and social backgrounds. Thus, its built-in assumption is that *race matters*. The approach is also quite sensitive to the ways racial systems are formed differently in different places, and the ways that movement between places requires immigrants to negotiate according to new racial rules, logics, and hierarchies. These founding assumptions very much help us to make sense of the experience of St. Domingue refugees leaving a Latinized racial system and being slowly integrated across generations into an increasingly Anglo-American racial system in southern Louisiana. The refugees were accustomed to the racial game of one American region and adapted this knowledge to cope with the new situation they found in Anglo-American Louisiana. None of these conditions applied to European immigrants leaving their home countries to come to the United States.

A growing number of scholars are calling for a fundamental transformation in the way we study immigration and race—a transformation that would de-emphasize the preoccupation with assimilation while making race and racialization central to our understanding of the reception and integration of people of color in the United States. Moon Kie Jung provides a thorough analysis and critique of the racial shortcomings of assimilation theory in a piece aptly titled "The Racial Unconscious of Assimilation Theory."[25] There he argues that though assimilation theorists attempt to address racial inequality, they rely on tools that continue to unconsciously reproduce normative assumptions that immigrants should aim to become more like the white mainstream. This racial unconscious predisposes such analysts to focus on how immigrants can become "more like us" and less on how racism inherent to the United States must be addressed in order to allow both immigrants and native-born persons of color to live and flourish on equal footing with their generally more advantaged white counterparts. Here the aim is not to be more like the white mainstream, but rather to have an equal chance to develop their own distinct lives and communities relieved of the burden of racial discrimination and bias. In contrast to this kind of race-sensitive approach, assimilation and segmented assimilation theorists continue to work within a fundamentally Eurocentric analytical framework that misses the centrality of race and racism in the daily experiences of people of color.

To correct assimilation theory's undertheorization of race and racism, Vilna Treitler argues that we need to shift to a racialized model of immigration. Her statement cuts to the heart of the contrast between an assimilation approach and one based on racialization:

> Assimilationism is modeled to see social agency as causal, either working to bring ethnic groups into the mainstream, or not. In contrast, the racialization model assumes that... racialized subjects... act to support their own interests in either dismantling or shoring up that racial system and act according to their knowledge of how the racial system works.[26]

What is key here is the way that newcomers either reinforce or challenge the existing racial system in order to bend it as much as possible to their needs and advantage. We certainly saw this with the Creole descendants of St. Domingue refugees. White descendants saw much earlier on the advantage of adopting an Anglo-American view of whiteness as purity, whereas those of color resisted the Anglo-American racial system as long as possible because it disadvantaged them. In the mid-nineteenth century, around the time *Les Cenelles* was published by French-speaking Creoles of color, there was little evidence that the poets saw themselves as sharing the lot of Anglo-black Americans. But by the 1860s when the relentless rise of the binary Anglo-American racial system exerted its presence, Creole intellectuals of African descent waged a civil rights movement where they clearly aligned themselves with Anglo-blacks. Today, a racialization framework that assumes the presence and significance of a racial palimpsest would lead us to ask questions about how lighter and darker skinned immigrants will ally themselves socially and politically, and would press us to acknowledge the stubborn persistence of racism and the need to commit more fully to dismantling the structures that support it.

But the tendencies of assimilation theory direct us away from thinking in terms of race and the persistence of racism. Instead, we are continually directed toward the underlying assumption that while there may be a few hiccups along the way, for the most part immigrants are more rather than less likely to integrate successfully if they put in the work to do so. For instance, in their book, *Remaking the American Mainstream*, Richard Alba and Victor Nee attempt to rehabilitate assimilation theory by emphasizing that assimilation occurs in different directions: immigrants to the mainstream and the mainstream to immigrants—with the result that what is considered to be "mainstream" changes from what it was before immigrants joined the United States.[27] They provide as examples the ways an initially marginalized religion like Catholicism has become part of the mainstream, and they discuss the ways immigrants' foodways have become integrated into US Americans' understandings of essential American cuisine. Their optimistic expectation is that most immigrant groups will successfully enter the mainstream. Their analysis does little, however, to address the experiences of immigrants of color who continue to be marginalized and stigmatized because of their darker skin.

This refusal to grapple with the significance of race and racism comes across in another work of Alba's, where he and his coauthors respond to Telles and Ortiz's account of Mexican American experiences. In their book *Generations of Exclusion*, Telles and Ortiz take a balanced approach to examining the integration experiences of Mexican Americans and Mexican immigrants over several generations. Although their findings lend support to assimilation theory for some Mexicans, they also find significant evidence of racialization. They explain:

> In many ways we show the glass as both half full and half empty. Some Mexican Americans have done well and most do better now than their parents did when they were young in the 1960s. Those are signs of partial assimilation. However, they continue to lag well behind their Anglo counterparts, which also reflects a process of racialization.[28]

Although these conclusions are quite balanced, and based on excellent intergenerational data, Alba et. al. argue that the authors are too tentative in their embrace of Mexican American assimilation when it comes to the issue of educational achievement.

They challenge Telles and Ortiz's findings on education by saying: "their conclusion that their 'evidence shows no educational assimilation', and that 'the third and fourth generation do worst of all suggesting downward assimilation in education' are too pessimistic a reading of their data."[29] Alba et. al.'s analysis of the same data paints a very different story of educational assimilation among Mexican Americans:

> This brief analysis points to the link between higher educational attainment, mixed ancestry, intermarriage and geographical mobility. As individuals distance themselves from the group's core by marrying non-Mexicans or moving

away from Mexican-American concentrations, their education rises—and vice versa.[30]

There is much to unpack in this response to Telles and Ortiz's work. Alba et. al. seem encouraged to find that distancing oneself by marrying non-Mexicans and leaving Mexican American neighborhoods leads to mainstream success. Essentially what they seem to be saying is that when Mexican Americans do everything they can to *stop* associating with other Mexican Americans, they will be educationally successful.

The quote from Alba et. al. clearly demonstrates Treitler's statement that the assimilation approach encourages us to see "social agency as causal" in determining successful integration. In this sense, Mexicans themselves are the ones to praise or blame for successful integration into US society. A different, racialized way to read what Alba and Nee are saying, however, is that continued racial inequality in access to opportunities and resources *within* Mexican communities makes it difficult for Mexican Americans to succeed educationally unless they attempt to shed this racialization by marrying non-Mexicans and leaving Mexican neighborhoods. The two interpretations are equally valid ways of making sense of the same data, but they are based on very different normative assumptions.

Alba et. al.'s embrace of educational upward mobility through shedding Mexican identity and community places value in becoming more like the white mainstream and, at least implicitly, recommends that other immigrants of color make similar choices. Scholars who call for the racialization of immigration study tend to place value instead on the cultivation of a more racially just society where it is not necessary to become more like the white mainstream in order to have access to resources and opportunities. The former is inherently conservative, whereas the latter challenges the racial status quo.

It is, I submit, the intrinsically Eurocentric history and nature of assimilation theory that causes it to be so relentlessly colorblind and conservative in orientation, and many other scholars agree. As Moon Kie Jung notes in his critique of old and new versions of assimilation, the problems with this approach lie at its core:

> If the sociological literature on race agrees on anything, it is that race is fundamentally about inequality and domination. Assimilation . . . would seem to be a mismatched conceptual tool with which to dissect racial dynamics. To be clear, I am not arguing that assimilation theories wholly ignore race or that they do not at all address inequality and domination. Rather, the concept of assimilation instills analytical tendencies to approach racial inequality and domination from an oblique angle that misses and distorts, as well as illuminates.[31]

It is my hope that *American Routes*, by bringing to light the submerged comparative histories of white immigrants and immigrants of color in nineteenth-century Louisiana, will help us to counter the tendency to rely on Eurocentric analytical tools when studying the integration of today's immigrants of color in the United States. The racial palimpsest concept attunes us to the necessity of developing in-depth and comparative analyses of different racial systems and of paying close attention to the ways immigrants and native-born locals negotiate layered racial systems as they engage in racial classification, identification, and integration. Having considered the implications of the palimpsest approach for scholarship on immigration and race, the concluding section of the book lays out the major takeaways of the palimpsest approach and the St. Domingue-Louisiana case study for everyday thinking and practice related to race and inequality in the United States.

RACIAL JUSTICE IN THE TIME OF THE PALIMPSEST

The emergence of a racial palimpsest requires new ways of thinking about race and racial justice in theory and practice. Under the Anglo-American system, all people of African descent are ranked at the bottom of a mainly two-tier society. This produces an all-or-nothing situation where one is either fully white or, if she has some African ancestry, she is fully black. Although this reality truncates many opportunities, it also makes the lines of social inequality and social struggle clear and establishes an incentive for solidarity among people of African descent—no matter how different they may be in terms of education, culture, and class.

Within the Latin/Caribbean system, however, solidarity with other people of African descent has not historically been something to strive for. This is because, within a Latin context, not all people of African descent are categorized in the same way. Instead, persons with nonwhite ancestry had the possibility of moving up the racial hierarchy by taking advantage of further education, smart marriage choices, or the capital afforded by light skin. In many ways, this has also been the situation among Creoles of color from Louisiana. Recall the stories of several interviewees in Chapter 6 who expressed their sense of being out of place because parents socialized them *not* to associate or equate themselves with African Americans. Recall as well the interviewees who shared difficult experiences with family members who denigrated their darker skin color. And finally, consider concerns among participants in the Creole Studies Conference who pushed their fellow Creoles of color to acknowledge deeply ingrained racism and colorism within their own community. Thus, the racial logic of a Latin/Caribbean system produces mixed results. On the one hand, there is more room to work hard to rise to the top—regardless of color. On the other, its logic often conceals the pernicious effects of racism and colorism behind the assumption that anyone can work his or her way up the social hierarchy regardless of color.[32]

The alternative social logic of the Latin/Caribbean racial system means that in areas like Miami where 51.3 percent of residents are foreign-born—many of them in Latin America—it will not be sufficient to fight racism with the tools developed in areas where traditional Anglo-American notions of race and inequality are dominant. It is necessary, rather, to enter into the kinds of stories we have heard in Chapter 6 to better understand the subtleties and complexities of a Latin/Caribbean approach to race and color inequality for persons of African descent. Consider, for instance, the following interview excerpt from Mary Waters's book *Black Identities*:

> It's different [than the United States] down in Jamaica . . . in Jamaica it's social class. And there was a way out of it, but it seems in America it does not matter how much money you have or how much education you have, race is still going to be an issue. In Jamaica if you were very black, very dark-skinned, you could always get a good education and gain the respect and admiration of everybody. That was it, nobody would ever again look at you or the color of your skin to ask where you came from . . . that would go once you got the education. Education and social class.[33]

Here we see a classic statement of the difference between the social valuing of dark-skinned people according to a Latin/Caribbean system compared to an Anglo-American racial system. In Jamaica, dark skin is—in the absence of any other mitigating factors—a disadvantage. But one can climb the social ladder by gaining education, cultural capital, money, and social status. Because West Indians are formed with these expectations, many look askance at black Americans and place them lower on the social ladder than they do blacks from the Caribbean. Consider the following excerpts from Waters's book:

> The blacks here should have more life—they don't try to promote themselves. They in too much drugs, on the streets, doing wrong things. . . . We West Indians do things a lot different. . . . We try hard work. But I feel that the majority of them they depend on someone to give them a hand out all the time.
>
> —Woman from St. Kitts[34]

[Black Americans] are just now striving to overcome many of the discriminations and what the whites have been doing to them over the period. You see, we West Indians came here with the idea that nobody was better than we are. It was not a matter of color in the Caribbean, it was a matter of haves and have-nots.
—Jamaican woman[35]

These excerpts, together with those from Kathia and Nelly from the beginning of this chapter, are quite similar to what we saw of Creoles' experiences in Chapter 6, and they are similar as well to the nuances and distinctions drawn between people of African descent in many parts of Latin America and the Caribbean. This is an approach to race that effectively dismisses racism as an issue and instead points to individual work as most important for getting ahead. But as the experience of the first Jamaican woman cited earlier makes clear, while West Indians may come to the United States with these ideas, the dynamics of the Anglo-American racial system produce a clash with reality on the ground. And though a Latin/Caribbean system may be the ascending layer of the racial palimpsest in several parts of the United States, the bedrock Anglo-American system will continue to exert its influence for the foreseeable future.

In regions like southern Louisiana, Miami, and other places where a racial palimpsest is established or is developing, conceptions of black and white are neither simple nor unidimensional, and dealing with race and inequality will require working simultaneously along the axes of the two overlapping racial systems. On the one hand, policies and programs devoted to breaking down barriers to equality will have to deal with the subtle and nuanced distinctions of color, class, and status that characterize the Latin/Caribbean system of racial ranking and, on the other, acknowledge and address the continued influence of the Anglo system's stark division of resources and opportunities between those who are black and those who are white according to its particular criteria.

To realize long-lasting progress toward racial justice, policies and programs will need to be cognizant of the characteristics of these contrasting racial systems while also working on multiple levels from the structural to the interpersonal in order to make lasting progress. At the structural level it is important to continue to address racial inequalities that persist in access to housing, education, and other resources. Equally important, however, is the need to break down obstacles to meaningful interpersonal engagement across lines of race and class.

At this interpersonal level, we must be attentive to the need to reimagine who we are as members of the same national community, and to thoroughly retrain ingrained habits that are obstacles to racial integration and racial justice. This requires us to rethink who the "we" is when we think of what it means to be American. This is a particularly pressing need given the racial and cultural diversification and internationalization of many of our cities and regions. Danielle Allen provides a model for this rethinking in her book *Talking to Strangers*, which grapples with the stubborness of racial distrust in the United States. She writes that we might do well to think in terms of a metaphor of "wholeness" rather than "oneness" when we think of what it means to be part of the United States.

> A focus on the wholeness of the citizenry rather than on its oneness, might allow for the development of forms of citizenship that focus on integration, not assimilation.... In short, the metaphor of wholeness can guide us into a conversation about how to develop habits of citizenship that can help a democracy bring trustful coherence out of division without erasing or suppressing difference. This ... epiphany prompts us to reimagine the very idea of "the people."[36]

Here Allen engages our social imagination, encouraging us to move away from the image of melting-pot assimilation and toward a vision that is both integrative and respectful of difference. Throughout the book, Allen discusses where our ingrained habits of racial distrust come from, how they inhibit the realization of full citizenship, and how we might form new habits and practices that are more conducive to racial integration and equity. This kind of work, which literally requires retraining our habits of thinking, seeing, and relating to the other is quite challenging, but it is also one of the most important tasks before us as we move deeper into the twenty-first century with its added racial complexities and persistent racial and class divisions.

As the Louisiana case has shown us, even in a community where people of color make up the majority, race, color, and class intertwine to continue to replicate entrenched inequalities. All indications are that we will continue to face these challenges across the United States whether we live in areas dominated by the Anglo-American racial system or those experiencing the more complex situation of overlapping racial systems. The difference will be in the tools we develop and deploy to manage and overcome these persistent inequalities. We must strive to forge tools that release us from the shackles that currently bind us, and that free us to imagine, think, and live in ways that promote a new vision of racial justice.

APPENDIX I

Notes on Methodology

The interview, archival, and observational data for *American Routes* were gathered in three waves, which can be described as preliminary, core, and supplementary. The sections that follow describe each stage and explain how the data gathered were brought together to create the narrative presented in the book.

PRELIMINARY STAGE: AUGUST 2003–JULY 2005

I moved to New Orleans in the summer of 2003 and began my position on August 1 in the sociology department of Loyola University–New Orleans. I arrived having recently completed a dissertation which examined contemporary Haitian immigrants' use of online forums for social networking and cultural identity expression. My move to New Orleans occurred during a propitious time—it was the bicentennial observance of the Louisiana Purchase of 1803 and the achievement of Haitian independence on January 1, 1804. I arrived, then, during a time when there was much discussion about the ties between Haiti and Louisiana.

It was also during the fall of 2003 that I learned that the Creole Studies Consortium—a partnership between Tulane University and Northwestern State University—would hold a conference entitled "Creole Legacies: The Current Status and Future Prospects of Creole Studies Research." This conference provided a wonderful introduction to the history and present of Louisiana Creoles. The talk that made the greatest impression on me and that helped to shape my project was the one by Wendy Gaudin. She discussed her work on Creoles of color and how they navigated the politics of racial segregation in the Jim Crow South. Overall, the tenor of her talk was quite positive, emphasizing the ways Creoles were able to subvert the worst indignities of segregation by maintaining their own network of community institutions and—when lightness of skin allowed—selectively engaging in situational passing in order to temporarily gain access to the privileges of whiteness. Gaudin's talk was followed by an intense and sometimes heated discussion among the Creole members of the audience who either questioned her account or pushed her to engage more deeply with the politics of color in their community. Observations from this conversation are reported in Chapter 6. That was the conversation where some participants drew a parallel between the experiences of Creoles of color and Hispanics in the United States—both groups felt out of place in the Anglo binary system that dominates the country. This was the beginning of my thinking about the parallels between these two groups.

The 2003 conference piqued my interest in learning more about Creoles of color. In the spring of 2004, I submitted an institutional review board application that would allow me to engage in participant observation with the Cajun/Creole discussion list. This list caught my attention when I was looking for online resources to understand Creole identity. I was also interested in observing discussion on that list because I had just finished a dissertation project which had shown me how effectively online discussion could be used for participants' exploration and expression of their cultural identity. In the earlier research I had studied the Rezo Entènet Kreyolis Aysiyen (REKA)—the Haitian Creole Internet Network. REKA was formed by a group of Haitian writers and intellectuals whose members were dispersed across the Americas, and who had a passion for the serious reading and study of scholarship and literature written in Haitian Creole. This part of my dissertation research had introduced me to the intricate politics of language and its many intersections with power, culture, and identity.

I spent the spring of 2004 monitoring discussion on the Cajun/Creole list, intermittently sending out a notice to the list that I was doing so. The list discussions provided a helpful entrée to the ways Creoles of color have experienced race in the United States. Many struggled to reconcile what it meant to be Creole with what it is to be black in the United States. Some of this discussion is presented in Chapter 6. After monitoring the group for several months, I conducted an online survey to learn more about the people on the list. Only twenty-three persons completed the survey, and it is unclear how many total members were on the list, so it is certainly not possible to say that the survey is representative of Cajun/

Creole members. These few surveys did, however, give me a place to start in learning more about the community. Survey results are provided in Appendix II.

My next step was selecting a subset of survey respondents with whom to conduct oral history interviews. I structured these in a way that focused on respondents' development of their racial and cultural identity over their lifetime. I began by asking each person to write down chapter titles that described each stage of their lives. Then, for each stage, I asked questions that helped to elicit their racial and cultural experience as members of the Creole community. Table A.1 is a list of Cajun/Creole interview respondents, presented as pseudonyms. I use pseudonyms because during this first group of interviews I had not yet developed a form that routinely asked respondents if they would prefer to use their true name or to have their name changed in published results. For the next two waves of data collection, I did this, and so I am able to provide true names for the majority of respondents. Though Table A.1 provides pseudonyms, it also includes useful information about the interviewees. There were two other interviews as well, but those respondents did not meet the criteria of being part of the Creole community. One was black but not Creole, and another was Trinidadian.

All of these were phone interviews because the respondents were spread out across the country. I recorded the interviews on cassette tape and also typed up summaries of their responses for each life chapter as they talked. I am extremely grateful that I have these typed summaries,

Table A.1 CAJUN/CREOLE INTERVIEWEES

Name	Age at Interview	Identification
Alexander	19	Black/Hispanic (later in interview describes his Creole heritage)
Diana	54	Not available
Stephanie	61	Black American-Creole ancestry
Allan	24	African American (has Creole heritage but does not feel he can make this public)
Nicholas	45	Black
Minette	23	Black and/or Creole depending on context
Rhon Barras*	31	Creole/African American
Terralyn	34	Black/Native American/Creole
Christopher	Not available	Black/Native American/French

*This is her real name. She is an exception to the rest of the Cajun/Creole interviews because she was also a St. Domingue descendant interviewee and agreed to have her true name used.

because as I report in the Acknowledgments, I had the traumatic experience in 2011 of having all of my interview cassette tapes and most of my paper documents soaked in water as our family drove from New Orleans up the coast to my sabbatical at the Institute for Advanced Study in Princeton. We started out under the literal cloud of a tropical storm, and the storm lingered over our car for the entire trip. When we got out for a stop at a hotel, just a day away from Princeton, I found the terrible water damage. My husband helped me to salvage the mess. At the time I prioritized saving the core interviews with St. Domingue descendants and did not focus on salvaging the Cajun/Creole interviews. It would not be clear to me for two more years that those Cajun/Creole interviews would also be of great use for telling the story that has unfolded in *American Routes*. By the time I turned back to these interviews, I was concerned about the fragile state of the cassettes and rather than risk destroying them entirely by trying to play them, I decided to rely on my written summaries instead. Although the summaries are not verbatim accounts, they are very faithful to what each respondent said because I typed as I listened rather than waiting until the end of an interview to write a summary. These summaries are therefore a running account of what respondents were saying as they were saying it.

During this preliminary period, I was also coming to know the members of the St. Domingue Special Interest Group (SIG)—a subset of the Jefferson Genealogical Society. This group, founded by Augusta Elmwood, helps members to trace their ancestry back to colonial St. Domingue. I began to attend these meetings because by late 2004 I had developed a preliminary focus on descendants of the Haitian Revolution whose ancestors had fled to Louisiana. This interest was first prompted by my chair at the time, Ed McCaughan, who had suggested that given my interest in Haiti I might want to explore the deep historical ties between Haiti and Louisiana. My time spent listening to Creoles of color had shown me that many were aware of the community's connections to Haiti. When I began to attend the SIG meetings, it was with the intent of finding members of African descent who were tracing their connection to revolutionary Haiti.

But, as I report in Chapter 1, the trajectory of the project was irrevocably changed by Mary Anne de Boisblanc's declaration of her forgiveness of Toussaint L'Ouverture for killing her white ancestors, and her apology for her ancestors' involvement with slavery. By the summer of 2005, I formally decided to engage in a comparative study of the white and black descendants of St. Domingue/Haiti.

CORE STAGE: INTERVIEWS AND OBSERVATIONS WITH ST. DOMINGUE/HAITI DESCENDANTS

August 2005–December 2011

I began this new stage of my research at the end of August 2005 by attending the LA Creole conference held that year. Just days later, Hurricane Katrina hit. This was devastating, on many levels. My family and I spent three months with family in New York City, waiting to see when and how we could return to New Orleans. We finally returned at the end of November.

In February 2006, the Historic New Orleans Collection (HNOC) moved forward with its *Common Routes* symposium and exhibit. This symposium consisted of a series of talks that examined the many historic connections between St. Domingue/Haiti and Louisiana. Before the symposium took place, I had arranged with John Lawrence, the director of museum programs at the HNOC, to have a small table where I would solicit interviewees for my project. I continue to be extremely grateful to him for working with me, for that symposium is where I gathered the bulk of the names of people who I would interview during this core stage of data collection.

Many people, black and white, came to visit my table, and I had nearly twenty names by the time the symposium was over. From there, I made calls and began to schedule interviews. I also told SIG and LA Creole members about my research and got several interviewees from those groups as well. During and after each interview I continually asked for recommendations of others I could interview. Several times I was able to make contact with respondent relatives who were also St. Domingue descendants so that I could include them in the study.

At this stage I carried out semistructured interviews that were focused on collecting information about respondents' ancestral connections to St. Domingue/Haiti. Each interview began with a question about how the respondent came to be interested in genealogical research and how he or she had begun to document the family connection to St. Domingue. Each interview also involved collecting information to fill in a family history tree going back as far as possible to the St. Domingue ancestors. Respondents varied in the level and kind of information they used to make the connection to St. Domingue. Some have extensive documentation that lies in local archives, while others have oral family history that connects their family to St. Domingue. As is to be expected given differences in power and privilege, white respondents tended to have the most extensive written documentation. When a respondent did have extensive documentation in local archives, I went to review that information and incorporated it into the study. Tables A.2 and A.3 list those interviewed during this core stage.

I had originally started this stage of data collection with the goal of creating a kind of dialogue between past and present where I would go back and forth between my respondents' lives today and their ancestors' lives in the nineteenth century. Very few respondents, however, had the kind of extensive archival documentation that would have allowed for this kind of temporal dialogue. Moreover, even in the case of those who did have extensive documentation, what was available in the archives did not lend itself to any kind of "dialogue" concerning issues of race, culture, and identity. In the end, I used archival data connected to my respondents mainly to describe their ancestors' fate during and after the revolution in St. Domingue. Documents connected to Jan Barry, Barry Navarre, and Jerry Gandolfo provided some of the most interesting and voluminous material for Chapter 3.

Table A.2 WHITE DESCENDANTS OF ST. DOMINGUE (19, TOTAL)

Name	Age at Interview	Interview Date
Jan Barry	57	March 2006
Eva Campos	43	April 2006
Loretta Capedeville Clark	87	February 2006
Richard C. (pseudonym)	68	March 2007
William Connick Jr.	67	March 2006
Alice C. Dixon-Dantro	59	May 2006
Mary Anne Pecot de Boisblanc	81	May 2006
Carolyn Feehan Dunn	Not available	February 2007
John C. Ellis	41	January 2006
Augusta B. Elmwood	59	October 2006
Gerald M. Gandolfo	54	March 2006
Lisa Ann Gourgues	53	May 2007
Michael L. (pseudonym)	42	February 2007
Harriet Hardin McCallum	65	December 2006
Renee Natell	51	October 2006
Barry Navarre	44	February 2006
Denise P. (pseudonym)	84	February 2007
Lydia Habliston Toso-Ozenberger	58	October 2007
Lois Willoz	57	September 2007

Table A.3 ST. DOMINGUE DESCENDANTS OF COLOR (21, TOTAL)

Name	Age at Interview	Interview Date
Harold Baquet	52	July 2010
Rhon Barras	32	June 2006
Annalise (pseudonym)	Not available	October 2007
Naydja Domingue Bynum	Not available	May 2006
Lolita Villavasso Cherrie	62	March 2008
Carla Cormier-Long	51	June 2006
Joan Dubrey-Ducre	58	March 2008
Ronald Dumas	45	October 2006
Amelie Durant (pseudonym)	66	September 2006
Velva Flot	66	May 2007
Gregory Osborn	42	July 2008
Percy Pierre	72	August 2011
Celine (pseudonym)	38	November 2006
Jacob Plique	54	February 2006
Mark Roudané	57	July 2008
Laura Rouzan	66	April 2006
Pat Schexnayder	64	March 2008
Barbara Trevigne	59	February 2006
Christina (pseudonym)	73	September 2010
Barbara Trevigne	59	February 2006
Naurine V. White	Not available	February 2007
Melanie (pseudonym for a person listed above)*	NA	NA
Amy (pseudonym for a person listed above)*	NA	NA

*In this case, although the respondent gave permission for me to use their true name, there were certain sensitive parts of the interview that they preferred not to have their names associated with, usually in order to protect other members of the family who were not comfortable with having their ancestry of color made known.

Supplementary Stage: 2013–2014

By 2010, I had collected what I thought were the final data for writing *American Routes*. The timing was good because I was eligible for a year-long sabbatical beginning in August 2011. I spent part of the 2010–2011 academic year visiting archives to examine the documentation of my interviewees whose ancestors had left extensive records. I then spent the 2011–2012 academic year writing the first few chapters of the book. When I returned from sabbatical in the fall of 2012, I continued writing but began to sense that I was missing a key segment of material to fill out the account of the Creole descendants of the St. Domingue refugees. This gap was most acute with the white respondents. As I went back to look at how they related to the idea of being Creole, I found that only nine of the nineteen had *any* connection at all to a Creole or even a French identity when they were growing up. Many had found the connection only as a result of doing their family history research. I realized then that I was seeing the effects of relatively thorough Anglo-American assimilation. This was when I decided that I needed to document the other part of the story—white Louisianans whose families had not fully assimilated and thus had not lost a self-conscious connection to their Creole roots.

The difficulty, however, was in locating white Louisianans who would be willing to identify publicly as Creole. I began by asking white St. Domingue interviewees who I knew to be comfortable with their Creole identity. Jan Barry was most receptive to this request, and I am indebted to her for helping me to find some of the persons interviewed during this stage. She agreed to circulate a call for new interviewees who also had Creole heritage. I worded this call very carefully, asking for white Louisianans who knew about and identified with their Creole heritage. Although the difference is slight, I refrained from asking to interview "white Creoles" and instead asked for those with "Creole heritage," This is because while few white Louisianans identify as Creoles, there are many who embrace their Creole ancestry going back to some of the early families of New Orleans. Sally Reeves, an expert on New Orleans history, was also indispensable in helping me to contact many of those who I successfully interviewed. I was eventually able to locate seven people who were willing to do the oral history. Although the number is small, these were very extensive interviews lasting 2–3 hours and they produced wonderfully rich and detailed material. Table A.4 lists those interviewed for this section of the study. The interview guide for these oral histories is included in Appendix IV.

Table A.4 ORAL HISTORIES WITH WHITE LOUISIANANS WITH CREOLE HERITAGE

Name	Age at Interview	Interview Date
Anne Bachman	56	January 2013
Angelique Bergeron	35	February 2013
Dorothy Carter	52	January 2013
Julie Livaudais	60	July 2014
Norman Marmillion	67	January 2013
Marcel Saussy	75	July 2014
Jeanne Williams	62	July 2014

Although I did not have the same problem with my St. Domingue descendants of color because most of them actively identified as Creole, I realized that the St. Domingue–Haiti interview instrument had not sufficiently emphasized the emergence and development of those respondents' racial and ethnic identities as these changed over time. The Cajun/Creole interviews were the perfect source of data for this focus on race and Creole identity because I had structured them as oral histories centered on identity formation. I thus made these interviews the oral history counterpart of the supplementary interviews I did with white Louisianans of Creole heritage.

It was also during this final supplementary stage that I decided to do the *Times-Picayune* newspaper analysis to see how Creoles have been portrayed in the public imagination. The results reported in Chapter 5 confirmed what I had found in my historical study: white Creoles had ceased to exist publicly. Where they were mentioned, it was always during or before the nineteenth century. Creoles of color, in contrast, were liberally represented as present-day members of the community.

MY SOCIAL AND CULTURAL LOCATION AS RESEARCHER

I am an outsider in just about every way when it comes to this research. I am an African American woman and am originally from Miami, Florida. I have no family connections to Louisiana or to Louisiana Creoles. When I moved to New Orleans in 2003, everything about Creoles was new to me. At that point, I had an understanding of Creoles very similar to that of the majority of persons in the country. I assumed that they were people of color of African descent and that there was no such thing as a white Creole. I also had a sense, by 2004, that there was a lot of tension surrounding the idea of being Creole. All of this was new to me as well. When I would mention to Anglo–African Americans what I was doing, many reacted negatively. As I got to the bottom of their reactions, I saw that Creoles were generally understood to be light-skinned persons who tried their best to distance themselves from the larger black community.

But then, as I came to know Creoles of color personally, as I went to their conferences and conducted interviews with them, I began to see that the reality was much more nuanced than many Anglo-black Americans understood. Given the fact that I am African American with chocolate-colored skin, certainly my Creole respondents of color would have been unlikely to tell me that they thought Creoles were of higher status than black Americans. Still, however, I overheard conversations that highlighted sensitivities to color in the Creole community and encountered some who I would describe as Creole cultural activists who were very determined to make a distinction between black Americans and Creoles. On the whole, however, I found that many Creoles of color thought of themselves as both black and Creole. The discussion in Chapter 6 reports on the variability I found in this community and helps to document the complexity of issues surrounding race and identity among Creoles of color.

My position as a black interviewer took on an entirely different significance when I interviewed white respondents. Many were good enough to invite me into their homes, and I could see in the aged portraits on the walls how deeply rooted they were in their ancestral history. The interview instrument used for the core interviews with St. Domingue descendants included sensitive questions about ancestors' racial status, their status as free or enslaved, and the kinds of property—including enslaved persons—that their ancestors owned. The specific questions asked are included in Appendix III. There were certainly pauses of discomfort in some cases, and I did my best to set respondents at ease. My position was not to make judgments, but rather to capture as well as possible the essence of the historical period I was researching. Although there was some discomfort around certain questions, on the whole these interviews went smoothly and well.

Finally, I had to think carefully about how I would present the data I collected. Unlike many researchers who do not live in the place where they carry out fieldwork and interviews, I live in New Orleans and expect to be here for many years to come. As this project has made clear, the issues surrounding what it means to be "Creole" are contentious and potentially explosive. As anyone who lives in New Orleans knows, this may be a city, but it feels and operates like a small town. Everyone is connected to everyone. I had no interest, therefore, in creating sensationalistic or insensitive portraits of the persons who were good enough to speak with me. My rootedness here, and my investment in being here for the long term, meant that I took great care to listen carefully and deeply and to produce as balanced an account as I possibly could. I took issues of confidentiality very seriously and gave every respondent the option of having a pseudonym for the published results. The vast majority, however, opted to use their true names. It is my hope that I have produced an account of the St. Domingue refugees and their Creole descendants that will shatter stereotypes and increase our understanding of the complex and beautiful social and cultural landscape that is southern Louisiana.

APPENDIX II

Cajun/Creole Survey Results

Note: All results presented here are based on twenty-three completed and returned surveys.

Sex
  Female: 14
  Male: 9

Age
  18–24 years: 6
  25–30 years: 5
  31–40 years: 6
  41–50 years: 2
  51–60 years: 2
  61–70 years: 2

Highest Level of Education Completed
  Less than high school   1
  High school   5
  Some college   2
  Associate's or technical 3
  Bachelor's degree   6
  Master's degree   3
  Doctoral degree   3

Country of Origin
  United States   20
  Ghana   1
  Trinidad   1
  Italy   1

Current Geographic Location

Louisiana	5
Texas	5
California	3
Mississippi	2
New York	2
Washington, DC	1
Oklahoma	1
Georgia	1
Illinois	1
New Jersey	1
Italy	1

Ethnic/Racial Identification: (Please note that there were no predetermined categories to choose from on the survey. Each respondent created his or her own description.)

Black/Creole or African American/Creole	7
Black or African American	5
Black/Native American/Creole	1
Black/Native American/French	1
Creole	1
Black/Hispanic	1
African American/Cajun	1
White	1
White/Cajun	1
White/Black	1
Hispanic	1
Italian	1
African	1

CREOLE-RELATED ORGANIZATIONS THAT MEMBERS SUPPORT

Note: Where available, the organizational website is included for easy reference and further information.

Creole Heritage Education and Research Society (C.H.E.R.S.): http://www.creolehistory.com/
Creole Preservation Society
St. Augustine Historical Society
Louisiana to Los Angeles Festival
Louisiana Creole Heritage Center: http://www.nsula.edu/creole/

CREOLE-RELATED WEBSITES FREQUENTLY VISITED BY MEMBERS

Frenchcreoles.com
Creolehistory.com
Cajun.net
Zouker.com
Gumbo LaLa (http://cat.xula.edu/gumbo/index.html)
Gazette Asteur (http://www.asteur.org/)
Louisiana Creole Heritage Center (http://www.nsula.edu/creole/)
Creole People (http://groups.yahoo.com/group/creolepeople/)
New Orleans Gens de Couleur-NOGDCR (http://groups.yahoo.com/group/NOGDCR/)
Cajun/Creole (http://groups.yahoo.com/group/cajuncreole/)
RadioLouisiane.com
Rounder Records (http://www.rounder.com/index.php?id=genres.php)

WHAT MEMBERS LIKE BEST ABOUT CAJUN/CREOLE

Learning More about Cajun/Creole Culture

"[I like] to learn more about my heritage and to revive the language of . . . my family.

[I] wasn't reared with much knowledge of my heritage; this site enlightens me on the way of my people." (Survey #11)

"[I like] to learn about an interesting, romantic, lovely, and unique culture and how I can preserve it. " (Survey #5)

"[It is] interesting to see the interest in LA Creole culture and learn about new websites and information every once in a while." (Survey #21)

Finding Others Who Share Their Background and Understand Them

"[I like] to connect and communicate with people of a similar background and upbringing as my own. This forum lets me know that I am not alone and that there are other people like me that I can share information." (Survey #7)

"I love interacting with people that understand who I am and don't expect me to apologize for it or make me feel ashamed of my culture." (Survey #8)

"There are people just like me out there. I get to learn about them while they learn about me and sometimes you get to see how [our] family lines cross each other." (Survey #9)

WHAT MEMBERS WOULD LIKE TO SEE MORE OF ON CAJUN/CREOLE

More Practice and/or Teaching of Louisiana Creole

"I would like to practice reading and writing the language. . . . Most importantly I want knowledge of how I can apply my love of the culture and the language to my life." (Survey #5)

"I think the Creole community needs to go back to the beginning and we should not have ever let [our] language fade away . . . I would like for there to be a language session. Or a day where those few who still speak Creole teach others how to speak it so we can revive our ancestors language." (Survey #9)

APPENDIX III

St. Domingue/Haiti-Louisiana Interview Instrument

Knowledge of St. Domingue/Haiti Family History

1) Please tell me how you became interested in researching your family history from St. Domingue/Haiti.
2) On the survey, in response to the question: "Where have you obtained your knowledge of your family history ties to St. Domingue/Haiti? Check as many as apply," you answered:

   _____Your own research
   _____Research done by other family members
   _____Stories passed down in your family
   _____Other (please specify)

   Please tell me more about what you learned of your family history from each of these sources.
3) On the survey, in response to the question: "On a scale of 1 to 10, how would you rate your knowledge of your ancestry in St. Domingue/Haiti?" you answered:

   On this scale, 1 means "very little" and 10 means "a great deal."

   Very Little

   1___
   2___
   3___
   4___

5___
6___
7___
8___
9___
10___

A Great Deal

Please tell me as much as you can about what you know of your family's connection to St. Domingue/Haiti.

4) Which parts of this history have you been able to document with written records?

Historical Relationship Between St. Domingue/Haiti and Louisiana

5) On the survey, in response to the question "On a scale of 1 to 10, how would you rate your knowledge of the events of the revolution in St. Domingue/Haiti?" you answered:

On this scale, 1 means "very little" and 10 means "a great deal."

Very Little

1___
2___
3___
4___
5___
6___
7___
8___
9___
10___

A Great Deal

Please tell me as much as you can about what you know concerning the revolution in Haiti.

6) On the survey, in response to the question: "On a scale of 1 to 10, how would you rate your knowledge of the significance of the revolution in St. Domingue/Haiti for Louisiana history and culture?" you answered:

On this scale, 1 means "very little" and 10 means "a great deal."

Very Little

1___
2___
3___
4___
5___
6___
7___
8___
9___
10___

A Great Deal

Please tell me as much as you can about how the revolution in St. Domingue/Haiti affected the history and culture of Louisiana.

7) How do you think the revolution in St. Domingue/Haiti affected the history and culture of New Orleans?

8) On the survey, in response to the question: "Where have you obtained your knowledge of the significance of the revolution in St. Domingue/Haiti for Louisiana history and culture? Check as many as apply," you answered:
_____Your own reading and/or research
_____Formal classes at an educational institution
_____Community events, exhibits, or forums
_____Informal discussion with friends or family
_____Other (please specify)

Please tell me more about what you learned from each and why you decided to participate in that activity.

9) Do you know anything about how your ancestors were involved in or affected by the revolution in Haiti?

   _____Yes

   _____No (if no, go to question # 12)

10) Please tell me what you know about how your ancestors were involved in or affected by the revolution.

11) What are your sources of information concerning your ancestors' activities during the revolution in Haiti?

    _____Your own research

    _____Research done by other family members

    _____Stories passed down in your family

    _____Other (please specify)

Connections Between the Past and the Present

12) On a scale of 0 to 10, how much would you say the past influence of St. Domingue/Haiti affects the society and culture of present-day Louisiana?

    Not at all

    0___
    1___
    2___
    3___
    4___
    5___
    6___
    7___
    8___
    9___
    10___

    A Great Deal

13) On a scale of 0 to 10, how much would you say the past influence of St. Domingue/Haiti affects the society and culture of present-day New Orleans?

    Not at all

    0___
    1___

2____
3____
4____
5____
6____
7____
8____
9____
10____

A Great Deal

14) When you consider how your ancestors may have been affected by the revolution in Haiti, how do you think their experiences and decisions shaped the generations of your family descended from those ancestors?

15) To the best of your knowledge, which of the following best expresses the social status of your ancestors from St. Domingue before the revolution? (check as many as apply)

_____ enslaved
_____ free people of color
_____ free whites
_____ property owner (specify what kind)
_____ other (please specify)

16) What sources of information have you used to determine the social status of your ancestors from St. Domingue before the revolution?

_____
_____
_____

17) Does the social status of your ancestors in St. Domingue affect the way you think about your family's past or present?

18) How do you think the social status of your family in St. Domingue before the revolution affected your family's social status for the generations descended from those ancestors?

Now I'm going to ask you some questions about your views concerning the relationship of the past to the present.

19) Consider the following statement:

Researching my family history has helped me to better understand my racial and ethnic background.

To what extent do you agree with this statement?
___strongly agree
___agree
___disagree
___strongly disagree

Please explain why you answer as you do.

20) Consider the following statement:

Researching my family history has helped me to better understand people from racial and ethnic groups other than my own.

To what extent do you agree with this statement?
___strongly agree
___agree
___disagree
___strongly disagree

Please explain why you answer as you do.

21) Consider the following statement:

"It is better not to think or speak too much about past social inequalities like race and class because this contributes to continued social divisions today."

To what extent do you agree with this statement?
___strongly agree
___agree
___disagree
___strongly disagree

22) **Question discontinued**

Consider the following statement: "It is better not to think or speak too much about past racial inequalities because this contributes to continued racial divisions today."

Now I'm interested in knowing something about your knowledge of present-day Haiti.

23) On a scale of 0 to 10, how much do you know about present-day Haiti?

Nothing at all

Appendix III (231)

0___
1___
2___
3___
4___
5___
6___
7___
8___
9___
10___

A Great Deal

24) Through which of the following sources have you obtained your knowledge about present-day Haiti: (check as many as apply)

_____ newspapers or magazines
_____ television news
_____ films or documentaries
_____ nonfiction books
_____ novels or short stories
_____ Internet websites or forums
_____ formal classes at an educational institution
_____ public events or exhibits
_____ informal discussion with friends or family
_____ other (please specify)

25) Of the sources you mentioned above, tell me which three you rely upon the most.

(Rank these in descending order)

_____
_____
_____

26) On a scale of 0 to 10, to what extent does your family's past connection to St. Domingue/Haiti affect your interest in present-day Haiti?

Not at all

0___
1___
2___
3___

4____
5____
6____
7____
8____
9____
10____

A Great Deal

27) Have you ever been involved in any group, association, or project related to Haiti?
    _____ Yes
    _____ No (skip to question #30)
28) Please tell me what the group(s) was/were and how you were involved.
    _____
    _____
    _____
29) Are you still involved in this group(s)?
    ____Yes
    ____No
30) Have you ever traveled to Haiti?
    ____Yes
    ____No (skip to question #32)
31) Please tell me when you traveled to Haiti and what you did while you were there.

(skip to question #35)

32) Do you have any interest in traveling to Haiti?
    ____Yes
    ____No (skip to question #35)
33) Why are you interested in going to Haiti?
34) When would you like to go to Haiti and what would you like to do when you get there?
35) On the survey, in response to the question: Please list the organizations to which you belong or events in which you participate where the focus is on:

    "Researching your family history AND/OR Appreciating your cultural heritage" you answered:

Please tell me more about your involvement in each of these.

36) On the survey, in answer to the question: "Please list any Internet sites or forums that you visit or belong to where the focus is on: Researching your family history AND/OR Appreciating your cultural heritage" you answered:

Please tell me how often you visit these sites, and why you like to visit each of them.

37) Has Hurricane Katrina affected your family history research? If yes, please explain.
38) Has Hurricane Katrina affected the way you think about your family history research? If yes, please explain.

APPENDIX IV

---ᴄᴧᴐ---

Creole Oral History Guide

The guide shown here provides a general outline for the kinds of questions to be asked in the oral history interviews. The topics provide a flexible guideline, but interviews may go in different directions depending on the subject's responses and life experiences.

- **Write an Outline of the Major Chapters in Your Life**
  - Give subject about 5 minutes to do this. Ask the subject to organize his or her life into chapters and provide a title or description for each chapter, as if writing a book about his or her life.
- **Family History**
  - Family tree as far back as can remember (name parents, grandparents, and so on for both sides of family)
  - Race, ethnicity of past family members
  - Stories heard about past family members growing up
  - Descriptions of family members personally known to subject
- **Local Geography at Each Life Stage**
  - Address where lived, if possible
  - Draw a map of your block/neighborhood; label as much as possible
  - Description of house inside and outside
  - Description of neighborhood
  - Racial, ethnic composition of neighborhood
  - Keeping of garden, farm, or livestock used for food (if yes, describe location of garden/farm, foods/animals raised, how used, why maintained)
- **Recreation at Each Life Stage**
  - Games played as a child

- Activities for fun as young adult
- Entertainment and social life in adulthood (e.g., film, dinner parties, family events, frequency of activities, etc.)

- **Family and Cultural Practices**
  - Types of food served or prepared on average day
  - Favorite foods
  - Foods subject associated with Creole community and culture
  - Celebration of holidays (which holidays observed; specific traditions; foods served; etc.)
  - Languages spoken
  - Funeral practices (e.g., location, traditions, etc; how these have changed over time, if at all within Creole community)
  - Wedding practices (e.g., location, traditions, etc.; how these have changed over time within Creole community)
  - Family reunions held? (If yes, describe how often and what is done)
  - Family heirlooms or scrapbooks (If yes, describe significance of these)
  - Baptism, First Communion, other significant religious events (e.g., location, traditions, etc; how these have changed over time, if at all, within Creole community)
  - Other social or cultural traditions important within Creole communities you have been part of

- **Community Life Outside of Household at Each Life Stage**
  - Participation in social or cultural events within church or religious community
  - Participation in holiday activities or festivals in neighborhood, town, or city
  - Sense of community within neighborhood (describe relationship with neighbors; social events; etc.)

- **Personal Identity**
  - Racial/ethnic identification (Has this changed over time? If so, how and why?)
  - Difficulties embracing or accepting this identity at any time? (If yes, explain why and provide examples or anecdotes to illustrate)

- **Hobbies at Each Life Stage**
  - Activities done for fun or skills pursued at amateur level (e.g., painting, music, reading, crocheting, gardening, etc.)
  - How introduced to activity or became interested in it
  - Social context within which practiced (e.g., in a group, alone, single sex, etc.)

- **Courtship and Marriage**
  - Dating or courtship practices

- Story of how met and came to marry spouse
- Stories passed down in family of how earlier family members courted, married
- **Education at Each Life Stage**
  - Name of educational institution
  - Dates attended each institution
  - Description of school (approx. number of students, physical appearance, racial/ethnic composition, sex composition, religious or nonreligious; etc.)
  - Teachers subject still remembers and why
  - General experience with school (e.g., tenor and quality of social relationships in terms of race, ethnicity, sex; subjects most enjoyed; quality of education, etc.)
  - At advanced levels, course(s) of study chosen and why
- **Childrearing Practices**
  - For subject, how parents raised him/her (e.g., discipline, chores, allowance, etc.)
  - For subject how raised own children and why (e.g., discipline, chores, allowance, etc.)
- **Work Experience at Each Life Stage**
  - Age when started
  - How got into the work or job, where/how learned skills for job
  - Type of work done (describe special tools or processes if these are relevant)
  - General experience and/or satisfaction with the work
- **Significant Historical Events**
  - How was subject impacted by significant events he/she lived through (e.g., WWI; WWII; assassinations of Kennedy, King; September 11th; etc.)

NOTES

INTRODUCTION

1. For the epigraph source, see Clarence Edwin Carter, ed., *The Territorial Papers of the United States, Vol. IX, The Territory of Orleans, 1803–1812* (Washington, DC: US Government Printing Office, 1940), 841–842.
2. The Territory of Orleans was the original name of what became the state of Louisiana.
3. See the following for examples of this kind of implicit or explicit reference to past European immigrants when discussing current immigrants of color: Joel Perlmann, *Italians Then, Mexicans Now: Immigrant Origins and Second-Generation Progress, 1890–Present* (New York: Russell Sage Foundation, 2005), 205; Roger Waldinger and Joel Perlmann, "Second Generations: Past, Present and Future," *Journal of Ethnic and Migration Studies* 24, no. 1 (1998): 5–24; Alejandro Portes and Ruben Rumbaut, "Introduction: The Second Generation and the Children of Immigrants Longitudinal Study," *Ethnic and Racial Studies* 28, no. 6 (2005): 983–999; Ruben Rumbaut, "The Crucible Within: Ethnic Identity, Self-Esteem, and Segmented Assimilation among Children of Immigrants," *International Migration Review* 28, no. 4 (1994): 748–794.
4. See the following on the ways different European groups went through the process of becoming "white" according to US standards: Noel Ignatiev, *How the Irish Became White* (New York: Routledge, 1995); Karen Brodkin, *How the Jews Became White Folks & What That Says about Race in America* (New Brunswick, NJ: Rutgers University Press, 1998); Matthew Frye Jacobson, *Whiteness of a Different Color: European Immigrants and the Alchemy of Race* (Cambridge, MA: Harvard University Press, 1999); David R. Roediger, *Working Toward Whiteness: How America's Immigrants Became White* (New York: Basic Books, 2005).
5. See the following for scholars who make this argument: Vilna Bashi Treitler, "Social Agency and White Supremacy in Immigration Studies," *Sociology of Race and Ethnicity* 1, no. 1 (2015): 153–165; Rogelio Sáenz and Karen Manges Douglas, "A Call for the Racialization of Immigration Studies: On the Transition of Ethnic Immigrants to Racialized Immigrants," *Sociology of Race and Ethnicity* 1, no. 1 (2015): 166–180; Joe R. Feagin and José Cobas, *Latinos Facing Racism: Discrimination, Resistance, and Endurance* (Boulder, CO: Paradigm Publishers, 2014).
6. Sáenz and Douglas, "A Call for the Racialization of Immigration Studies," 167.
7. Segmented assimilation theorists have attempted to integrate race into their models, but with limited effectiveness. Segmented assimilation is a concept that

is meant to acknowledge that immigrants of color may not blend into the US mainstream. According to segmented assimilation theorists, immigrants take one of three paths: blend into the mainstream while mostly shedding their ethnic distinctiveness; keep their ethnic distinctiveness as a resource to help them cope with the challenges of integration; or assimilate to the social and economic margins of the United States, sharing the lot of lower income African Americans and others who have been unable to enter the middle-class mainstream.

For early statements on segmented assimilation, see Alejandro Portes and Min Zhou, "The New Second Generation: Segmented Assimilation and Its Variants," *The Annals of the American Academy of Political and Social Science* 530 (1993): 74–96, and Min Zhou, "Segmented Assimilation: Issues, Controversies, and Recent Research on the New Second Generation," *International Migration Review* 31, no. 4 (1997): 975–1008; Rubén Rumbaut, "Assimilation and Its Discontents: Between Rhetoric and Reality," *International Migration Review* 31, no. 4 (1997): 923–960.

8. US Census 2010 American Community Survey.
9. See, for instance, the discussion of the different racial schemas immigrants from the Hispanic Caribbean bring with them to the United States, and the ways they use these schemas in different contexts as they negotiate the racial terrain in the United States in Wendy Roth, *Race Migrations: Latinos and the Cultural Transformation of Race* (Stanford, CA: Stanford University Press, 2012).
10. These figures come from an American Community Survey Brief by Yesenia D. Acosta and G. Patricia de la Cruz, "The Foreign Born from Latin America and the Caribbean: 2010" (September 2011), accessed June 3, 2016, http://www.census.gov/prod/2011pubs/acsbr10-15.pdf.
11. US Census Quick Facts 2013, accessed July 30, 2015, http://quickfacts.census.gov/qfd/index.html.
12. For more work on the idea of an emerging black/nonblack color line, see Frank D. Bean, Jennifer Lee and James D. Bachmeier, "Immigration and the Color Line at the Beginning of the Twenty-First Century," *Daedalus* 142, no. 3 (2013): 123–140. In addition to this, also see a large stream of work in a similar vein by the same authors: Jennifer Lee and Frank D. Bean, *The Diversity Paradox: Immigration and the Color Line in Twenty-First Century America* (New York: Russel Sage, 2010); Jennifer Lee and Frank D. Bean, "Reinventing the Color Line: Immigration and America's New Racial/Ethnic Divide," *Social Forces* 86, no. 2 (2007): 561–586; Jennifer Lee and Frank D. Bean, "America's Changing Color Lines: Immigration, Race/Ethnicity and Multiracial Identification," *Annual Review of Sociology* 30 (2004): 221–242.

For work on the emergence of a triracial system, see Eduardo Bonilla-Silva, "We Are All Americans! The Latin Americanization of Racial Stratification in the U.S.A.," *Race and Society* 5 (2002): 3–16.
13. For some examples of how today's immigrants are resisting the Anglo-American racial system, see Jessica M. Vasquez, "The Whitening Hypothesis Challenged: Biculturalism in Latino and Non-Hispanic White Intermarriage," *Sociological Forum* 29, no. 2 (2014): 386–407; Tanya Golash-Boza and William Darity Jr., "Latino Racial Choices: The Effects of Skin Colour and Discrimination on Latinos' and Latinas' Racial Self-Identifications," *Ethnic and Racial Studies* 31, no. 5 (2008): 899–934; Sonya M. Tafoya, "Shades of Belonging: Latinos and Racial Identity," *Harvard Journal of Hispanic Policy* 17 (2004/2005): 58–78; John R. Logan, "How Race Counts for Hispanic Americans," Lewis Mumford Center for Comparative Urban and Regional Research, University at Albany, July 14, 2003,

accessed April 16, 2016, http://mumford.albany.edu/census/BlackLatinoReport/BlackLatinoReport.pdf.
14. Table adapted from Paul La Chance, "The 1809 Immigration of Saint-Domingue Refugees to New Orleans: Reception, Integration, and Impact," in *The Road to Louisiana: The Saint-Domingue Refugees 1792–1809*, eds. Carl A. Brasseaux and Glenn R. Conrad (Lafayette, LA: The Center for Louisiana Studies, 1992), 247.
15. While there were populations of free people of color in other US cities, they were nowhere as large a percentage of the population as they had been in colonial St. Domingue, and they did not exercise a comparable amount of political power. Chapter 1 will provide a comparison of the free people of color populations in the United States and other parts of the Americas.
16. This image is courtesy of the Cornell University Library, "Making of America" Digital Collection.
17. Jerah Johnson, *Congo Square in New Orleans* (New Orleans: Louisiana Landmarks Society, 2011), 36.
18. Ibid.
19. It must be acknowledged, however, that whereas white Creoles were more accustomed to this reality, this did not always mean that they liked it. In colonial St. Domingue, for instance, there were tensions between petty bourgeois whites and free people of color because they sometimes competed for the same occupational positions as overseers on plantations. In addition, as free people of color grew in wealth and prominence in St. Domingue, white Creoles grew more resentful of their success. Despite these issues, however, it is still fair to say that white Creoles were less shocked and horrified by the presence and flourishing of free people of color than were the Americans who had no experience dealing with such a group of racially subordinate yet social and economically empowered people.
20. Many thanks to Ed McCaughan who was my chair at that time and made the excellent suggestion that led to the creation of this book.
21. Throughout the book the term "Anglo-black" or "Anglo–African American" is used when referring to black Louisianans who have Anglo rather than Creole heritage. These terms are also used interchangeably with "black" or "African American." The "Anglo" qualifier is used to provide a contrast to the history and experience of Creoles of African descent.
22. I would like to have had more oral histories with white Creoles, but because of the racial controversies surrounding the idea of being Creole, it is somewhat difficult to find white Louisianans who will publicly identify as having Creole heritage. That said, the seven oral histories were combined with nine St. Domingue descendant interviewees who were aware of their Creole heritage to provide sixteen in-depth accounts to illustrate this population's struggles with the Anglo-American racial system.
23. For a fuller discussion of the study's methods, see the Methodological Appendix.
24. See R. L. Desdunes, "A Few Words to Dr. DuBois with Malice Toward None," March 1907, 13. The Amistad Research Center A. P. Tureaud Collection, Box 77, Folder 38.

CHAPTER 1

1. Darryl Fears, "People of Color Who Never Felt They Were Black: Racial Label Surprises Many Latino Immigrants," *The Washington Post*, December 26, 2002, accessed February 10, 2016, https://www.washingtonpost.com/archive/politics/

2002/12/26/people-of-color-who-never-felt-they-were-black/071e165f-48b7-4aaa-9d86-23e907cfbc7f/.
2. Given the scope of the discussion to follow, which ranges from the mid-sixteenth through the nineteenth century, the discussion is necessarily a comparative summary that highlights major transitions in the Anglo-American and Latin/Caribbean racial systems. It is not, therefore, a comprehensive analysis. This relatively brief comparative-historical discussion is necessary, however, for clarifying the historical foundations and current characteristics of the two racial systems.
3. Mara Loveman, *National Colors: Racial Classification and the State in Latin America* (New York: Oxford University Press, 2014), 68.
4. Charles Mills, *The Racial Contract* (Ithaca, NY: Cornell University Press, 1997), 11.
5. "Exclusive access" here should be understood as de facto rather than de jure access to full membership rights. Although all persons may legally be entitled to be treated equally, the historical record as well as current events continue to demonstrate that what one is legally entitled to does not overlap neatly with what one actually experiences.
6. Lourdes Martinez-Echazabal, "Mestizaje and the Discourse of National/Cultural Identity in Latin America: 1845–1959," *Latin American Perspectives* 25, no. 3 (1998): 28.
7. Loveman, *National Colors*, 148.
8. Edward Telles, *Race in Another America: The Significance of Skin Color in Brazil* (Princeton, NJ: Princeton University Press, 2004), 26.
9. Ibid., 27.
10. Loveman, *National Colors*, 125.
11. Ariela Gross and Alejandro de la Fuente, "Slaves, Free Blacks, and Race in the Legal Regimes of Cuba, Louisiana and Virginia: A Comparison," *North Carolina Law Review* 91, no. 5 (2013): 1750.
12. Laura Foner, "The Free People of Color in Louisiana and St. Domingue: A Comparative Portrait of Two Three-Caste Slave Societies," *Journal of Social History* 3, no. 4 (1970): 415.
13. Edward Telles and René Flores, "Not Just Color: Whiteness, Nation and Status in Latin America," *Hispanic American Historical Review* 93, no. 3 (2013): 416.
14. Although there was internal debate among intellectuals about the social effects of race mixture—with some embracing racially determinist views which saw it as a problem which held their countries back—the majority who prevailed argued forcefully that race mixture brought positive social development and a generally whiter population. For more on this debate, see Loveman, *National Colors*, 128–132.
15. Loveman, *National Colors*, 131.
16. Michael Omi and Howard Winant, *Racial Formation in the United States*, 4th ed. (New York: Routledge, 2015), 56.
17. Telles, *Race in Another America*, 28.
18. Loveman, *National Colors*, 155.
19. Mara Loveman, "Whiteness in Latin America: Measurement and Meaning in National Censuses," *Journal de la Société des Américanistes* 95, no. 2 (2009): 221.
20. Martinez-Echazabal, "Mestizaje and the Discourse of National/Cultural Identity in Latin America," 34.
21. Ibid., 33.
22. Loveman, *National Colors*, 232.
23. Telles and Flores, "Not Just Color," 418.

Notes (243)

24. Gilberto Freyre, *The Masters and the Slaves: A Study in the Development of Brazilian Civilization*, 2nd English language edition, revised, trans. Samuel Putnam (New York: Alfred A. Knopf, 1956), 278.
25. Telles, *Race in Another America*, 5.
26. I must be careful to note here that the embrace of African ancestry is *not* a defining characteristic of racial systems across all of Latin America and the Caribbean. The Dominican Republic, for instance, has developed a national understanding that depends on a negative contrast with Haiti. Haiti is seen as black and African, whereas the Dominican Republic is, in many ways, constructed as being non-Haitian. In this sense, neither blackness nor Africanness is embraced even at the ideological level. Even in this strong case where blackness is explicitly excised from national understanding, having visible black ancestry is not a problem because "blackness" is not based simply on having African ancestry. Instead, there are a variety of racial categories between black and white to which a person with African ancestry might belong without being categorized as "black." Here, as across much of Latin America and the Caribbean, categorization based on appearance allows for a good deal of flexibility.
27. Telles and Flores, "Not Just Color," 416.
28. I noted with a good deal of interest and surprise that some of my white interviewees were nervous about the idea that they might have had a black ancestor in just *one* of their family lines as far back as two hundred years ago. What if they had? Even with the US history of the "one-drop rule," someone with an African ancestor in 1804 would still be considered white today given the fact that the African connection was so long ago and the family history is overwhelmingly white. And yet this self-consciousness remains. Part of the reason for the concern could possibly lie in the fact that nonwhite racial heritage could still bring negative social outcomes today for a white person who has an interest in joining elite organizations that are based on proving one's genealogical connection to early founders of the United States or of various states and cities in the United States (e.g., Daughters of the American Revolution). To the extent that the gatekeepers of such organizations continue to care about "pure" white ancestry, there is indeed cause for concern if one has documented nonwhite ancestors and yet desires entrance into such an exclusive group. Although some of these elite organizations do allow black members who can prove their connection to relevant historical events and figures, many white Americans of elite background continue to harbor concerns with the idea of being publicly connected to African ancestors—particularly if these ancestors were enslaved.
29. For more on the history of the one-drop rule in the United States, see F. James Davis, *Who Is Black? One Nation's Definition* (University Park: The Pennsylvania State University Press, 1991).
30. Frank Tannenbaum, *Slave and Citizen: The Negro in the Americas* (New York: Vintage Books, 1946).
31. See the following for some authors critical of Tannenbaum's thesis: James Sweet, "The Iberian Roots of American Racist Thought," *The William and Mary Quarterly* 44, no.1 (1997): 143–166; David Rankin, "The Tannenbaum Thesis Reconsidered: Slavery and Race Relations in Antebellum Louisiana," *Southern Studies* 18, no. 1 (1979): 5–31; Donald G. Eder, "Time under the Southern Cross: The Tannenbaum Thesis Reappraised," *Agricultural History* 50, no. 4 (1976): 600–614.
32. Tannenbaum, *Slave and Citizen*, 42. The emphasis here is mine.

33. Ariela Gross and Alejandro de la Fuente, "Slaves, Free Blacks, and Race in the Legal Regimes of Cuba, Louisiana and Virginia: A Comparison," *North Carolina Law Review* 91, no. 5 (2013): 1724.
34. For critiques of an overreliance on law in understanding the treatment of the enslaved: Thomas N. Ingersoll, *Mammon and Manon in Early New Orleans: The First Slave Society in the Deep South, 1718–1819* (Knoxville: University of Tennessee Press, 1999); Marvin Harris, *Patterns of Race in the Americas* (New York: Walker and Company, 1964); David Brion Davis, *The Problem of Slavery in Western Culture* (Ithaca, NY: Cornell University Press, 1966); Gwendolyn Midlo Hall, *Social Control in Slave Plantation Societies: A Comparison of St. Domingue and Cuba* (Baltimore: Johns Hopkins University Press, 1971).
35. Gross and de la Fuente, "Slaves, Free Blacks, and Race in the Legal Regimes of Cuba, Louisiana and Virginia," 1714–1716.
36. Ibid., 1716.
37. Ibid., 1720.
38. Ibid., 1721. There were a few exceptions to this 1705 law. "Turks and Moors in amity with her majesty" and others who could prove that they had been Christians arriving from a Christian country were exempted from automatic enslavement.
39. Ibid., 1723–1724.
40. Although the Spanish technically ruled Louisiana in 1763 as a result of its territorial gains during the Seven Years' War, it took several years for it to gain de facto control through an effective government in 1769.
41. Tannenbaum, *Slave and Citizen*, 61.
42. Rev. Abiel Abbott, *Letters Written in the Interior of Cuba: Between the Mountains of Arcana to the East and of Cusco to the West* (Boston: Bowles and Dearborn, 1829), 97, accessed March 23, 2016, https://archive.org/stream/letterswritteni00abbogoog#page/n7/mode/2up.
43. Ibid.
44. Ibid., 98.
45. Alejandro de la Fuente, "Slave Law and Claims-Making in Cuba: The Tannenbaum Debate Revisited," *Law and History Review* 22, no. 2 (Summer 2004): 358.
46. Kimberly S. Hanger, *Bounded Lives, Bounded Places: Free Black Society in Colonial New Orleans, 1769–1803* (Durham, NC: Duke University Press, 1997), 12.
47. Ibid., 22–23.
48. Ibid., 25.
49. Hanger is clear that although the practice was technically available throughout Louisiana, in practice it was most likely to occur in New Orleans where the seat of Spanish government was concentrated and where its legal reach was strongest. Achieving manumission through *coartación* was not as easy in the countryside.
50. Hanger, *Bounded Lives, Bounded Places*, 42.
51. Ibid., 43.
52. Ibid., 49.
53. For more on Berlin's comparative discussion of free blacks in different parts of the United States, see Section III "Slave and Free" in Ira Berlin, *Many Thousands Gone: The First Two Centuries of Slavery in North America* (Cambridge, MA: Harvard University Press, 1998); also see Ira Berlin, "Southern Free People of Color in the Age of William Johnson," *Southern Quarterly* 43, no. 2 (2006): 9–17.
54. Though Milteer does not give an exact date for the time period he is describing here, the article focuses mainly on the 1790s through the 1850s. For more, see Warren E. Milteer, Jr. "Life in a Great Dismal Swamp Community: Free People of

Color in Pre-Civil War Gates County, North Carolina," *The North Carolina Historical Review* 91, no. 2 (2014): 153.
55. Richard C. Rohrs, "The Free Black Experience in Antebellum Wilmington, North Carolina: Refining Generalizations about Race Relations," *The Journal of Southern History* 78, no. 3 (2012): 623.
56. Ibid., 626–627.
57. Ira Berlin, *Slaves Without Masters: The Free Negro in the Antebellum South* (New York: Oxford University Press, 1974), 344.
58. John Hope Franklin, *The Free Negro in North Carolina, 1790–1860* (Chapel Hill: University of North Carolina Press, 1943): 212–213.
59. Tommy L. Bogger, *Free Blacks in Norfolk, Virginia, 1790–1860: The Darker Side of Freedom* (Charlottesville: University Press of Virginia, 1997): 169.
60. Ibid., 171.
61. Franklin, *The Free Negro in North Carolina*, 219.
62. Rebecca J. Scott, *Degrees of Freedom: Louisiana and Cuba after Slavery* (Cambridge, MA: Harvard University Press, 2005), 16.
63. Foner, "The Free People of Color in Louisiana and St. Domingue," 427.
64. For examples of repression against free people of color, see John D. Garrigus, "Redrawing the Color Line: Gender and the Social Construction of Race in Pre-Revolutionary Haiti," *Journal of Caribbean History* 30, no. 1&2 (1996a): 28–50; and Laura Foner, "The Free People of Color in Louisiana and St. Domingue," 426–427.
65. For more on La Escalera, see Michele Reid-Vasquez, *The Year of the Lash: Free People of Color in Cuba and the Nineteenth-Century Atlantic World* (Athens: University of Georgia Press, 2011).
66. Ibid., 8.
67. David Sartorius, *Ever Faithful: Race, Loyalty and the Ends of Empire in Spanish Cuba* (Durham, NC: Duke University Press, 2013), 87.
68. There are, however, more pessimistic views of La Escalera and its impact on the free colored population of Cuba. Aline Helg, for instance, argues that the repression was so significant that it transformed the racial landscape into one that was quite similar to the US division between "black" and "white" with little in between. She argues that following the alleged conspiracy, races were effectively divided between whites and a "raza de color" (race of color) or "clase de color" (class of color), which included both blacks and mulattoes. This interpretation of Cuba as being very similar to the United States is, however, an unusual one, as Cuba is generally believed to racially fall closer to the other parts of Latin America and the Caribbean in having a more flexible approach to definitions of whiteness and blackness than is the case in the United States. See Aline Helg, "Race and Black Mobilization in Colonial and Early Independent Cuba: A Comparative Perspective," *Ethnohistory* 44, no.1 (Winter 1997): 53–74.
69. Emily Clark, *The Strange History of the American Quadroon: Free Women of Color in the Revolutionary Atlantic World* (Charlotte: University of North Carolina Press, 2013), 6.
70. Ibid., 9.
71. For more on the evolution of racial politics in the making of the US Census, see Sharon M. Lee, "Racial Classifications in the U.S. Census: 1890–1990," *Ethnic and Racial Studies* 16, no. 1 (1993): 75–94; Melissa Nobles, *Shades of Citizenship: Race and the Census in Modern Politics* (Stanford, CA: Stanford University Press, 2000). On the solidification of the "one-drop rule," which strengthened the stark division

between black and white, see chapter 4, "The Rule Becomes Firm," in F. James Davis, *Who Is Black*.

72. I write this while fully acknowledging that there were pockets in the United States where people of African descent did resist this dualistic racial categorization. Indeed, Louisiana, and New Orleans in particular, is one of those areas and we will see in Chapters 4 and 6 how Creoles of color resisted categorization as "black." That said, however, unless they engaged in racial passing, the overwhelming majority of people of African descent in the United States during this period were categorized as black and identified as black according to the criteria of the one-drop rule.
73. H. Hoetink, " 'Race' and Color in the Caribbean," in *Caribbean Contours*, ed. Sidney W. Mintz and Sally Price (Baltimore: Johns Hopkins University Press, 1985), 61.
74. Ibid.
75. For an analysis that explicitly compares pre-Revolutionary St. Domingue and pre-Purchase Louisiana as areas characterized by tripartite racial systems, see Laura Foner, "The Free People of Color in Louisiana and St. Domingue."
76. The exact terms he uses here are "African Negroid" for black, "European Caucasoid" for white, and "Amerindian of Mongolian derivation" for Indian. See Charles Wagley, "On the Concept of Social Race in the Americas," in *Contemporary Societies and Cultures in Latin America*, ed. Dwight B. Heath and Richard N. Adams (New York: Random House, 1965), 531–545.
77. Here Wagley includes the following countries: Mexico, Guatemala, Ecuador, Peru, and Bolivia.
78. Wagley, "On the Concept of Social Race in the Americas," 541.
79. Ibid., 540–541.
80. Ibid., 537.

CHAPTER 2

1. For epigraph 1, see Carolyn E. Fick, *The Making of Haiti: The Saint Domingue Revolution from Below* (Knoxville: University of Tennessee Press, 1990), 93. For epigraph 2, see Laurent Dubois, *Avengers of the New World: The Story of the Haitian Revolution* (Cambridge, MA: Harvard University Press, 2004), 95.
2. We will meet his descendant, John Ellis, in Chapter 5.
3. We will meet his descendant, Mark Charles Roudanez, in Chapter 6.
4. For an extensive discussion of the St. Domingue refugees' many social and cultural contributions to New Orleans, see Nathalie Dessens, *From Saint-Domingue to New Orleans: Migration and Influences* (Gainesville: University Press of Florida, 2007).
5. Moreau de St. Méry, *Description topographique, physique, civile, politique, et historique de la partie francaise de l'isle Saint-Domingue* (Philadelphia, 1797), 371, accessed June 6, 2016, http://www.archive.org/details/descriptiontopog00more.
6. Ibid., 370.
7. Ibid., 371.
8. Dessens, *From Saint-Domingue to New Orleans*, 119–120.
9. Bernard Camier, "Les concerts dans les capitals de Saint-Domingue à la fin du XVIIIe siècle," *Revue de Musicologie* 2007, T. 93 (1): 75–98.
10. St. Méry, *Description topographique, physique, civile, politique, et historique de la partie francaise de l'isle Saint-Domingue*, 361.
11. Ibid., 365.
12. Ibid., 364–365.

13. For more on the lives of the free colored elite in colonial St. Domingue, see John D. Garrigus, "Colour, Class and Identity on the Eve of the Haitian Revolution: Saint-Domingue's Free Colored Elite as *Colons Americaines*," *Slavery and Abolition* 17, no. 1(April 1996): 19–43.
14. St. Méry's manuscript was published in 1797, but it is a retrospective of St. Domingue before the revolution.
15. Garrigus, "Redrawing the Color Line," 28.
16. Foner, 426–427.
17. This concern with white racial purity seems to conflict with the contrast drawn in the first chapter between the Latin/Caribbean and Anglo-American racial systems where purity was only at issue in the latter. Although it is true that the early colonial histories in parts of Latin America and the Caribbean featured strict concerns about white purity, this approach to race did not endure in most places. The lack of endurance is due, in part, to the fact that there was a much smaller population of whites compared to the United States, so that maintaining white racial purity became more and more challenging.
18. For more on this see Foner, "The Free People of Color in Louisiana and St. Domingue," 427, and John D. Garrigus "Colour, Class and Identity on the Eve of the Haitian Revolution," 26.
19. Tulane University, Lambert Family Papers, Collection 244. The source of translation is Jan Barry, and I checked it against the original document I photographed and reviewed at the Tulane collection. Barry is one of the St. Domingue descendants I interviewed for this project.
20. For more on the attempts of free people of color to achieve their rights, see Garrigus, "Colour, Class and Identity on the Eve of the Haitian Revolution"; chapter 3 of Fick, *The Making of Haiti*; and chapter 3 of DuBois, *Avengers of the New World*.
21. Laurent DuBois writes that Chavannes was interested in allying with slaves and that, while Ogé was not, he apparently confessed before he died that there were free people of color throughout the colony who were considering such an alliance. See DuBois, *Avengers of the New World*, 88.
22. Much of the discussion here relies on Fick, *The Making of Haiti*, 93. Also, concerning precise dates for the August assembly and start of the revolution, see Fick Appendix B, pp. 260–266, as there is some question about the precision of dates, though the week of August 14–22 is the one in which these events took place.
23. Ibid., 96.
24. See Lambert Family Papers, note 48. The "fatal blow of Dessalines" refers to the wave of massacres of whites that Dessalines ordered after he rose to power. For more on this, see Jeremy D. Popkin, "A Survivor of Dessalines's Massacres in 1804," in *Facing Racial Revolution: Eyewitness Accounts of the Haitian Insurrection* (Chicago: University of Chicago Press, 2007), 336–362.
25. We will meet their descendant, Jerry Gondolfo, later on in Chapter 5.
26. Quoted in Gabriel Debien, "The Saint-Domingue Refugees in Cuba," in *The Road to Louisiana: The Saint-Domingue Refugees 1792–1809*, ed. Carl A. Brasseaux and Glenn R. Conrad (Lafayette: The Center for Louisiana Studies, University of Southwestern Louisiana, 1992), 54–55.
27. Thanks to Jerry Gandolfo, their descendant, who pointed me toward the Rivet collection at the Historic New Orleans Collection (HNOC). The discussion to follow relies on documents I examined from this collection.

28. See Folder 20 from HNOC's Rivet collection for this letter; also, for more on the St. Domingue delegation which was set up at Baracoa to determine the legitimacy of marine seizures, see Paul LaChance, "Were St. Domingue Refugees a Distinctive Cultural Group in Antebellum New Orleans? Evidence from Patterns and Strategies of Property Holding," *Revista/Review Interamericana* 29, no. 1–4 (1999): 181.
29. The letter explains that they were sailing on "le corsair La Téméraire." "Corsair" is French for privateer and the Téméraire was a class of warships created by the French for its territories abroad.
30. French practice was to allow privateers to keep just a portion of what they captured. There is not enough in the documents to determine what exactly happened, but there must have been some disagreement about how much Daubert and the others kept.
31. See Folder 35 HNOC from the Rivet Collection
32. Folder 36 HNOC from the Rivet Collection.
33. See Folder 37 for the February letter and Folder 40 for the April letter from the HNOC Rivet Collection.
34. Quoted in Debien, "The Saint-Domingue Refugees in Cuba," 91–92.
35. Quoted in Debien, "The Saint-Domingue Refugees in Cuba," 96.
36. See letter addressed to Judge James Pitot, provided by the brothers Victor and Jean Navarre. The letter provides their testimony of their family's migration from St. Domingue to Cuba and then to New Orleans and also discusses Justine's travel back to St. Domingue and news they received of her death after several years of not hearing from her. This letter is included in the Succession of Justine de Carle, Louisiana Division of the New Orleans Public Library, mf VCH280 1805-1846, Orleans Parish, LA Court of Probate. Succession and Probate Records: 1805–1848. This is an ancestor of respondent Barry Navarre who provided meticulously researched documentation along with scans of original documents accompanied by French transcriptions and English translations, all of which I reviewed and verified by retrieving the documents at the New Orleans Public Library.
37. Ibid.
38. Letter from Justine de Carle to Mr. Guillotte in September 1810 where Justine gives him charge of her slaves and advises him to rent them out as needed for income. This letter is also included in the Succession of Justine de Carle, Louisiana Division of the New Orleans Public Library, mf VCH280 1805-1846, Orleans Parish, LA Court of Probate. Succession and Probate Records: 1805–1848.
39. Ibid.
40. For more on this, see Dessens, *From St. Domingue to New Orleans*, 98.
41. See note 38.
42. On the legend of the faithful slave, see Dessens, *From St. Domingue to New Orleans*, 133–134; also see Paul LaChance, "St. Domingue Émigrés in New Orleans, 1800–1830," lecture presented at the Eleventh Annual Williams Research Center Symposium, New Orleans, Louisiana, February 4, 2006, 7–9. In addition, the tale of the faithful slave is also one I have encountered in some of my interviews with white St. Domingue descendants.
43. Discussion here relies on Dessens, *From St. Domingue to New Orleans*, 41–45.
44. See Emancipation Petition with A. Guillotte representing Widow Carl Navarre, September 18, 1816. The LSU Libraries website entitled "Free People of Color in Louisiana: Revealing an Unknown Past," accessed August 2, 2015, http://www.lib.lsu.edu/special/fpoc/collections.html#NOPL.

CHAPTER 3

1. Letter from Benjamin Morgan to Chandler Price from New Orleans, August 11, 1803, Carter, *The Territorial Papers of the United States*, 8.

    The biographical information for Benjamin Morgan is taken from *Interim Appointment: W.C.C. Claiborne Letter Book, 1804–1805*, edited with Biographical Sketches, by Jared William Bradley (Baton Rouge: Louisiana State University Press, 2002), 282–298. Bradley notes that Morgan moved to New Orleans from Philadelphia, where he had been a businessman. In New Orleans he continued in business and also served in politics. He was considered to be a person of integrity and discernment. Because of this, and because of his father's distinguished military service, he had a reputation as someone to be trusted. His observations about Louisiana were sought out by officials in Louisiana and Washington, and he provided critical advice to both concerning whom to appoint to office and what factors to consider in the task of governing the new territory.

2. Letter from Benjamin Morgan to Chandler Price from New Orleans, August 11, 1803, and letter from Benjamin Morgan to Chandler Price from New Orleans, August 18, 1803, Carter, *The Territorial Papers of the United States*, 8–9.
3. Governor Claiborne to the President, Near Natchez, August 24, 1803, Carter, *The Territorial Papers of the United States*, 21–22. The numbers preceding the questions represent their order among the thirty-six Jefferson posed to Claiborne.
4. Governor Claiborne to the President, Near Natchez, August 24, 1803, Carter, *The Territorial Papers of the United States*, 21.
5. Daniel Clark to the Secretary of State, New Orleans, 8 September 1803, Carter, *The Territorial Papers of the United States*, 38.
6. For more on the various groups of "foreign French," see Paul LaChance, "The Foreign French," in *Creole New Orleans: Race and Americanization*, ed. Arnold Hirsch and Joseph Logsdon (Baton Rouge: Louisiana State University Press, 1992), 101–130.
7. Although there were undoubtedly national prejudices at work here, there is an element of truth. The Louisiana that the Americans encountered in 1803 was economically stagnant and bereft of cultural resources such as theaters, operas, daily newspapers, and plentiful schools. This situation began to change significantly with the arrival of the St. Domingue émigrés who arrived in 1809. This group brought a number of cultural establishments to the territory.
8. John Pintard to the Secretary of the Treasury, New Rochelle, September 14, 1803, Clark, *The Territorial Papers of the United States*, 51.
9. In her work, Ellene Lowe notes that Claiborne's second marriage to a French woman and his third to a Spanish woman may have helped to smooth over his cultural differences with the Creoles. See Ellene Lowe, "Administrative Problems of W.C.C. Claiborne, First Anglo-American Governor of Louisiana" (Master's thesis, University of North Texas, 1939).
10. Governor Claiborne to the President, Near Natchez, September 29, 1803, Clark, *The Territorial Papers of the United States*, 58.
11. For more on how different European groups went through the process of becoming "white" according to US standards, see Noel Ignatiev, *How the Irish Became White* (New York: Routledge, 1995); Karen Brodkin, *How the Jews Became White Folks & What that Says about Race in America* (New Brunswick, NJ: Rutgers University Press, 1998); Matthew Frye Jacobson, *Whiteness of a Different Color: European Immigrants and the Alchemy of Race* (Cambridge, MA: Harvard University Press,

1999); David R. Roediger, *Working Toward Whiteness: How America's Immigrants Became White* (New York: Basic Books, 2005).
12. See more on this in Joseph Tregle, Jr. "Creoles and Americans," in *Creole New Orleans: Race and Americanization*, ed. Arnold R. Hirsch and Joseph Logsdon (Baton Rouge: Louisiana State University Press, 1992), 143.
13. Memorial to Congress from Merchants of New Orleans, January 9, 1804, Carter, *The Territorial Papers of the United States*, 157–158.
14. Governor Claiborne and James Wilkinson to the Secretary of State, New Orleans, February 7, 1804, Carter, *The Territorial Papers of the United States*, 177–180.
15. LaChance, "The Foreign French."
16. Dessens, *From St. Domingue to New Orleans*, 48–49.
17. See the following for more discussion of the Café des Refugiés: Dessens, *From St. Domingue to New Orleans*, 49.
18. For more on the refugees' endogamy during their earliest years in New Orleans see Dessens, *From St. Domingue to New Orleans*, 50–51 and LaChance, "Were St. Domingue Refugees a Distinctive Cultural Group in Antebellum New Orleans?"
19. St. Gême Family Papers, Historic New Orleans Collection, Folder 164, p. 12. The translation in the text is my own.
20. St. Gême Family Papers, Historic New Orleans Collection, Folder 180, p. 4, February 1831. The translation in the text is my own.
21. St. Gême Family Papers, Historic New Orleans Collection, Folder 188, p. 415, 1831. The translation in the text is my own.
22. This section benefits from Joseph G. Tregle's analysis in "Creoles and Americans," especially pp. 153–155.
23. Dessens, *From Saint Domingue to New Orleans*, 55.
24. Carl A. Brasseaux and Glenn Conrad, *The Road to Louisiana: The Saint-Domingue Refugees, 1792–1809*. trans. David Cheramie (Lafayette: Center for Louisiana Studies, University of Southwestern Louisiana, 1992), xvi.
25. LaChance, "Were St. Domingue Refugees a Distinctive Cultural Group in Antebellum New Orleans?" 192.
26. Tregle, "Creoles and Americans," 155.
27. Ibid., 156.
28. New Orleans Public Library, accessed April 6, 2012, http://nutrias.org/exhibits/charter/normanmap.htm. Courtesy of the Louisiana Division/City Archives, New Orleans Public Library.
29. Tregle, "Creoles and Americans," 156–157.
30. Virginia Dominguez, *White by Definition: Social Classification in Creole Louisiana* (New Brunswick, NJ: Rutgers University Press, 1986), 118. Dominguez notes the source of this information as coming from the *New Orleans Daily Orleanian*, October 18, 1850, and the *New Orleans Daily Crescent*, February 9, 1850.
31. Garrigus, "Redrawing the Colour Line," 36.
32. For more on *plaçage* and on the position of the *ménagère* in St. Domingue, see Clark, *The Strange History of the American Quadroon*. Chapter 4 in *American Routes* contains a more sustained discussion of the mixed-race *ménagère* which describes how these women lost a certain amount of power and respect when they got to Louisiana where this social position was not recognized.
33. For more on *plaçage* in Louisiana, see Joan M. Martin, "*Plaçage* and the Louisiana Gens de Couleur Libre: How Race and Sex Defined the Lifestyles of Free Women of Color," in *Creole: The History and Legacy of Louisiana's Free People of Color*, ed. Sybil Kein (Baton Rouge: Louisiana State University Press, 2000), 57–70.
34. Dessens, *From Saint-Domingue to New Orleans*, 98.

35. Ibid., 99.
36. Ibid., 100.
37. Tregle, "Creoles and Americans," 139.
38. Ibid.
39. Ibid., 171.
40. Ibid., 173.
41. Dominguez, *White by Definition*, 141.
42. "White versus Black: The Coming Issue," *The Opelousas Journal*, Friday, April 17, 1874, 3. Accessed March 13, 2015, http://www.chroniclingamerica.loc.gov.
43. Ibid.
44. Ibid., 2.
45. See Jackson's defense of himself and his response to Lewis's attack at the meeting. This appears on the editorial page under the title "Reform Dr. Lewis and His Party," *The Opelousas Journal*, Friday, May 1, 1874, accessed June 8, 2015, http://www.chroniclingamerica.loc.gov.
46. See "The Meeting Last Monday," *The Opelousas Courier*, May 2, 1874, 1, accessed March 13, 2015, http://www.chroniclingamerica.loc.gov.
47. For Lewis's thank you see "The White League," *The Opelousas Courier*, May 9, 1874, 1, accessed March 13, 2015, http://www.chroniclingamerica.loc.gov. For the announcement about the *Courier* editorial page being taken over by the White League, see the front page of the edition published on May 30, 1874, accessed June 8, 2015, http://www.chroniclingamerica.loc.gov.
48. Dominguez, *White by Definition*, 291. This English language translation is taken from the endnotes. The original French appears on p. 137.
49. This discussion relies on Dominguez, *White by Definition*, 137.
50. Dominguez, *White by Definition*, 294. This English language translation is taken from the endnotes. The original French appears on p. 141. This is taken from *Le Carillon*, August 3, 1873, p. 1.
51. See The "Creole" Defined, *The New Orleans Bulletin*, Sunday, August 1, 1875, 6, accessed June 8, 2015, http://www.chroniclingamerica.loc.gov. A search of previous issues of the paper failed to discover the original letter from P. S. Moran that prompted Dimitry's response.
52. George Washington Cable, *The Grandissimes* (Gretna, LA: Pelican Publishing Company, 2001). The original was published in 1880 by Charles Scribner's Sons.
53. *New Orleans Item*, September 27, 1880, p. 2.
54. *L'Abeille*, March 15, 1885, 4. The translation in the text is my own.
55. *L'Abeille*, March 15, 1885, 4. The translation in the text is my own.
56. Whereas Boré was the first mayor of American New Orleans, James Pitot—who was mentioned earlier in the chapter—was the first mayor following the incorporation of the city.
57. Charles Gayarré, "The Creoles of History and the Creoles of Romance" (lecture delivered at Tulane University), April 25, 1880.
58. Dominguez, *White by Definition*, 122.
59. See excerpts from this interview in M. J. O'Neill, *How Does He Do It: Sam T. Jack, Twenty Years a King in the Realm of Burlesque* (Whitefish, MT: Kessinger Publishing, 2007): 69–70.
60. *St. Landry Clarion*, Saturday October 21, 1893, accessed March 13, 2015, http://www.chroniclingamerica.loc.gov.
61. The New York editorial was reprinted in the *Lafayette Advertiser*, November 4, 1893, accessed March 13, 2015, http://www.chroniclingamerica.loc.gov.
62. Ibid.

63. Tregle, "Creoles and Americans," 184.
64. Tregle, "Creoles and Americans," 185.
65. Rien Fertel, *Imagining the Creole City: The Rise of Literary Culture in Nineteenth-Century New Orleans* (Baton Rouge, LA: Louisiana State University Press, 2014), 98.
66. Pierre Nora, "Between Memory and History: Les Lieux de Mémoires," *Representations*, no. 26, Special Issue: Memory and Counter-Memory (Spring 1989): 12.
67. See more on the significance of Grace King's work in Fertel, *Imagining the Creole City*, chapter 5.
68. Grace King, *Creole Families of New Orleans* (New York: Macmillan Company, 1921), vii. The emphasis placed in the quote is my own.
69. Nora, "Between Memory and History," 12.
70. See more on the local-color movement and its many female authors in chapter 5 of Fertel, *Imagining the Creole City*.
71. The columns were collected together and published in Henry C. Castellanos, *New Orleans As It Was: Episodes of Louisiana Life* (Baton Rouge: Louisiana State University Press, 2006). The original collection was published in 1895.
72. For more on Anastazie Desarzant's true story, see the Prologue in Shirley Elizabeth Thompson, *Exiles at Home: The Struggle to Become American in Creole New Orleans* (Cambridge, MA: Harvard University Press, 2009); and Shirley Elizabeth Thompson, "'Ah Toucoutou, Ye Conin Vou': History and Memory in Creole New Orleans," *American Quarterly* 53, no. 2 (2001): 232–266.
73. Edward Laroque Tinker, *Toucoutou* (New York: Dodd, Mead and Company, 1930), 7.
74. Saenz and Douglas, "A Call for the Racialization of Immigration Studies."

CHAPTER 4

1. Carter, *The Territorial Papers of the United States*, 7.
2. Though the ethnic distinctiveness of refugees of color lasted a bit longer than it did for white refugees, refugees of African descent did largely merge with the local Creole community during the antebellum period. For instance, while LaChance acknowledges that refugees of color married endogamously a bit longer than did white refugees, he concludes his paper on the subject by noting: "To the extent that one can identify distinctive ethnic groups in New Orleans, Saint-Domingue refugees of color have a stronger claim to classification as such than white refugees. In the final analysis, however, it may be better to abandon the paradigm of a society stratified into culturally distinct and competitive groups for the alternative paradigm of a cosmopolitan city in which individuals ... intermarried, and produced a new generation that would in its turn interact and intermarry with the next cohort of immigrants," in LaChance, "Were St. Domingue Refugees a Distinctive Cultural Group in Antebellum New Orleans?," 192.

    Nathalie Dessens also notes that while refugees of color married endogamously for a longer period of time than white refugees, those of color showed "an increasing trend to marry into the free Creole population of color" (56).
3. James Brown to John Breckinridge, September 17, 1805, Clark, *The Territorial Papers of the United States*, 510.
4. Clark, *The Strange History of the American Quadroon*, 64. In this section, Clark relies heavily on the work of Dominique Rogers, in particular her dissertation entitled: "Les libres de couleur dans les capitals de Saint-Domingue: fortune,

mentalités et integration à la fin de l'Ancien Régime (1776–1789)." Ph.D. diss., L'université Michel de Montaigne, Bourdeaux III, 1999.
5. Ibid., 66.
6. Governor Claiborne to the President, August 24, 1803, Clark, *The Territorial Papers of the United States, Vol. IX*, 18.
7. Ibid., 59. Governor Claiborne to the President, September 29, 1803.
8. Ibid., 160, James Wilkinson to the Secretary of War, January 11, 1803 [1804].
9. Ibid., 174–175, Address from the Free People of Color, January 1804.
10. Ibid., 561, Governor Claiborne to the Secretary of State, January 8, 1806.
11. For a more in-depth discussion of the Creoles of color and their struggle to have a recognized militia, see chapter 2, "The Republican Cause and the Afro-Creole Militia," in Caryn Cossé Bell, *Revolution, Romanticism and the Afro-Creole Protest Tradition in Louisiana 1718–1868* (Baton Rouge: Louisiana State University Press, 1997).
12. "Legal Transplants: Slavery and the Civil Law in Louisiana," USC Legal Studies Research Paper No. 09-16 by Ariela Gross, p. 6. Accessed November 28, 2014, http://weblaw.usc.edu/centers/class/class-workshops/usc-legal-studies-working-papers/documents/09_16_paper.pdf.
    The original text along with the rest of the Black Codes of 1806 can be accessed at http://louisdl.louislibraries.org/cdm/ref/collection/lapur/id/25266.
13. See Bell, *Revolution, Romanticism and the Afro-Creole Protest Tradition in Louisiana*, 76–77.
14. Edward Maceo Coleman, ed., *Creole Voices: Poems in French by Free Men of Color*, first published in 1845 (Washington, DC: Associated Publishers, 1945), xviii.
15. The discussion in this section relies on Henry Louis Gates, *Loose Canons: Notes in the Culture Wars* (New York: Oxford University Press, 1992), 24–25.
16. Ibid.
17. Thomas Haddox, "The 'Nous' of Southern Catholic Quadroons: Racial, Ethnic, and Religious Identity in *Les Cenelles*," *American Literature* 73, no. 4 (2001): 757.
18. Ibid., 759.
19. R. L. Desdunes, *Our People and Our Culture: Fifty Creole Portraits* (Baton Rouge: Louisiana State University Press, 1973), 12.
20. Armand Lanusse, ed., *Les Cenelles: Choix de poésies indigenes* (Shreveport, LA: Les Cahiers de Tintamarre, 2013), 21. The translation is my own.
21. Ibid., 208. The translations are my own.
22. There is one poem, "Epigramme," which denounces the practice of *placage*, condemning the practice as a sin while also recognizing the desperation that drives some to engage in the practice. See this poem on p. 47.
23. For a recent exploration of the historical and present significance of the Declaration of Independence for all Americans, see Danielle Allen, *Our Declaration: A Reading of the Declaration of Independence in Defense of Liberty* (New York: W.W. Norton & Co, 2014).
24. This changes with the advent of *La Tribune*, which is bilingual and includes separate French and English sections of the paper. In reporting on the French sections of the paper quoted in this chapter, all translations are mine unless otherwise noted.
25. This first edition of *L'Union* was accessed at http://www.genealogybank.com on November 29, 2014. The left-hand column, which contains the exchange between Hertelou and Hugo, is partly cut off and partly blurred so that it is impossible to read the left-most words of each sentence. A full French transcription of Hertelou's letter is available, however, in the essay cited here. That essay does not, however,

have a transcription of Hugo's response. The response noted in that essay does not match what is published in *L'Union*. For more, see the essay by Léon-François Hoffmann, "Victor Hugo, John Brown et les Haitiens," *Nineteenth-Century French Studies* 16, no. 1–2 (1987–1988): 47–58.

26. *New Orleans Tribune*, July 21, 1864, accessed November 29, 2014, http://www.genealogybank.com.
27. French section, *New Orleans Tribune*, August 4, 1864, 3. Accessed November 29, 2014, http://www.genealogybank.com. I was alerted to this particular entry by David Rankin, "The Politics of Caste: Free Colored Leadership in New Orleans During the Civil War," in *Louisiana's Black Heritage*. Edited by Robert R. MacDonald, John R. Kemp, and Edward F. Haas (New Orleans: Louisiana State Museum, 1979), 133.
28. English section and p. 3 of the French section in *New Orleans Tribune*, November 10, 1864, accessed November 29, 2014, http://www.genealogybank.com.
29. This reading of the *Tribune* is affirmed by other accounts that come at the subject from opposite perspectives. In *Revolution and Romanticism*, Caryn Cossé Bell argues strongly that the Creoles discussed here were inspired by a French republican tradition of equality that motivated them to fight on behalf of all people of color. At the other end of the spectrum, David Rankin's "The Politics of Caste" provides a much less charitable reading of *L'Union* and the *Tribune* as he argues that the Creoles of color acted as a caste. Even Rankin, however, admits that the *Tribune* writers did, more consistently than not, fight on behalf of all people of African descent and not just their own group.
30. R. L. Desdunes, "A Few Words to Dr. DuBois with Malice Toward None," March 1907, 13. The Amistad Research Center A. P. Tureaud Collection, Box 77.
31. *New York Times* online, February 18, 1907, accessed December 28, 2013, http://query.nytimes.com/mem/archive-free/pdf?res=F00D15F83D5A15738DDDA10994DA405B878CF1D3.
32. *New Orleans Item*, February 24, 1907.
33. Accessed June 30, 2015, http://www.ourdocuments.gov/doc.php?flash=false&doc=52.
34. Accessed June 30, 2015, http://www.pbs.org/wnet/jimcrow/stories_events_plessy.html.
35. Accessed June 30, 2015, http://www.inmotionaame.org/print.cfm;jsessionid=f830773701435688785133?migration=5&bhcp=1.
36. Michel Laguerre, *Diasporic Citizenship: Haitians in Transnational America* (New York: St. Martin's Press, 1998).
37. Rebecca Scott, "The Atlantic World and the Road to *Plessy v. Ferguson*." *Journal of American History* 94, no. 3 (2007): 731–732.
38. For more on this approach of putting Louisiana into a larger Gulf of Mexico and Atlantic context, see Rebecca Scott and Jean Hébrard, *Freedom Papers: An Atlantic Odyssey in the Age of Emancipation* (Cambridge, MA: Harvard University Press, 2012).
39. Scott, "The Atlantic World and the Road to *Plessy v. Ferguson*," 727. Along similar lines, concerning the strong record of St. Domingue émigrés when it came to fighting for their rights, also see Dessens, *From St. Dommingue to New Orleans*, especially chapter 6, and Caryn Cosse Bell, *Revolution and Romanticism*.
40. Desdunes, *Our People and Our Culture*, 147.
41. Ibid., 18.

42. Wendy Ann Gaudin, "Autocrats and All Saints: Migration, Memory, and Modern Creole Identities" (Ph.D. diss., New York University, 2005), 57.
43. Ibid., 58.
44. Ibid., 96.
45. Ibid., 84.
46. I must be clear here in saying that this is not an argument that *all* Creoles of color made a distinction between themselves and Anglo-blacks that placed Anglo-blacks lower than themselves in the racial hierarchy. There were certainly many Creoles who simply held on to Creole identity because it was important to them. Still, however, even if they did not make an active calculation that keeping Creole identity would place a buffer between themselves and Anglo-blacks, Creole identification did not disadvantage them the way it did for white Creoles. This in itself made it a viable choice to maintain Creole identification.

CHAPTER 5

1. The respondents with whom I did oral histories were not necessarily descendants of St. Domingue. They were chosen for their explicit identification as whites with Creole heritage. That said, their Louisiana ancestors would have withstood all the same kinds of social and cultural pressures to become Anglicized as their St. Domingue refugee counterparts did.
2. There are two among these interviewees who would identify as Cajun or Acadian rather than as Creole. Many of the dynamics concerning loss of language and identity are similar, however, for Cajuns and Creoles both faced the onslaught of a fairly aggressive Anglo-Americanization in the late nineteenth and early to mid-twentieth centuries.
3. Reference is made to James Pitot in Chapter 3.
4. Renee is a St. Domingue descendant.
5. Jerry Gandolfo is a St. Domingue descendant. His ancestors, Germain Daubert and Marie Claude Rigaud, were discussed in Chapter 2.
6. Alice Dantro is a St. Domingue descendant.
7. Loretta Clark is a St. Domingue descendant.
8. Marcel Saussy is one of the seven white oral history respondents.
9. The discussion in this section relies on information provided at the CODOFIL website: http://www.crt.state.la.us/cultural-development/codofil/about/french-in-louisiana/legal-status/index. CODOFIL is an initiative of the state of Louisiana and stands for the *Conseil Pour le Developpement du Francais en Louisiane*. It was established in 1968 in an attempt to rescue and preserve the state's French language heritage.
10. Dorothy Carter is one of the seven white oral history respondents.
11. Both Angelique Bergeron and Julie Livaudais are white oral history respondents.
12. Alcée Fortier, *A History of Louisiana*, vol. IV, The American Domination Part II, 1861–1908 (New York: Manzi, Joyant & Co., 1904), 259–260.
13. *L'Abeille*, February 6, 1856, p. 3. The translation in the text is my own.
14. Samuel Kinser, *Carnival, American Style: Mardi Gras at New Orleans and Mobile* (Chicago: University of Chicago Press, 1990), 89.
15. Perry Young, *The Mistick Krewe: Chronicles of Comus and His Kin* (Shreveport: Louisiana Heritage Press, 1969), 62–63.
16. Kinser, *Carnival, American Style*, 91.
17. William Connick is a St. Domingue descendant.
18. Dominguez, *White by Definition*, 177.

19. Ibid., 181.
20. The family name mentioned in the interview is removed in order to protect the privacy of the family. Throughout the interviewing process it was not uncommon when interviewing white Louisianans to be told that I must report certain things anonymously. This also occurred when I was interviewing Creoles of color where one branch of the family had passed as white.
21. Mary Waters discusses this phenomenon of white Americans selectively choosing which European heritages to identify with in her book *Ethnic Options: Choosing Identities in America* (Berkeley: University of California Press, 1990).
22. It is important to note here that the Baltimore ancestry is not at all separate from the St. Domingue ancestry. Many St. Domigue refugees initially went to ports along the Eastern seaboard—many went to Baltimore. Some of these later made their way down to New Orleans.
23. Richard is a pseudonym because this respondent requested that his name be changed.
24. Denise is a pseudonym. This respondent requested that her name be changed.
25. There were references to this family's history in Chapter 2, starting at the section that shares a portion of a letter written by Madame Lambert as she observes the Revolution swirling around her in St. Domingue.
26. Benedict Anderson, *Imagined Communities: Reflections on the Origin and Spread of Nationalism* (New York: Verso Press, 1983).
27. Of course, all of this is changing in the digital age, where newspapers are fighting for their lives. Until quite recently, however, the newspaper significantly defined a community's sense of itself.
28. When a code says that race is "identified," this means that there was an explicit reference or the person in question is a public figure whose race is generally known. When a code says that the race is "signaled," this means that certain kinds of historical, cultural, or class references are made that make it nearly certain that the family being discussed is from a particular racial group.
29. R. Stephanie Bruno, "Holy Cross Houses Are a Breath of Fresh Air," *The Times-Picayune*, Saturday, January 29, 2011.
30. Linda Treash, "Creole vs. Cajun: St. Martinville Historical Site Sorts It Out," *The Times-Picayune*, Friday, October 22, 1999.
31. Jill Anding, "Newcomb Pottery Brings Record Price," *The Times-Picayune*, Saturday, July 4, 2009.
32. Dave Walker, "Family Stories—Digging into History Reveals Some Rewarding Surprises," *The Times-Picayune*, Tuesday, January 13, 2015.
33. Sharon Edwards, "Live Music, Fun on Tap for Live It Up Rally—Event Sheds Light on Suicide Prevention," *The Times-Picayune*, Thursday, November 11, 2010.
34. Judy Walker, "Creole Queen—Gallons of Gumbo Later, Leah Chase Is Still in the Kitchen and Now in Her Own Gallery at the Southern Food and Beverage Museum," *The Times-Picayune*, Thursday, July 2, 2009.
35. Angela Aleiss, "Touching Base," *The Times-Picayune*, Saturday, November 1, 1997.

CHAPTER 6

1. This is true even with the rise of what some call "post-blackness." The argument made by advocates of post-blackness is that there is no longer—if there ever was—any dominant way of being black. Black people are so diverse that it is unreasonable to think in terms of "blackness" as being constituted by some set of core attributes. Even those who argue that we are in a state of post-blackness,

however, do not suggest that some people of African descent are not black. There is still a basic understanding about who is considered to be black, but there is increased pushback against the idea that there is one typical way to be black. The term "post-black" came out of the art world and initially referred to debate concerning what constitutes black art. For more on the varied dimensions of post-blackness, see Christine Kim, Franklin Sirmans, and Thelma Golden, eds., *Freestyle: The Studio Museum in Harlem* (New York: Studio Museum in Harlem, 2001); Touré, *Who's Afraid of Post-Blackness? What It Means to Be Black Now* (New York: Atria Books, 2012); Paul C. Taylor, "Post-Black, Old Black," *African American Review* 41, no. 4 (2007): 625–640. Similar themes that resonate with this discussion of post-blackness are to be found in the following pieces: Trey Ellis, "The New Black Aesthetic," *Callaloo* (Winter 1989): 233–243; Malin Pereira, "The Poet in the World and the World in the Poet: Cyrus Cassells's and Elizabeth Alexander's Versions of Post-Soul Cosmopolitanism," *African American Review* 41, no. 4 (2007): 709–725.
2. Terralyn is a pseudonym. All of the respondents recruited from the Cajun/Creole list have had their names changed. I conducted these interviews before I introduced the use of a form that I asked respondents to sign indicating whether or not they would like me to use their true name in published results. All other interviewees after those from the Cajun/Creole list gave explicit permission for me to use their true name or specifically asked not to use their true name.
3. Interview conducted with Terralyn, March 2005. Recruited from the Cajun/Creole online discussion forum.

Methodological note: Comments shared from this interview, and all of the Cajun/Creole interviews were done in 2005, very early on in the work for this study and were recorded on cassette tapes. They were not originally part of the St. Domingue-Louisiana project. It was only several years later that it became clear to me that in order to tell the story of how the St. Domingue immigrants of color adapted to the Anglo-American system, I needed to tell the larger story of Creoles of color in Louisiana, whether or not they had established St. Domingue ancestry.

The value of the Cajun/Creole interviews is that they focus intensively on the respondent's development of a racial and ethnic identity in a more concentrated way than do the St. Domingue descendant interviews. Much as the oral histories with white Creoles who did not have St. Domingue ancestry helped to tell a deeper and richer story of how both groups coped with Anglo-Americanization, the Cajun/Creole interviews help to supplement accounts from respondents of color who are St. Domingue descendants. Throughout the chapter, there is a clear indication in the endnotes describing whether the respondent was a Cajun/Creole interviewee or a St. Domingue descendant. As becomes clear, the racial and ethnic experiences of the two groups overlap nearly completely.

Given their importance to the study, I am extremely grateful that the Cajun/Creole interviews made it into the book at all. In 2011, on my way to a year-long sabbatical at Princeton, all of my cassettes were doused in water when the back of our minivan leaked water, succumbing to the force of a fierce storm system that started out with us in New Orleans and hovered over us as we made our way up the East Coast into Princeton, New Jersey. I was devastated. On the way to a dream year of focused writing, it appeared that my writing was over before it had started. My sound engineer husband wisely advised me to immediately blow-dry all of the cassettes and set them aside to dry out completely. I did this, and I was able to salvage almost everything. With his assistance, I quickly made digital copies. But the significance of the Cajun/Creole interviews was still not clear to me, and it would not become a priority until I was working on this chapter in late 2014—three years after the dousing. Concerned about what shape the nearly ten-year-old, water-damaged cassettes would be in, I decided to rely on the typed notes I had wisely taken in 2005 while carrying out the interviews. Because of those notes, I have much of the content of those interviews. But because these were typed notes, what is reported here for all of the Cajun/Creole interviews are summaries of interviewee comments, though I did try as much as possible at the time of the interview to get exact wording down. They cannot, however, be considered direct quotes.

4. Interview with Terralyn, March 2005.
5. Interview conducted with "Allan"—who requested that his real name not be used. Conducted in March 2005, recruited from the Cajun/Creole list. The emphasis in the quote is my own.
6. Amelie is a St. Domingue descendant. She did not consent to the use of her true name. For this reason, a pseudonym has been chosen and used here.
7. Interview conducted with Stephanie in March 2005. Recruited from the Cajun/Creole list.
8. Diana is a pseudonym.
9. Interview conducted with Diana in March 2005. Recruited form the Cajun/Creole list.
10. Velva Flot is a St. Domingue descendant.
11. Posted by "QN33," April 1, 2004, https://groups.yahoo.com/neo/groups/cajun-creole/conversations/topics/769, accessed December 3, 2014.
12. Posted by "MissPettyNoir," April 1, 2004, 10:07 a.m., https://groups.yahoo.com/neo/groups/cajuncreole/conversations/topics/769, accessed December 4, 2014.
13. Alexander is a pseudonym. He was recruited from the Cajun/Creole list.
14. Christopher is a pseudonym. He was recruited from the Cajun/Creole list.
15. Laura is a St. Domingue descendant.
16. Rhondale is a St. Domingue descendant.
17. Celine is a St. Domingue descendant. Celine is a pseudonym because she asked that her name be changed.
18. Both Christina and Mark are St. Domingue descendants.
19. St. Domingue descendant interview with Christina—not her real name. She asked that her name be changed because some members of her family are still choosing to be white without identifying their black ancestry.
20. Stephanie is a Cajun/Creole interviewee
21. Both Barbara and Harold are St. Domingue descendants.
22. Jacob is a St. Domingue descendant.
23. Although it is true that several respondents made this geographical connection between California and racial passing, what I report here should not be seen as a blanket assertion that all or even most Creoles in California were trying to pass as white. Diana's story earlier on in this chapter provides a good example of the many Afro-Creole families who were open about and proud of being Creoles of color and who regularly and openly visited Creole family in Louisiana.
24. Pat is a St. Domingue descendant.
25. Amy is a St. Domingue descendant. The name Amy is a pseudonym used to protect the identities of extended family members who do not want it known that they have black ancestry.

26. Melanie is a pseudonym used to protect family members who desire to be known as white. Melanie's true name was used in another part of the book, but the pseudonym is being used in this section. She is a St. Domingue descendant.
27. Naurine is a St. Domingue descendant.
28. Naydja is a St. Domingue descendant.
29. At the time of the interview Ronald was working to document his St. Domingue ancestry.

CHAPTER 7

1. Rachel L. Swarns, "Hispanics Resist Racial Grouping by Census," *New York Times*, October 24, 2004, accessed June 6, 2016, http://www.nytimes.com/learning/teachers/featured_articles/20041025monday.html.
2. For more on the significance of ethnic replenishment in shaping a group's integration experience, see Tomás R. Jimenez, *Replenished Ethnicity: Mexican Americans, Immigration, and Identity* (Berkeley: University of California Press, 2010).
3. Sandra L. Colby and Jennifer M. Ortman, "Projections of the Size and Composition of the U.S. Population: 2014 to 2060," March 2015, accessed April 15, 2016, http://www.census.gov/content/dam/Census/library/publications/2015/demo/p25-1143.pdf.
4. In addition, the size of the Hispanic population may also be affected by the fact that the US Census office is considering a change in the way the question about race is worded so that "race" is never even mentioned. Instead, respondents would be asked to choose which group best describes them. Potential choices include the following: white (e.g., German, Irish, Italian); Hispanic (e.g., Mexican, Cuban, Puerto Rican); black or African American (e.g., African American; Haitian, Jamaican). Changes in the wording of the question about race could change the way people answer the question and in turn change official statistics about race and racial groups in the United States. For more on this, see D'Vera Cohn, "Census Considers New Approach to Asking about Race—By Not Using the Term at All," accessed April 15, 2016, http://www.pewresearch.org/fact-tank/2015/06/18/census-considers-new-approach-to-asking-about-race-by-not-using-the-term-at-all/.
5. Karen Humes, Nicholas A. Jones, and Roberto R. Ramirez, "Overview of Race and Hispanic Origin 2010," 2010 Census Briefs, p. 6. Accessed April 15, 2016, http://www.census.gov/prod/cen2010/briefs/c2010br-02.pdf.
6. For an analysis that reads the "some other race" choice as a declaration that Hispanic is a race, see Ian Haney Lopez, "Race on the 2010 Census: Hispanics and the Shrinking White Majority," *Daedalus* 134, no. 1 (2005): 46.
7. Jessica M. Vasquez, "The Whitening Hypothesis Challenged: Biculturalism in Latino and Non-Hispanic White Intermarriage," *Sociological Forum* 29, no. 2 (2014): 404.
8. See the following on symbolic ethnicity: Mary Waters, *Ethnic Options* and Herbert Gans, "Symbolic Ethnicity: The Future of Ethnic Groups and Cultures in America," *Ethnic and Racial Studies* 2, no. 1 (1979): 1–20.
9. Vasquez, "The Whitening Hypothesis Challenged," 404.
10. Tanya Golash-Boza and William Darity Jr., "Latino Racial Choices: The Effects of Skin Colour and Discrimination on Latinos' and Latinas' Racial Self-identifications," *Ethnic and Racial Studies* 31, no. 5 (2008): 916.
11. For more on bi- and multiracial individuals and their forms of racial identification, see the following: Lauren D. Davenport, "Beyond Black and White: Biracial

Attitudes in Contemporary U.S. Politics," *American Political Science Review* 110, no. 1 (2016): 52–67; David Brunsma, Daniel Delgado, and Kerry Ann Rockquemore, "Liminality in the Multiracial Experience: Towards a Concept of Identity Matrix," *Identities* 20, no.5 (2013): 481–502; Sarah S. M. Townsend, Clara L. Wilkins, Stephanie A. Fryberg, Hazel Rose Markus, "Being Mixed: Who Claims a Biracial Identity?," *Cultural Diversity and Ethnic Minority Psychology* 18, no. 1 (2012): 91–96; Nikki Khanna, "Ethnicity and Race as 'Symbolic': The Use of Ethnic and Racial Symbols in Asserting a Biracial Identity," *Ethnic and Racial Studies* 34, no. 6 (2011): 1049–1067; Kerry Ann Rockquemore and David Brunsma, "Socially Embedded Identities: Theories, Typologies and Processes of Racial Identity Among Black/White Biracials," *Sociological Quarterly* 43, no. 3 (2002): 335–357.

12. While none of the authors to be discussed here comes out and says that they mean for their discussion of a new color line to apply to every part of the United States, this is certainly the implicit understanding with which they write. They cite the black-white color line as historically structuring US race relations and then ask if a new color line is emerging to take its place. There is no attempt to nuance the argument based on place or region within the United States.

13. Frank D. Bean, Jennifer Lee, and James D. Bachmeier, "Immigration and the Color Line at the Beginning of the Twenty-First Century," *Daedalus* 142, no. 3 (2013): 123–140. In addition to this, also see a large stream of work in a similar vein by the same authors: Jennifer Lee and Frank D. Bean, *The Diversity Paradox: Immigration and the Color Line in Twenty-First Century America* (New York: Russel Sage, 2010); Jennifer Lee and Frank D. Bean, "Reinventing the Color Line: Immigration and America's New Racial/Ethnic Divide," *Social Forces* 86, no. 2 (2007): 561–586; Jennifer Lee and Frank D. Bean, "America's Changing Color Lines: Immigration, Race/Ethnicity and Multiracial Identification," *Annual Review of Sociology* 30 (2004): 221–242.

14. In addition to the voluminous work by Lee and Bean, also see Helen B. Marrow, "New Immigrant Destinations and the American Colour Line," *Ethnic and Racial Studies* 32, no. 6 (2009): 1037–1057.

15. Although money does not necessarily recategorize a person as white in Latin America, more money can socially whiten a person in that he or she will be considered to be acceptable in white social circles.

16. Reanne Frank, Ilana Resdstone Akresh, and Bo Lu, "Latino Immigrants and the U.S. Racial Order: How and Where Do They Fit In?" *American Sociological Review* 75, no. 3 (2010): 378–401.

17. Ibid., 389.

18. Ibid., 391.

19. Wendy Roth adroitly addresses the complexities in the ways individuals perceive, read, and label themselves and others racially. Such reading and labeling vary from individual to individual and are also shaped by the ethnic and racial composition of the community in which an individual lives. Thus, we must pay attention both to the multiple dimensions of race and the ways these dimensions are differently configured in varied places. For more on distinguishing between different dimensions of race and how this affects the racial identification and classification of self and other, see Wendy D. Roth, "Racial Mismatch: The Divergence Between Form and Function in Data for Monitoring Racial Discrimination of Hispanics," *Social Science Quarterly* 91, no. 5 (2010): 1288–1311; and Wendy D. Roth, "The Multiple Dimensions of Race," *Ethnic and Racial Studies* 39, no. 8 (2016): 1310–1338.

20. Tafoya, "Shades of Belonging: Latinos and Racial Identity," 65.

21. The emphasis in the quotation is mine. John R. Logan, "How Race Counts for Hispanic Americans," Lewis Mumford Center for Comparative Urban and Regional Research, University at Albany, July 14, 2003, accessed April 16, 2016, http://mumford.albany.edu/census/BlackLatinoReport/BlackLatinoReport.pdf, 11.
22. See the following texts for classic statements on assimilation: Robert E. Park, "Racial Assimilation in Secondary Groups with Particular Reference to the Negro," *American Journal of Sociology* 19, no. 5 (1914): 606–623; see Robert E. Park, "Assimilation" in *Introduction to the Science of Sociology*, ed. Robert E. Part and Ernest Burgess (Chicago: University of Chicago Press, 1921), 756–784; Robert E. Park, "Social Assimilation," in *Encyclopaedia of the Social Sciences*, vol. 2 (New York: Macmillan, 1930), 281–283; William Isaac Thomas, Robert E. Park and Herbert A. Miller, *Old World Traits Transplanted* (New York: Harper Brothers, 1921); W. Lloyd Warner and Leo Srole, *The Social Systems of American Ethnic Groups* (New Haven, CT: Yale University Press, 1947); Milton Gordon, *Assimilation in American Life: The Role of Race, Religion and National Origins* (New York: Oxford University Press, 1964).
23. The literature on assimilation and segmented assimilation is too voluminous to summarize here, but the following discussion offers a larger context for understanding the significance of the segmented assimilation concept. In the 1990s, work on the second generation of post-1965 immigrants began to sound a new, less positive note about the powers of assimilation. In works published during this time, Herbert Gans, "Second-Generation Decline: Scenarios for the Economic and Ethnic Futures of the Post-1965 American Immigrants," *Ethnic and Racial Studies* 15, no. 2 (1992): 173–192, signaled the pressures black and Hispanic immigrants had to conform to the social and cultural perspectives of poor people of color native to the United States. In a 1993 article, Alejandro Portes and Min Zhou introduced a new, more flexible conceptualization of assimilation that took this reality into account: "segmented assimilation." Here see Alejandro Portes and Min Zhou, "The New Second Generation: Segmented Assimilation and its Variants," *The Annals of the American Academy of Political and Social Science* 530 (1993): 74–96. The innovation of segmented assimilation is that it raises the important question of what immigrants are assimilating into. Earlier work had assumed that all immigrants would eventually assimilate into the US Anglo-American core. Even if the assumption was that some cultural diversity would remain—as it was with Park—the assumption was that immigrants would be able to merge in most ways into the Anglo-American mainstream.

The work emerging from the 1990s, based on the experience of the children of immigrants coming to the United States after 1965, signaled that immigrant children were indeed assimilating, but into different American streams. In their work, Portes and Zhou examined the outcomes of young people from three different kinds of immigrant backgrounds: Mexican, Caribbean, and South Asian. What they found was that the young people who adhered most closely to their parents' culture were the ones who had the best social and educational outcomes. This stood the long-term discussion of assimilation on its head. Rather than assimilating to US standards, immigrants of color might do better to keep their ethnic cultures as a strategy for getting ahead in the United States.

See the following for more on segmented assimilation: Min Zhou, "Segmented assimilation: Issues, Controversies, and Recent Research on the New Second Generation," *International Migration Review* 31, no. 4 (1997): 975–1008. For an account which comes to some of the same conclusions about the protective force

of keeping ethnic identity, but without invoking the term "segmented assimilation," see Rubén Rumbaut, "Assimilation and Its Discontents: Between Rhetoric and Reality," *International Migration Review* 31, no. 4 (1997): 923–960.
24. Robert Park does, however, deal to some extent with the situation of black Americans. In general, he believed that black Americans would also eventually assimilate. See Robert E. Park, "Racial Assimilation in Secondary Groups with Particular Reference to the Negro."
25. Moon Kie Jung, "The Racial Unconscious of Assimilation Theory," *Du Bois Review* 6, no. 2 (2009): 375–395.
26. Vilna Bashi Treitler, "Social Agency and White Supremacy in Immigration Studies," *Sociology of Race and Ethnicity* 1, no. 1 (2015): 162.
27. Richard Alba and Victor Nee, *Remaking the American Mainstream: Assimilation and Contemporary Immigration* (Cambridge, MA: Harvard University Press, 2003).
28. Edward E. Telles and Vilma Ortiz, *Generations of Exclusion: Mexican Americans, Assimilation, and Race* (New York: Russel Sage Foundation, 2009), 17.
29. Richard Alba, Tomás R. Jiménez, and Helen B. Marrow, "Mexican Americans as a Paradigm for Contemporary Intra-Group Heterogeniety," *Ethnic and Racial Studies* 37, no. 3 (2014): 456.
30. Ibid., 458.
31. Jung, "The Racial Unconscious of Assimilation Theory," 381.
32. Consider Maritza Quiñones Rivera's very personal analysis of dealing with these complex dynamics in the Latin/Caribbean racial system of Puerto Rico. See Maritza Quiñones Rivera, "From Trigueñita to Afro-Puerto Rican: Intersections of the Racialized, Gendered, and Sexualized Body in Puerto Rico and the U.S. Mainland," *Meridians: Feminism, Race, Transnationalism* 7, no. 1 (2006): 162–182.
33. Mary C. Water, *Black Identities: West Indian Immigrant Dreams and American Realities* (New York: Russell Sage Foundation, 1999), 166.
34. Ibid., 65.
35. Ibid., 68.
36. Danielle S. Allen, *Talking to Strangers: Anxieties of Citizenship Since Brown v. Board of Education* (Chicago: University of Chicago Press, 2004), 20.

BIBLIOGRAPHY

PRIMARY SOURCES
Digital Collections
Chronicling America: Historic American Newspapers http://www.chroniclingamerica. loc.gov
Genealogy Bank http://www.genealogybank.com
LSU Libraries "Free People of Color in Louisiana: Revealing an Unknown Past" http:// www.lib.lsu.edu/special/fpoc/collections.html#NOPL

Onsite Archives
Historic New Orleans Collection, Rivet Collection
Historic New Orleans Collection, St. Gême Family Papers
Tulane University, Amistad Research Center, A. P. Tureaud Collection
Tulane University, Lambert Family Papers, Collection 244

Printed Primary Source
The Territorial Papers of the United States, Vol. IX, The Territory of Orleans, 1803–1812, Clarence Edwin Carter, ed. Washington, DC: U.S. Government Printing Office, 1940.

Secondary Sources
Abott, Rev. Abiel. *Letters Written in the Interior of Cuba: Between the Mountains of Arcana to the East and of Cusco to the West*. Boston: Bowles and Dearborn, 1829. Accessed March 23, 2016, https://archive.org/stream/letterswritteni00abbogoog#page/n7/mode/2up.

Acosta, Yesenia D., and G. Patricia de la Cruz. "The Foreign Born from Latin America and the Caribbean: 2010." *American Community Survey Brief*, September 2011. Accessed June 3, 2016, http://www.census.gov/prod/2011pubs/acsbr10-15.pdf

Alba, Richard Tomás, R. Jiménez, and Helen B. Marrow. "Mexican Americans as a Paradigm for Contemporary Intra-Group Heterogeneity." *Ethnic and Racial Studies* 37, no. 3 (2014): 446–466.

Alba, Richard, and Victor Nee. *Remaking the American Mainstream: Assimilation and Contemporary Immigration*. Cambridge, MA: Harvard University Press, 2003.

Allen, Danielle. *Our Declaration: A Reading of the Declaration of Independence in Defense of Liberty*. New York: W.W. Norton & Co., 2014.

Allen, Danielle S. *Talking to Strangers: Anxieties of Citizenship Since Brown v. Board of Education*. Chicago: University of Chicago Press, 2004.

Anderson, Benedict. *Imagined Communities: Reflections on the Origin and Spread of Nationalism*. New York: Verso Press, 1983.
Bean, Frank D., Jennifer Lee, and James D. Bachmeier. "Immigration and the Color Line at the Beginning of the Twenty-First Century." *Daedalus* 142, no. 3 (2013): 123–140.
Bell, Caryn Cossé. *Revolution, Romanticism and the Afro-Creole Protest Tradition in Louisiana 1718–1868*. Baton Rouge: Louisiana State University Press, 1997.
Berlin, Ira. *Many Thousands Gone: The First Two Centuries of Slavery in North America*. Cambridge, MA: Harvard University Press, 1998.
Berlin, Ira. *Slaves Without Masters: The Free Negro in the Antebellum* South. New York: Oxford University Press, 1974.
Berlin, Ira. "Southern Free People of Color in the Age of William Johnson." *Southern Quarterly* 43, no. 2 (2006): 9–17.
Bogger, Tommy L. *Free Blacks in Norfolk, Virginia, 1790–1860: The Darker Side of Freedom*. Charlottesville: University Press of Virginia, 1997.
Bonilla-Silva, Eduardo. "We Are All Americans! The Latin Americanization of Racial Stratification in the U.S.A." *Race and Society* 5 (2002): 3–16.
Bradley, Jared William, Ed. *Interim Appointment: W.C.C. Claiborne Letter Book, 1804–1805, with Biographical Sketches*. Baton Rouge: Louisiana State University Press, 2002.
Brasseaux, Carl A., and Glenn Conrad, *The Road to Louisiana: The Saint-Domingue Refugees, 1792–1809*. Translated by David Cheramie. Lafayette, Center for Louisiana Studies: University of Southwestern Louisiana, 1992.
Brodkin, Karen. *How the Jews Became White Folks & What That Says about Race in America*. Brunswick, NJ: Rutgers University Press, 1998.
Brunsma, David, Daniel Delgado, and Kerry Ann Rockquemore. "Liminality in the Multiracial Experience: Towards a Concept of Identity Matrix." *Identities* 20, no. 5 (2013): 481–502.
Camier, Bernard. "Les concerts dans les capitals de Saint-Domingue à la fin du XVIIIe siècle." *Revue de Musicologie*. T. 93, no. 1 (2007): 75–98.
Castellanos, Henry C. *New Orleans As It Was: Episodes of Louisiana Life*. Baton Rouge: Louisiana State University Press, 2006.
Clark, Emily. *The Strange History of the American Quadroon: Free Women of Color in the Revolutionary Atlantic World*. Charlotte: University of North Carolina Press, 2013.
Cohn, D'Vera. "Census Considers New Approach to Asking about Race—By Not Using the Term at All." June 18, 2015. Accessed April 15, 2016, http://www.pewresearch.org/fact-tank/2015/06/18/census-considers-new-approach-to-asking-about-race-by-not-using-the-term-at-all/
Colby, Sandra L., and Jennifer Ortman. "Projections of the Size and Composition of the U.S. Population: 2014 to 2060, March 2015. Accessed April 15, 2016, http://www.census.gov/content/dam/Census/library/publications/2015/demo/p25-1143.pdf
Coleman, Edward Maceo, Ed. *Creole Voices: Poems in French by Free Men of Color*. Washington, D.C.: Associated Publishers, 1945.
Davenport, Lauren D. "Beyond Black and White: Biracial Attitudes in Contemporary U.S. Politics." *American Political Science Review* 110, no. 1 (2016): 52–67.
Davis, David Brion. *The Problem of Slavery in Western Culture*. Ithaca, NY: Cornell University Press, 1966.

Davis, F. James. *Who Is Black? One Nation's Definition*. University Park: The Pennsylvania State University Press, 1991.

Debien, Gabriel. "The Saint-Domingue Refugees in Cuba." In *The Road to Louisiana: The Saint-Domingue Refugees 1792–1809*, edited by Carl A. Brasseaux and Glenn R. Conrad, 31–112. Lafayette, LA: The Center for Louisiana Studies, University of Southwestern Louisiana, 1992.

de la Fuente, Alejandro. "Slave Law and Claims-Making in Cuba: The Tannenbaum Debate Revisited." *Law and History Review* 22, no. 2 (Summer 2004): 339–369.

Desdunes, R.L. *Our People and Our Culture: Fifty Creole Portraits*. Baton Rouge: Louisiana State University Press, 1973.

Dessens, Nathalie. *From Saint-Domingue to New Orleans: Migration and Influences*, Gainesville: University Press of Florida, 2007.

Dominguez, Virginia. *White by Definition: Social Classification in Creole Louisiana*. New Brunswick, NJ: Rutgers University Press, 1986.

Dubois, Laurent. *Avengers of the New World: The Story of the Haitian Revolution*. Cambridge, MA: Harvard University Press, 2004.

Eder, Donald G. "Time under the Southern Cross: The Tannenbaum Thesis Reappraised." *Agricultural History* 50, no. 4 (1976): 600–614.

Ellis, Trey. "The New Black Aesthetic." *Callaloo* (Winter 1989): 233–243.

Feagin, Joe R., and José Cobas, *Latinos Facing Racism: Discrimination, Resistance, and Endurance*. Boulder, CO: Paradigm Publishers, 2014.

Fears, Darryl. "People of Color Who Never Felt They Were Black: Racial Label Surprises Many Latino Immigrants." *The Washington Post*, December 26, 2002. Accessed February 10, 2016, https://www.washingtonpost.com/archive/politics/2002/12/26/people-of-color-who-never-felt-they-were-black/071e165f-48b7-4aaa-9d86-23e907cfbc7f/.

Fertel, Rien. *Imagining the Creole City: The Rise of Literary Culture in Nineteenth-Century New Orleans*. Baton Rouge: Louisiana State University Press, 2014.

Fick, Carolyn E. *The Making of Haiti: The Saint Domingue Revolution from Below*. Knoxville: University of Tennessee Press, 1990.

Foner, Laura. "The Free People of Color in Louisiana and St. Domingue: A Comparative Portrait of Two Three-Caste Slave Societies." *Journal of Social History* 3, no. 4 (1970): 406–430.

Fortier, Alcée. *A History of Louisiana*, vol. IV, The American Domination Part II, 1861–1908. New York: Manzi, Joyant & Co., 1904.

Frank, Reanne, Ilana Resdstone Akresh, and Bo Lu. "Latino Immigrants and the U.S. Racial Order: How and Where Do They Fit In?" *American Sociological Review* 75, no. 3 (2010): 378–401.

Franklin, John Hope. *The Free Negro in North Carolina, 1790–1860*. Chapel Hill: University of North Carolina Press, 1943.

Freyre, Gilberto. *The Masters and the Slaves: A Study in the Development of Brazilian Civilization*. 2nd English language edition, revised. Translated by Samuel Putnam. New York: Alfred A. Knopf, 1956.

Gans, Herbert. "Second-Generation Decline: Scenarios for the Economic and Ethnic Futures of the Post-1965 American Immigrants." *Ethnic and Racial Studies* 15, no. 2 (1992): 173–192.

Gans, Herbert. "Symbolic Ethnicity: The future of Ethnic Groups and Cultures in America." *Ethnic and Racial Studies* 2, no. 1 (1979): 1–20.

Garrigus, John D. "Colour, Class and Identity on the Eve of the Haitian Revolution: Saint-Domingue's Free Colored Elite as *Colons Americaines*." *Slavery and Abolition* 17, no. 1(April 1996): 19–43.

Garrigus, John D. "Redrawing the Colour Line: Gender and the Social Construction of Race in Pre-Revolutionary Haiti." *Journal of Caribbean History* 30, no. 1 & 2 (1996a): 28–50.

Gates, Henry Louis. *Loose Canons: Notes in the Culture Wars*. New York: Oxford University Press, 1992.

Gaudin, Wendy Ann. "Autocrats and All Saints: Migration, Memory, and Modern Creole Identities." Ph.D. diss., New York University, 2005.

Golash-Boza, Tanya, and William Darity Jr. "Latino Racial Choices: The Effects of Skin Colour and Discrimination on Latinos' and Latinas' Racial Self-Identifications." *Ethnic and Racial Studies* 31, no. 5 (2008): 899–934.

Gordon, Milton. *Assimilation in American Life: The Role of Race, Religion and National Origins*. New York: Oxford University Press, 1964.

Gross, Ariela. "Legal Transplants: Slavery and the Civil Law in Louisiana," USC Legal Studies Research Paper No. 09-16. Accessed November 28, 2014, http://weblaw.usc.edu/centers/class/class-workshops/usc-legal-studies-working-papers/documents/09_16_paper.pdf.

Gross, Ariela, and Alejandro de la Fuente. "Slaves, Free Blacks, and Race in the Legal Regimes of Cuba, Louisiana and Virginia: A Comparison." *North Carolina Law Review* 91, no. 5 (2013): 1699–1756.

Haddox, Thomas. "The 'Nous' of Southern Catholic Quadroons: Racial, Ethnic, and Religious Identity in *Les Cenelles*." *American Literature* 73, no. 4 (2001): 757–778.

Hall, Gwendolyn Midlo. *Social Control in Slave Plantation Societies: A Comparison of St. Domingue and Cuba*. Baltimore: Johns Hopkins University Press, 1971.

Hanger, Kimberly S. *Bounded Lives, Bounded Places: Free Black Society in Colonial New Orleans, 1769–1803*. Durham, NC: Duke University Press, 1997.

Harris, Marvin. *Patterns of Race in the Americas*. New York: Walker and Company, 1964.

Helg, Aline. "Race and Black Mobilization in Colonial and Early Independent Cuba: A Comparative Perspective." *Ethnohistory* 44, no.1 (Winter 1997): 53–74.

Hoetink, H. *Caribbean Race Relations: A Study of Two Variants*. New York: Oxford University Press, 1967.

Hoetink, H. " 'Race' and Color in the Caribbean." In *Caribbean Contours*, edited by Sidney W. Mintz and Sally Price, 55–84. Baltimore: Johns Hopkins University Press, 1985.

Hoffmann, Léon-François. "Victor Hugo, John Brown et les Haitiens." *Nineteenth-Century French Studies* 16, no. 1-2 (1987–1988): 47–58.

Humes, Karen, Nicholas A. Jones, and Roberto R. Ramirez, "Overview of Race and Hispanic Origin 2010," 2010 Census Briefs. Accessed April 15, 2016, http://www.census.gov/prod/cen2010/briefs/c2010br-02.pdf.

Ignatiev, Noel. *How the Irish Became White*. New York: Routledge, 1995.

Ingersoll, Thomas N. *Mammon and Manon in Early New Orleans: The First Slave Society in the Deep South, 1718–1819*. Knoxville: University of Tennessee Press, 1999.

Jacobson, Matthew Frye. *Whiteness of a Different Color: European Immigrants and the Alchemy of Race*. Cambridge, MA: Harvard University Press, 1999.

Jimenez, Tomás R. *Replenished Ethnicity: Mexican Americans, Immigration, and Identity*. Berkeley: University of California Press, 2010.

Johnson, Jerah. *Congo Square in New Orleans*. New Orleans: Louisiana Landmarks Society, 2011.

Jung, Moon Kie. "The Racial Unconscious of Assimilation Theory." *Du Bois Review* 6, no. 2 (2009): 375–395.
Khanna, Nikki. "Ethnicity and Race as 'Symbolic': The Use of Ethnic and Racial Symbols in Asserting a Biracial Identity." *Ethnic and Racial Studies* 34, no. 6 (2011): 1049–1067.
Kim, Christine, Franklin Sirmans and Thelma Golden, Editors. *Freestyle: The Studio Museum in Harlem*. New York: Studio Museum in Harlem, 2001.
King, Grace. *Creole Families of New Orleans*. New York: Macmillan Company, 1921.
Kinser, Samuel. *Carnival, American Style: Mardi Gras at New Orleans and Mobile*. Chicago: University of Chicago Press, 1990.
La Chance, Paul. "The Foreign French." In *Creole New Orleans: Race and Americanization*, edited by Arnold Hirsch and Joseph Logsdon, 101–130. Baton Rouge: Louisiana State University Press, 1992.
La Chance, Paul. "The 1809 Immigration of Saint-Domingue Refugees to New Orleans: Reception, Integration, and Impact." In *The Road to Louisiana: The Saint-Domingue Refugees 1792–1809*, edited by Carl A. Brasseaux and Glenn R. Conrad, 245–284. Lafayette, LA: The Center for Louisiana Studies, 1992.
La Chance, Paul. "St. Domingue émigrés in New Orleans, 1800–1830." Lecture presented at the Eleventh Annual Williams Research Center Symposium, New Orleans, Louisiana, February 4, 2006.
La Chance, Paul. "Were St. Domingue Refugees a Distinctive Cultural Group in Antebellum New Orleans? Evidence from Patterns and Strategies of Property Holding." *Revista/Review Interamericana* 29, no. 1-4 (1999): 171–192.
Laguerre, Michel. *Diasporic Citizenship: Haitians in transnational America*. New York: St. Martin's Press, 1998.
Lanusse, Armand, Editor. *Les Cenelles: Choix de poésies indigenes*. Shreveport, LA: Les Cahiers de Tintamarre, 2013.
Lee, Jennifer, and Frank D. Bean. "America's Changing Color Lines: Immigration, Race/Ethnicity and Multiracial Identification." *Annual Review of Sociology* 30 (2004): 221–242.
Lee, Jennifer, and Frank D. Bean. *The Diversity Paradox: Immigration and the Color Line in Twenty-First Century America*. New York: Russell Sage, 2010.
Lee, Jennifer, and Frank D. Bean. "Reinventing the Color Line: Immigration and America's New Racial/Ethnic Divide." *Social Forces* 86, no. 2 (2007): 561–586.
Lee, Sharon M. "Racial Classifications in the U.S. Census: 1890–1990." *Ethnic and Racial Studies* 16, no. 1 (1993): 75–94.
Logan, John R. "How Race Counts for Hispanic Americans." Lewis Mumford Center for Comparative Urban and Regional Research, University at Albany, July 14, 2003, accessed April 16, 2016, http://mumford.albany.edu/census/BlackLatinoReport/BlackLatinoReport.pdf.
Lopez, Ian Haney. "Race on the 2010 Census: Hispanics and the Shrinking White Majority." *Daedalus* 134, no. 1 (2005): 42–52.
Loveman, Mara. *National Colors: Racial Classification and the State in Latin America*. New York: Oxford University Press, 2014.
Loveman, Mara. "Whiteness in Latin America: Measurement and Meaning in National Censuses." *Journal de la Société des Américanistes* 95, no. 2 (2009): 207–234.
Lowe, Ellene. "Administrative Problems of W.C.C. Claiborne, First Anglo-American Governor of Louisiana." Master's thesis, University of North Texas, 1939.
Marrow, Helen B. "New Immigrant Destinations and the American Colour Line." *Ethnic and Racial Studies* 32, no. 6 (2009): 1037–1057.

Martin, Joan M. "*Plaçage* and the Louisiana Gens de Couleur Libre: How Race and Sex Defined the Lifestyles of Free Women of Color." In *Creole: The History and Legacy of Louisiana's Free People of Color*, edited by Sybil Kein, 57–70. Baton Rouge: Louisiana State University Press, 2000.

Martinez-Echazabal, Lourdes. "Mestizaje and the Discourse of National/Cultural Identity in Latin America: 1845–1959." *Latin American Perspectives* 25, no. 3 (1998): 21–42.

Mills, Charles. *The Racial Contract*. Ithaca, NY: Cornell University Press, 1997.

Milteer, Jr., Warren E. "Life in a Great Dismal Swamp Community: Free People of Color in Pre-Civil War Gates County, North Carolina." *The North Carolina Historical Review* 91-2 (2014): 144–170.

Nobles, Melissa. *Shades of Citizenship: Race and the Census in Modern Politics*. Stanford, CA: Stanford University Press, 2000.

Nora, Pierre. "Between Memory and History: *Les Lieux de Mémoires*." *Representations*. 26, Special Issue: Memory and Counter-Memory (Spring 1989): 7–24.

Omi, Michael, and Howard Winant. *Racial Formation in the United States*, 4th ed. New York: Routledge, 2015.

O'Neill, M. J. *How Does He Do It: Sam T. Jack, Twenty Years a King in the Realm of Burlesque*. Whitefish, MT: Kessinger Publishing, 2007.

Park, Robert E. "Assimilation" in *Introduction to the Science of Sociology*, edited by Robert E. Part and Ernest Burgess, 756–784. Chicago: University of Chicago Press, 1921.

Park, Robert E. "Racial Assimilation in Secondary Groups with Particular Reference to the Negro." *American Journal of Sociology* 19, no. 5 (1914): 606–623.

Park, Robert E. "Social Assimilation." In *Encyclopaedia of the Social Sciences*, vol. 2, 281–283. New York: Macmillan, 1930.

Pereira, Malin. "The Poet in the World and the World in the Poet: Cyrus Cassells's and Elizabeth Alexander's Versions of Post-Soul Cosmopolitanism." *African American Review* 41, no. 4 (2007): 709–725.

Perlmann, Joel. *Italians Then, Mexicans Now: Immigrant Origins and Second-Generation Progress, 1890–Present*. New York: Russell Sage Foundation, 2005.

Popkin, Jeremy D. "A Survivor of Dessalines's Massacres in 1804." In *Facing Racial Revolution: Eyewitness Accounts of the Haitian Insurrection*, 336–362. Chicago: University of Chicago Press, 2007.

Portes, Alejandro, and Min Zhou. "The New Second Generation: Segmented Assimilation and Its Variants." *The Annals of the American Academy of Political and Social Science* 530 (1993): 74–96.

Portes, Alejandro, and Ruben Rumbaut. "Introduction: The Second Generation and the Children of Immigrants Longitudinal Study." *Ethnic and Racial Studies* 28, no. 6 (2005): 983–999.

Rankin, David. "The Politics of Caste: Free Colored Leadership in New Orleans During the Civil War." In *Louisiana's Black Heritage*, edited by Robert R. MacDonald, John R. Kemp, and Edward F. Haas, 107–146. New Orleans: Louisiana State Museum, 1979.

Rankin, David. "The Tannenbaum Thesis Reconsidered: Slavery and Race Relations in Antebellum Louisiana." *Southern Studies* 18, no.1 (1979): 5–31.

Reid-Vasquez, Michele. *The Year of the Lash: Free People of Color in Cuba and the Nineteenth-Century Atlantic World*. Athens: University of Georgia Press, 2011.

Rivera, Maritza Quiñones. "From Trigueñita to Afro-Puerto Rican: Intersections of the Racialized, Gendered, and Sexualized Body in Puerto Rico and the U.S. Mainland." *Meridians: Feminism, Race, Transnationalism* 7, no. 1 (2006): 162–182.

Rockquemore, Kerry Ann and David Brunsma. "Socially Embedded Identities: Theories, Typologies and Processes of Racial Identity among Black/White Biracials." *Sociological Quarterly* 43, no. 3 (2002): 335–357.

Roediger, David R. *Working Toward Whiteness: How America's Immigrants Became White*. New York: Basic Books, 2005.

Rogers, Dominique. "Les libres de couleur dans les capitals de Saint-Domingue: fortune, mentalités et integration à la fin de l'Ancien Régime (1776–1789)." Ph.D. diss., L'université Michel de Montaigne, Bourdeaux III, 1999.

Rohrs, Richard C. "The Free Black Experience in Antebellum Wilmington, North Carolina: Refining Generalizations about Race Relations." *The Journal of Southern History* 78, no. 3 (2012): 615–638.

Roth, Wendy D. "The Multiple Dimensions of Race." *Ethnic and Racial Studies* 39, no. 8 (2016): 1310–1338.

Roth, Wendy D. *Race Migrations: Latinos and the Cultural Transformation of Race*. Stanford, CA: Stanford University Press, 2012.

Roth, Wendy D. "Racial Mismatch: The Divergence Between Form and Function in Data for Monitoring Racial Discrimination of Hispanics." *Social Science Quarterly* 91, no. 5 (2010): 1288–1311.

Rumbaut, Rubén. "Assimilation and Its Discontents: Between Rhetoric and Reality." *International Migration Review* 31, no. 4 (1997): 923–960.

Rumbaut, Rubén. "The Crucible Within: Ethnic Identity, Self-Esteem, and Segmented Assimilation among Children of Immigrants." *International Migration Review* 28, no. 4 (1994): 748–794.

Sáenz, Rogelio, and Karen Manges Douglas. "A Call for the Racialization of Immigration Studies: On the Transition of Ethnic Immigrants to Racialized Immigrants." *Sociology of Race and Ethnicity* 1, no. 1 (2015):166–180.

Sartorius, David. *Ever Faithful: Race, Loyalty and the Ends of Empire in Spanish Cuba*. Durham, NC: Duke University Press, 2013.

Scott, Rebecca. "The Atlantic World and the Road to *Plessy v. Ferguson*." *Journal of American History* 94, no. 3 (2007): 726–733.

Scott, Rebecca J. *Degrees of Freedom: Louisiana and Cuba after Slavery*. Cambridge, MA: Harvard University Press, 2005.

Scott, Rebecca, and Jean Hébrard. *Freedom Papers: An Atlantic Odyssey in the Age of Emancipation*. Cambridge, MA: Harvard University Press, 2012.

St. Méry, Moreau de. *Description topographique, physique, civile, politique, et historique de la partie française de l'isle Saint-Domingue*. Philadelphia, 1797. Accessed June 6, 2016, http://www.archive.org/details/descriptiontopog00more.

Swarns, Rachel L. "Hispanics Resist Racial Grouping by Census." *New York Times*, October 24, 2004. Accessed June 6, 2016, http://www.nytimes.com/learning/teachers/featured_articles/20041025monday.html.

Sweet, James. "The Iberian Roots of American Racist Thought." *The William and Mary Quarterly* 44, no. 1 (1997): 143–166.

Tafoya, Sonya M. "Shades of Belonging: Latinos and Racial Identity." *Harvard Journal of Hispanic Policy* 17 (2004/2005): 58–78.

Tannenbaum, Frank. *Slave and Citizen: The Negro in the Americas*. New York: Vintage Books, 1946.

Taylor, Paul C. "Post-Black, Old Black." *African American Review* 41, no. 4 (2007): 625–640.

Telles, Edward. *Race in Another America: The Significance of Skin Color in Brazil*. Princeton, NJ: Princeton University Press, 2004.

Telles, Edward, and René Flores. "Not Just Color: Whiteness, Nation and Status in Latin America." *Hispanic American Historical Review* 93, no. 3 (2013): 411–449.

Telles, Edward E., and Vilma Ortiz. *Generations of Exclusion: Mexican Americans, Assimilation, and Race*. New York: Russel Sage Foundation, 2009.

Thompson, Shirley Elizabeth. "'Ah Toucoutou, Ye Conin Vou': History and Memory in Creole New Orleans." *American Quarterly* 53, no. 2 (2001): 232–266.

Thompson, Shirley Elizabeth. *Exiles at Home: The Struggle to Become American in Creole New Orleans*. Cambridge, MA: Harvard University Press, 2009.

Tinker, Edward Laroque. *Toucoutou*. New York: Dodd, Mead and Company, 1930.

Touré. *Who's Afraid of Post-Blackness? What It Means to Be Black Now*. New York: Atria Books, 2012.

Townsend, Sarah S. M., Clara L. Wilkins, Stephanie A. Fryberg, and Hazel Rose Markus. "Being Mixed: Who Claims a Biracial Identity?" *Cultural Diversity and Ethnic Minority Psychology* 18, no. 1 (2012): 91–96.

Tregle, Jr., Joseph. "Creoles and Americans." In *Creole New Orleans: Race and Americanization*, edited by Arnold R. Hirsch and Joseph Logsdon, 131–188. Baton Rouge: Louisiana State University Press, 1992.

Treitler, Vilna Bashi. "Social Agency and White Supremacy in Immigration Studies." *Sociology of Race and Ethnicity* 1, no. 1 (2015): 153–165.

Vasquez, Jessica M. "The Whitening Hypothesis Challenged: Biculturalism in Latino and Non-Hispanic White Intermarriage." *Sociological Forum* 29, no. 2 (2014): 386–407.

Wagley, Charles. "On the Concept of Social Race in the Americas." In *Contemporary Societies and Cultures in Latin America*, edited by Dwight B. Heath and Richard N. Adams, 531–545. New York: Random House, 1965.

Waldinger, Roger, and Joel Perlmann. "Second Generations: Past, Present and Future." *Journal of Ethnic and Migration Studies* 24, no. 1 (1998): 5–24

Warner, W. Lloyd, and Leo Srole. *The Social Systems of American Ethnic Groups*. New Haven, CT: Yale University Press, 1947.

Waters, Mary C. *Black Identities: West Indian Immigrant Dreams and American Realities*. New York: Russell Sage Foundation, 1999.

Waters, Mary C. *Ethnic Options: Choosing Identities in America*. Berkeley: University of California Press, 1990.

Young, Perry. *The Mistick Krewe: Chronicles of Comus and His Kin*. Shreveport, LA: Louisiana Heritage Press, 1969.

Zhou, Min. "Segmented Assimilation: Issues, Controversies, and Recent Research on the New Second Generation." *International Migration Review* 31, no. 4 (1997): 975–1008.

INDEX

Abbott, Abiel: on *coartación*, 35; on freedom, 35; on manumission, 36
L'Abeille, 133
African ancestry: as blackness, 45–46, 156; Creoles of, 152–53; Freyre on, 27; identity of, 155–56, 256n1; Latin/Caribbean racial system of, 206–8; *limpieza de sangre* influenced by, 28, 243n26; "one-drop rule" of, 29
Afro-Creole. *See* Creoles of color
Alba, Richard, 204–205
Allen, Danielle, 209
American Quarter, 78, 79f
Americans: Anglo-Americans as, 124; Creoles perception by, 7, 249n7; in Faubourg St. Mary, 77; *See also* Anglo-Americans; Mexican Americans
ancestry, *See;* Anglo-Americans and, 145–46; of Creoles, 11–12, 86, 143, 152–53, 241n21; social distance by, 49; of St. Domingue, 215–16; of white Creoles, 220; whiteness by, 140. *See also* African ancestry
Anderson, Benedict, 148
Anglo-American racial system: against Creoles, 78; for Creoles of color, 188; Creoles of color influenced by, 118, 155–56, 188–89; Latin/Caribbean racial system and, 5, 20, 80, 139, 165, 190, 193, 200, 207, 242n2; for Latinos, 192–93; of Louisiana, 97–98; for purity, 82–83; racial palimpsest and, 21, 46, 47t, 189–90, 199, 206; for St. Domingue refugees, 186–87, 202; whiteness by, 92, 115, 183
Anglo-Americans: as Americans, 124; ancestry and, 145–46; Boze on, 76; Creoles and, 14, 72–73, 123, 126; against free people of color, 95; French language and, 1–2; of Louisiana, 6; Louisiana Purchase by, 7; Mistick Krewe of Comus by, 133–34; *Plessy v. Ferguson* influenced by, 112; white Creoles and, 15–16, 69, 95, 121–22, 255n2; whiteness and, 69, 92–93
Anglo-blacks: Creoles of color and, 13, 107, 109, 114, 219–20; identity of, 156; *La Tribune de la Nouvelle Orleans* for, 107
assimilation theory: for Eurocentrism, 201, 205; for immigrants, 3–4, 203–4; *See also* downward assimilation; educational assimilation; segmented assimilation
Athénée Louisianais, 128–29

Bean, Frank, 195–96
Berlin, Ira: on free people of color, 38; *Slaves without Masters* by, 40
Black Codes: Section 28 of, 107; for slavery, 100
Black Identities (Waters), 207–8
blackness: African ancestry as, 45–46, 156; of Creoles, 87–88, 135–37; of Creoles of color, 183; Creoles of color and, 166–67; in Cuba, 32; freedom and, 31–32; free people of color and, 29; slavery determined by, 32–34, 244n38; of United States, 29; in Virginia, 33; *Xavierite* on, 117–18
black/nonblack color line, 193, 195–96
black/white color line, 200
Bogger, Tommy, 41–42
Bonaparte, Napoleon: Louisiana Purchase from, 11; revolution from, 6–7

Bonilla-Silva, Eduardo: triracial system by, 194–95, 195t
Boze, Jean, 75–76
Brazil: race in 20-28; racial system in 48

Cable, George Washington: Canonge against, 86–87; *The Grandissimes* by, 85–86, 138–39
Canal Street: division of, 124–25; of New Orleans, 78
Canonge, Placide, 86–87
Cap-Français, 60
Cap-Français theater: black women at, 55; dances at, 53; free people of color at, 54–55; St. Méry on, 52–53, 55
Catholics, 8, 10
Les Causeries de Lundi, 129
Les Cenelles (The Holly Berries): poetry of, 101; by racial palimpsest, 103
Census Bureau, 192. *See also* Latin American census
Chavannes, Jean-Baptiste, 58
Christianity, 33–34
citizenship, 73–74
civil rights: Creoles of color for, 105, 111, 117; *Crusader* for, 115
Civil War: Creole of color activists during 105-109; Creoles of color affected by 28, 41–42; Scott on, 42; white Creoles influenced by, 80-82, 88, 91, 138, 153; whiteness influenced by, 46, 88
Claiborne, W. C. C.: on civil trial, 70; on Creoles, 72; on French immigrants, 74; as governor, 1, 72, 249n9; Jefferson and, 70; on militia, 98–100
Clark, Daniel, 71
Clark, Emily: on *ménagère*, 96–97; on quadroon, 45, 98
coartación: Abbott on, 35; legal doctrine of, 34–35; in Louisiana, 36–37; Tannenbaum on, 36
Coin Coin, Marie, 163–64
Coleman, Edward: on free people of color, 101–2; triracial system and, 103
colons Américaines, 58
Comité des Citoyens, 115
Compromise of 1850, 39–40
Congo Square, 8, 9f
Creole Burlesque Company, 88–90
Creole Families of New Orleans (King), 91

Creole language, 165
Creoles: of African ancestry, 152–53; Americans perception of, 7, 249n7; ancestry of, 11–12, 86, 143, 152–53, 241n21; Anglo-American racial system against, 78; Anglo-Americans and, 14, 72–73, 123, 126; blackness of, 87–88, 135–37; Boze on, 75; *Les Causeries de Lundi* for, 129; citizenship for, 73–74; Claiborne on, 72; identity of, 13; organizations for, 222; race of, 184; racial palimpsest of, 160; racial passing by, 115–16; racial system of, 10, 241n19; whiteness and, 10. *See also* Creoles of color; white Creoles
Creoles of color: Anglo-American racial system for, 188; Anglo-American racial system influence on, 118, 155–56, 188–89; Anglo-blacks and, 13, 107, 109, 114, 219–20; blackness and, 166–67; blackness of, 183; for civil rights, 105, 111, 117; Hispanic and, 199, 211–12; identity of, 116, 118–19, 154–55, 166, 255n46; organizations for, 16–17; *Plessy v. Ferguson* influenced by, 111–12; racial palimpsest of, 109–10; racial passing of, 172–73; racial system of, 16, 153; *L'Union* for, 105–6; white Creoles and, 17, 137, 141–42; whiteness and, 177
Crusader, 115
Cuba: blackness in, 32; free people of color in, 32–33, 43; against French immigrants, 62–63; racial mixing of, 24; whiteness for, 22

Dalcour, P., 104–5, 253n22
Darity, William, 192
Depression era, 116
Desarzant, Anastasie, 91–92
descendants, 16, 67, 119, 145–46, 214–16, 216t–217t
Desdunes, Rodolphe Lucien: on "Chant d'Amour," 104; "A Few Words to Dr. DuBois with Malice Toward None" by, 109; letter by, 16; *Our People and Our History* by, 115; political activism by, 110–11; on racial oppression, 103–4

Dessens, Nathalie: on racial mixing, 81–82; on social bonds, 74–75; on white Creoles, 54
Dominguez, Virginia: on American Quarter, 78; *White by Definition* by, 82, 148–49; on white Creoles, 137
downward assimilation, 201, 261n23
DuBois, W. E. B., 110
Dutty, Boukman, 59, 247n22

educational assimilation, 204–5
1850s, 42
L'Essai sur l'Inégalités des Races Humaines (Gobineau), 22–23
eugenics, 26
Eurocentrism: assimilation theory for, 201, 205
European immigrants, 3, 22

family: of Creoles of color, 151–52; racial passing and, 174–75, 178; of *Times-Picayune*, 149, 150t
family history: of St. Domingue/Haiti-Louisiana, 225–33
Faubourg Marigny (Third Municipality), 78, 79f
Faubourg St. Mary (Second Municipality), 77–78, 79f
"A Few Words to Dr. DuBois with Malice Toward None" (Desdunes), 109
Fick, Carolyn, 59
First Municipality. *See* French Quarter
Foner, Laura, 24, 56
Fortier, Alcée, 128–29
France: revolution in, 57
Franklin, John Hope, 41
freedom: Abbott on, 35; of Anglo-American racial system, 37–38; blackness and, 31–32; of free people of color, 34; of Luisa, 37; L'Ouverture for, 58–59; by payment installments, 36
free people of color: Anglo-Americans against, 95; Berlin on, 38; blackness and, 29; at Cap-Français theater, 54–55; in Cuba, 32–33, 43; dwindling freedom of, 34; 1850s for, 42; for French National Assembly, 58; hopes of, 99; legal regimes influence on, 21, 30; literature by, 100–101; militia by, 41, 99; in New Orleans, 55–56, 98; North Carolina against, 38–39; political activism by, 40–41; racial systems and, 96; of St. Domingue, 7, 54, 93, 96, 114, 241n15; in United States, 42–43
French government, 61–62, 248n28–30
French immigrants: Claiborne on, 74; Cuba against, 62–63; slavery by, 63–64; of St. Domingue, 56
French language: Anglo-Americans and, 1–2; *Athénée Louisianais* for, 128–29; of Louisiana, 127; of public schools, 127, 255n9; *L'Union* in, 106; of white Creoles, 126–27.
French National Assembly, 58
French Quarter (First Municipality), 78, 79f
Freyre, Gilberto, 27
Fugitive Slave Act, 39–40

Garrigus, John: on race, 56; on racial mixing, 80
Gates, Henry Louis, 103
Gaudin, Wendy, 183–84; on Creoles of color, 211–12; on segregation, 165–66
Gayarré, Charles: "The Creoles of History and the Creoles of Romance" by, 87; funeral of, 90; for white Creoles, 87, 251n56
Gobineau, Arthur Compte de, 22–23
Golash-Boza, Tanya, 192
The Grandissimes (Cable): *New Orleans Item* review of, 86; racial mixture in, 138–39; social critique by, 85–86

Haddox, Thomas, 102–3
Haiti: ancestry in 139–140, 178, 185, 214–215; Louisiana and, 11; as part of French Atlantic world for Creoles of color 106–107; revolution resulting in 1, 6, 11, 57–60, 95, St. Domingue as, 1–2, 60–61, 239n2; also see St. Domingue
Hanger, Kimberly, 36–37, 244n49
Hispanic: Creoles of color and, 199, 211–12; identity of, 184; in Latin/Caribbean racial system, 197–98, 260n19; Latinos as, 192; whiteness of, 190–91
Historic New Orleans Collection (HNOC), 215; "Common Routes" symposium of, 12
A History of Louisiana (Fortier), 128–29

HNOC. *See* Historic New Orleans Collection
Hoetink, H., 46–47
The Holly Berries. *See Les Cenelles*
Hugo, Victor, 106, 253n24–25

identity: of African ancestry, 155–56, 256n1; of Anglo-blacks, 156; of Creoles, 13; of Creoles of color, 116, 118–19, 154–55, 166, 255n46; of Hispanic, 184; of Latinos, 190, 259n4; in mixed marriage, 191; race and, 165; in racial system, 184; of St. Domingue refugees, 75, 94–95, 252n2; of white Creoles, 90, 121, 130–31, 134–35, 141–43, 148, 153, 217–18
immigrants: assimilation theory for, 3–4, 203–4; concentration of, 4–5; racial system influenced by, 203; *See also* European immigrants; French immigrants; white immigrants
immigration, 4–5, 239n7, 240n9

Jack, Sam T., 88–89
Jefferson, Thomas, 70
Johnson, Jerah, 8, 10
Jung, Moon Kie: on assimilation theory, 202-203, 205

King, Grace: *Creole Families of New Orleans* by, 91; on white Creoles, 120–21
Kinser, Samuel, 133–34

LaChance, Paul, 76–77
Laguerre, Michel, 113
Latin America, 24–25, 242n14
Latin American census, 23–24
Latin/Caribbean populace: cultural practices of, 6; migration by, 17–18
Latin/Caribbean racial system: of African ancestry, 206–8; Anglo-American racial system and, 5, 20, 80, 139, 165, 190, 193, 200, 207, 242n2; categories of, 185; countries of, 20; Hispanic in, 197–98, 260n19; racial palimpsest of, 46, 47t; by St. Domingue refugees, 5
Latinos: Anglo-American racial system for, 192–93; as Hispanic, 192; identity of, 190, 259n4. *See also* Hispanic
Latrobe, Benjamin, 8
Lee, Jennifer, 195–96

legal regimes: free people of color influenced by, 21, 30; manumission from, 31; slavery influenced by, 31; of United States, 44–45
lieux de mémoire (memory sites), 90–91
limpieza de sangre: African ancestry influence on, 28, 243n26; whiteness and, 21
literature: by free people of color, 100–101; as *lieux de mémoire*, 90–91
Logan, John, 198–99, 261n21
Louisiana: Anglo-Americans of, 6; Anglo-American racial system of, 97–98; *coartación* in, 36–37; French language of, 127; Haiti and, 11; immigration of, 4–5, 240n9; for manumission, 37; mixed marriage in, 34; racial palimpsest of, 2; Reconstruction-era influence on, 82; St. Domingue migration for, 2, 5–7, 15, 66, 186; St. Domingue refugees in, 7, 52. *See also* Louisiana Purchase; St. Domingue/Haiti-Louisiana
Louisiana Purchase, 7, 11
Loveman, Mara: on Latin American census, 23–24; *National Colors* by, 23–24; on racial mixing, 24–25

manumission: in Anglo-American Louisiana, 42; in Cuba 32; in French Louisiana 34; from legal regimes, 30-31; Louisiana for, 37; in Spanish Louisiana 37; in the United States, 42
Martinez-Echazabal, Lourdes, 26–27
memory sites. *See lieux de mémoire*
ménagère, 80–81, 96–97
mestizaje, 25
Mexican Americans, 204–5
militia: Claiborne on, 98–100; by free people of color, 41, 99; purity in, 56–57, 247n17; Spain for, 44, 245n68
Mills, Charles, 21–22, 242n5
mixed marriage: identity in, 191; LaChance on, 76–77; in Louisiana, 34;
Morgan, Benjamin: on free people of color, 95; Price letter from, 69–70, 249n1; on quadroon, 94

Nee, Victor, 203–204
New Orleans: Canal Street of, 78; Congo Square of, 8; Creole language of, 165;

free people of color in, 55–56, 98; move to, 211; municipalities of, 77, 79f; Pitot of, 51–52, 54; quadroon influence on, 45; racial system of, 189; St. Domingue refugees of, 7t; White League of, 84–85

New Orleans Item, 86, 110

newspaper: Anderson on, 148; Creoles of color in, 151–52; race in, 150; of Roudanez, 51–52, 246n3–4; white Creoles in, 149–51

North Carolina, 38–39

Ogé, Vincent, 58, 247n21

Ohio, 106–7

"one-drop rule," 29

The Opelousas Courrier, 84

Our People and Our History (Desdunes), 115

L'Ouverture, Toussaint, 58–59, 178

Pitot, James: of New Orleans, 51–52, 54

plaçage: *of The Grandissimes*, 138–39; of St. Domingue, 80–81, 250n32

placée, 97

Plessy v. Ferguson: Anglo-American influence on, 112; Creoles of color influence on, 111–12; Scott on, 113–14; St. Domingue/Haiti ancestry of activists for 111-114; for whiteness, 46, 246n72

political activism: Boze on, 75–76; by Desdunes, 110–11; by free people of color, 40–41; of St. Domingue refugees, 113

Price, Chandler, 69–70, 249n1

privateering, 61–62, 247n27

public schools: French language of, 127, 255n9

purity: Anglo-American racial system for, 82–83; of Anglo-Americans, 122; by militia, 56–57, 247n17; whiteness as, 28, 44–45, 56–57, 243n28

quadroon: Clark, E., on, 45, 98; Morgan on, 94; New Orleans influenced by, 45

"Quadroon Bill," 108–9, 254n29

race: on Census Bureau, 192; of Creoles, 184; racial palimpsest and, 2–3, 208; segmented assimilation for, 201–2, 262n24

racial inequality, 205, 209

racial democracy (Brazil): 27, 140, 200

racial mixing: of Cuba, 24; democracy influence on, 26–27; in Brazil, 27–28, 140, 200; of Latin America, 24–25, 242n14; *mestizaje as*, 25; of United States, 30; whiteness by, 25–26

racial palimpsest: of Anglo-American racial system, 21, 46, 47t, 189–90, 199, 206; *Les Cenelles* by, 103; of Creoles, 160; of Creoles of color, 109–10; of Latin/ Caribbean racial system, 46, 47t; race and, 2–3, 208; racial histories of, 49–50; of racial system, 2, 5, 46, 50, 196–97; shifting by, 103; of St. Domingue refugees, 200

racial passing: by Creoles, 115–16; of Creoles of color, 172–73; family and, 174–75, 178; *See also* situational passing

racial system: of black/white color line, 200; of Creoles, 10, 241n19; of Creoles of color, 16, 153; definition of, 19–20; DuBois on, 110; free people of color and, 96; historical context of, 20–21; identity in, 184; immigrants influence on, 203; of New Orleans, 189; of origin country, 197; racial justice of, 208; racial palimpsest of, 2, 5, 46, 50, 196–97; responses to, 155; of St. Domingue refugees, 66, 94–95, 193, 199; white Creoles influenced by, 16–17. *See also* Anglo-American racial system; Latin/Caribbean racial system; triracial system

Raimond, Julien, 58

Reconstruction-era, 82, 84

Reid-Vasquez, Michelle, 43–44

Remaking the American Mainstream (Alba and Nee), 203–4

revolution: from Bonaparte, 6–7; Dutty leading of, 59, 247n22; in France, 57-58; impact on Louisiana 95, 97, 99, 114; of St. Domingue, 1, 6–7, 11, 15, 51, 54, 57, 59, 61, 63–66, 95

Roth, Wendy, 191

Roudanez, Louis Charles: newspaper of, 51–52, 246n3–4; Roudané from, 170, 182; *L'Union* by, 105

Sartorius, David, 43–44
Schomburg Center for Research in Black Culture, 112–13
Scott, Rebecca: on Civil War, 42; on *Plessy v. Ferguson*, 113–14; on political activism, 114
Second Municipality. *See* Faubourg St. Mary
segmented assimilation, 201–2, 261n23, 262n24
segregation: Creoles of Color and, 66, 94, 100, 113, 117-118, 157, 160, 166, 183, 212; Jim Crow, 21, 66, 88, 212; in St. Domingue 57; of United States, 46
situational passing, 174
Slave and Citizen (Tannenbaum), 30
slavery: Black Codes for, 100; by blackness, 32–34, 244n38, 244n40; Christianity and, 33–34; by French immigrants, 63–64; leasing for, 64; legal regime influence on, 31; of St. Domingue, 58–59
Slaves without Masters (Berlin), 40
social bonds, 57, 74–75
social race, 48–49, 246n76
Spain, 44, 245n68
St. Domingue: ancestry of, 11-14, 111-113, 139-140, 147, 178, 215–16; free people of color of, 7, 54, 93, 96, 114, 241n15; French immigrants of, 56; as Haiti, 1, 60–61, 239n2; Louisiana migration from, 2, 5–7, 15, 66, 186; *ménagère of*, 80–81; *plaçage of*, 80–81, 250n32; Raimond representation for, 58; revolution of, 1, 6–7, 15, 51; slavery of, 58–59; social bonds of, 57; triracial system of, 47–48; white immigrants in, 43
St. Domingue/Haiti-Louisiana: family history of, 225–26; historical relationship of, 226–28
St. Domingue refugees: Anglo-American racial system for, 186–87, 202; descendants of, 16, 67, 119, 145–46, 214–16, 216t–217t; dissolution of, 76–77; Faubourg Marigny for, 78; HNOC on, 12; identity of, 75, 94–95, 252n2; Latin/Caribbean racial system by, 5; in Louisiana, 7, 52; of New Orleans, 7t; political activism of, 113; racial palimpsest of, 200; racial system of, 66, 94–95, 193, 199; social bonds of, 74–75; white Creoles of, 54–55, 68
St. Domingue Special Interest Group (SIG), 12, 214
St. Méry, Moreau de, 52–53, 55

Tafoya, Sonya, 198
Tannenbaum, Frank, 30–31, 36
Telles, Edward: on eugenics, 26; *Generations of Exclusion* by, 204; *Race in Another America* by, 22–23
Third Municipality. *See* Faubourg Marigny
Times-Picayune: family of, 149, 150t; on white Creoles, 122, 148–49, 153, 219
Tinker, Edward Laroque, 91–92
Toucoutou (Tinker), 91–92
Tregle, Joseph G., 77, 81–82
Treitler, Vilna, 203
La Tribune de la Nouvelle Orleans: for Anglo-blacks, 107; against "Quadroon Bill," 108-9, 254n29; on voting rights, 107–8
triracial system: by Bonilla-Silva, 194–95, 195t; Coleman and, 103; Haddox and, 103; Hoetink on, 46–47; of racial system, 160; of St. Domingue, 47–48; transition by, 193, 260n12

L'Union, 105–6
United States: Anglo-Americans expectations of, 1–2; blackness of, 29; free people of color in, 42–43; legal regime of, 44–45; racial flexibility of, 28–29; racial mixing of, 30; segregation of, 46; social race of, 48–49

Vasquez, Jessica, 191–92
Virginia, 33
voting rights, 107–8

Wagley, Charles, 48, 246n76
Waters, Mary, 207–8
White by Definition (Dominguez), 82, 148–49
white Creoles: ancestry of, 220; Anglo-Americans and, 15–16, 69, 95, 121–22, 255n2; *Le Carillon* for, 84; Civil War influence on, 80, 138;

colonial rule of, 53; Creoles of color and, 17, 137, 141–42; cultural impact of, 68; Dessens on, 54; Dominguez on, 137; French language of, 126–27; Gayarré for, 87, 251n56; identity of, 90, 121, 130–31, 134–35, 141–43, 148, 153, 217–18; King on, 120–21; in newspaper, 149–51; racial system influence on, 16–17; of St. Domingue refugees, 54–55, 68; *Times-Picayune* on, 122, 148–49, 153, 219; Tregle on, 81–82

white immigrants, 43

White League, 83–85

whiteness: by ancestry, 140; by Anglo-American racial system, 92, 115, 183; by Anglo-Americans, 69, 92–93; by appearance, 28; Civil War influence on, 88; Creoles and, 10; Creoles of color and, 177; for Cuba, 22; of European immigrants, 3, 22; of Hispanic, 190–91; indigenous populations and, 24; *limpieza de sangre* and, 21; by money, 194–95, 260n15; *Plessy v. Ferguson* for, 46, 246n72; as purity, 28, 44–45, 56–57, 243n28; by racial mixing, 25–26; situational passing of, 174;

white/nonwhite color line, 193–94, 260n12

Xavierite, 117–18